The GROUCHO PHILE

An Illustrated Life

by

GROUCHO MARX

with an Introduction by

HECTOR ARCE

designed by Jacques Chazaud

A WALLABY BOOK

PUBLISHED BY POCKET BOOKS NEW YORK

THE GROUCHO PHILE

Bobbs-Merrill edition published 1976

WALLABY edition published September, 1977

This WALLABY edition includes every word contained in the original,
higher-priced edition. It is printed from brand-new plates.
WALLABY editions are published by
POCKET BOOKS,
a Simon & Schuster Division of
GULF & WESTERN CORPORATION
1230 Avenue of the Americas,
New York, N.Y. 10020.
Trademarks registered in the United States
and other countries.

ISBN: 0-671-79002-1.
Library of Congress Catalog Card Number: 76-11630.

Printed in the U.S.A.

Tell 'em
Groucho sent you

Acknowledgments

May I? . . . May I? . . . May I? . . .

Had I known that it would take me twenty-two letters just to get permission to talk about my severe hangnail in 1938, I might have dropped my ballpoint and taken up needlepoint.

"Clear the rights . . . get the permissions." Publishers can be such bores, they're so persnickety, and isn't Raquel Welch looking lovely these days?

But I digress. There are many people to thank for the memories, and to recognize for their contributions to this book.

For permission to use their material, I would like to thank the following friends: Goodman Ace, Irwin Allen, Steve Allen, Irene Atkins, Candice Bergen, Irving Berlin, Mrs. William (Toby) Garson, Mrs. Larry Gelbart, Bert and Charlotte Granet, E. Y. "Yip" Harburg, Hugh Hefner, Al Hirschfeld, Nunnally Johnson, Bil Keane, Goddard Lieberson, my grandson Andy Marx, my son Arthur Marx, Russell Myers, Peter Shore, E. B. White, Arthur Whitelaw and Thomas Wilhite. These friends, however, all owe me dinner invitations. In lieu of breaking bread with them at this time, I thank them for allowing me to make some of my own.

Special thanks go to Steve Schapiro, photographer extraordinaire, for much of the original photography, and to Steve Stoliar, my archivist-secretary, who so efficiently put his finger on much of the older material. (Actually, he's all thumbs.)

My gratitude also to those who helped with the research: Shaun Considine, New York; Bob Cooper, San Francisco; John Tefteller, Los Angeles; Henry Golas, Alonso Gonzales, Allan Held, Dave Lipschultz, Dan Paris, John Stanley and Steve Wolf.

For permission to use photographs, film stills and television frame blowups, I want to thank the following: Herbert Schlosser and Tod A. Roberts of the National Broadcasting Company; the Bell Telephone Co.; Columbia Pictures; Walt Disney Productions; Patricia A. Healy and Karla Davidson of the Metro-Goldwyn-Mayer Legal Department; Donald Havens, Jr., and Larry Adelman, National Telefilm Associates, Inc.; RKO Radio Pictures Inc.; Erwin H. Ezzes and Helen Killeen, United Artists Television Inc.; Julian Fowles and Joseph DiMuro, Universal City Studios.

I'm also grateful to the following for permission to use their photographs: *In the Know* magazine, Ellen Berman, Richard Cuskelly, Lester Glassner, Hal Kaufman, Ralph Levy, Howard Rosenberg and Richard Shear.

To show how ridiculous things got, I even had to get permission to quote from my own material. Milton Berle never had to get permission to quote from my own material. Keeping it legal, here are the copyright lines supplied by the publishers of my six previous books:

Beds, by Groucho Marx. Reprinted with the permission of Bobbs-Merrill Co., Inc.,© 1930 by Julius H. Marx, copyright renewed 1958 by Julius H. Marx, copyright 1976 by Julius H. Marx.

Contents

Introduction

Every day, when the hands on the clock point straight up, a slight, elderly man gets into a black limousine with his pretty brunette nurse at the wheel. The car wends its way down the sinuously curving grades of Trousdale Estates and comes to a stop at a public park in the flatlands of Beverly Hills, where the two will be taking their daily constitutional.

Quite often, a group of youngsters are at curb side, awaiting their Pied Piper. He may arrive in the guise of a retired banker, wearing a $600 Eric Ross suit which is punctuated by the ever-present beret. Gone forever is the trademark cigar. The black greasepaint mustache has given way to his grey, bristled one. A major heart attack and a series of small strokes have slowed down and curiously straightened up that distinctive bent-over gait, and the eyebrows no longer wiggle at sixty miles an hour. The fans, nevertheless, recognize the essence that is the man. And even if they didn't, they would know after the millions of words written about him that he's a creature of habit. Like mad dogs and Englishmen, Groucho Marx goes out in the noonday sun.

If regrets are voiced that he no longer affects the Captain Spaulding pith helmet and jodhpurs to protect him from the blazing elements, the fans may be taking comfort that Groucho also doesn't sport a whip with which to keep the more zealous of them at bay. His indifference to the way he's lionized and revered can no longer be feigned.

He may go through the predictable motions. A fan might say, "Groucho, I'm so and so." He'll quickly respond, "That's your problem."

Yet after a lifetime of divine and devastating rudeness—misdemeanors to which he still persists in pleading "not guilty"—his marshmallow core is occasionally exposed. Later at lunch, he'll describe with relish—and low-sodium salt substitute—his encounters of the hour before. And if there happened to be a pretty girl in the group who insisted on a kiss, what was a fellow to do? A clear case of mutual victimization.

It's the same type of relationship he's had with the world all his life, and that he hasn't worn out his welcome after seventy years before the public eye is one of the wonders of the universe. That the world hasn't worn out its welcome in *his* eyes proves that the rest of us must be doing *something* right, contrary to the view of *The Mikado* that "virtue is triumphant only in theatrical performances."

During my association with Groucho, one of the many revelations about him was that W. Somerset Maugham is one of his favorite writers. I see in Maugham the shallow theatrics of the drawing room, whereas Groucho sees much more: Maugham, the world traveler, finding human drama everywhere, describing human bondage in its various forms with depth and empathy.

Maugham offered a valedictory to the world when *A Writer's Notebook* was published in 1949. He wrote:

. . . I am like a passenger waiting for his ship at a war-time port. I do not know on which day it will sail, but I am ready to embark at a moment's notice. I leave the sights of the city unvisited. I do not want to see the fine new speedway along which I shall never drive, nor the grand new theatre, with all its modern appliances, in which I shall never sit. I read the papers and flip the pages of a magazine, but when someone offers to lend me a book I refuse because I may not have the time to finish it, and in any case with this journey before me I am not of a mind to interest myself in it. I strike up acquaintances at the bar or the card-table, but I do not try to make friends with people from whom I shall so soon be parted. I am on the wing.

Maugham lived for sixteen more years, if one can label *living* his cynical, arrogant conclusion that he'd seen and done all. That's a long time to put one's life on hold, and sixteen years of limbo must have been hell. He might have taken some lessons from Groucho in hope and indomitability.

I don't have to ask Groucho what he thinks of Maugham's words. They're the antithesis of what he is today: the first-nighter and bon vivant, the entertaining host, the nurturer of young talent, the voracious reader, the funny bone in the body politic, the living legend. ("Not to mention," he might add, "my legendary liver.")

In Hollywood, nothing seems to work as originally planned. The man who comes to dinner stays on to run the studio, and the modest little Western is inflated into next year's hyperbolic exercise in demonology. It's like the jacket blurb on Groucho's second book, *Many Happy Returns*, which "was written during a sandstorm at Palm Springs and started out as a serious novel. Sand kept flying into Mr. Marx's typewriter. To his surprise, he discovered that the finished manuscript was a book on the income tax."

And so it was with Groucho and me. I had come to his house to discuss the introduction he would write for a book by a mutual friend of ours, and stayed for over a year to work with him on several other projects.

There was nothing in my background to suggest that I was the ideal collaborator for Groucho. I wasn't a particularly devout follower of the Marx Brothers. Blame this on my awkward age, too young to see the films in their original incarnation and too old to be a part of the college crowd which took them up with such cultish fervor in the early 1970s.

Nor was I a Groucho Marx fan. I'd seen his quiz show and didn't find his baiting humor that funny. I have four older brothers and have been on the receiving end of that type of humor all my life.

I'd briefly met Groucho several years previously, at a big party celebrating the fact that *The Odd Couple* television series would be filmed before a live audience, starting with the 1971 season. The producers had invited friends and press to the first filming and hosted a huge cocktail buffet on an adjoining soundstage later. Groucho, sitting in the front row during the filming, intruded himself into all the proceedings. At first, the other guests laughed at his barbs. But he was "on" too long, and the exchanges between Groucho and long-suffering director Jerry Paris became a touch embarrassing. In his effort to prove something to himself, Groucho was doing what he'd rarely done before. He was pressing. The audience was a cow gone dry, but he persisted in milking them. It wasn't his finest hour, as Groucho himself finally realized, and he gave up the fight, allowing the show to continue. He was strangely subdued later at the party, where we were introduced by a mutual friend, and left early with his pretty date.

Some four years later, I arrived at his front door, loaded down with my tape recorder and my preconceptions, for my first actual meeting with the great man.

He was at first a grey silhouette against the glass window wall, seated at the grand piano, coaxing out a familiar tune. The vast expanse and the comparative darkness of the living room gave the fleeting impression that here was the living movie cliché, the piano player rehearsing in an empty nightclub.

The establishing shot, however, was off kilter. There were no wooden chairs upended on stamp-sized tables. The setting was lushly casual, with a throwaway chic only a very expensive interior designer could create. The sounds emanating from the piano also gave the lie to the first impression—they were tentative, exploring, unaccomplished.

I'd been ushered in without introduction and stood a few feet away, waiting to be acknowledged. Groucho continued his playing of "Take Me Out to the Ball Game." Curious, I thought; this pitcher is a southpaw, playing the melody with his left hand and the primitive chords with his right. (I was later to find out that Groucho's boyhood musical training had been minimal, primarily consisting of standing behind the spinet at that now famous house on East Ninety-third Street in New York and watching as his older brother Leonard practiced. His hands became the mirror image of his brother's, and consequently he'd trained himself to play the melody with his left hand and the chords with his right. Of such human little touches are classic comedy bits made, such as the mirror scene in *Duck Soup*. Now, seventy-five years later, Groucho was again picking up with his piano self-taught.)

Seated by the window, he looked frail and vulnerable. Decades seemed to have passed since the last time I'd seen him. Here, despite the glory and the immortality that is Groucho Marx, was a far older man than even the world's intrusive press had led me to believe. Had Time committed the final indignity, sticking out its leg and tripping up that famous nimble wit?

Then he looked up. "Who are you?" he growled.

The sheepish identification was made. Alert eyes did their sizing up. He nodded, then in surprisingly cordial tones said, "Shall we have lunch?"

The California spring weather had suddenly taken a change for the better, and outside, on the terrace by the pool, the wrought iron dining table was set for four. Erin Fleming, the catalyst who'd brought us together, called out a hello as she climbed out of the pool. Presently, Steve Stoliar, Groucho's archivist, joined us.

Lunch was to consist of broiled fish and Groucho's deviled tongue. If his serving up of verbal victuals was considerably slower than I'd remembered, it was no less delicious. He'd shown his fallibility at our first meeting. Now, with his eighty-five years weighing heavily on him, he was showing his vulnerability too. Underneath that crusty exterior was an endearing old man.

When the tape of our discussion was typed up a few days later, I discovered that Groucho had extemporized a solid first draft of the book introduction he'd be writing, replete with puns and non sequiturs. Another meeting to polish the material, and that should have been that.

I didn't know as yet that several publishers had approached Groucho about writing his recollections of *You Bet Your Life*, the most successful comedy-quiz show in television history. Because Groucho tires easily, and the publisher whose bid was ultimately selected had given him a six-month deadline, he didn't feel that he was up to writing the whole book himself. At that point, Erin—in her capacity as Groucho's personal manager—discussed with me the possibility of my serving as his collaborator. Within days, contracts were signed, the publisher's advance was paid, and I was part of Groucho's professional family.

During those few months I met his colleagues on the show and taped their reminiscences, all of which were filtered through Groucho. We were trying to create the same interplay that Groucho experienced with the contestants on the show.

It was *Rashomon* time all over again. *Variety*, in its review of the book, singled out "the various dicta and 'contradicta,' opinions, obstructions, obfuscations and just plain nonsensical waffling that whirl and swirl and commingle into just the right

show at just the right time, which is just what *You Bet Your Life* turned out to be and, apparently, still is."

Every morning, Andy Marx, Groucho's grandson, would run old films of the show for Steve Stoliar and me. We would tape significant exchanges which would be used in the appendix of the book.

In the afternoon, I'd hole up with Groucho in his bedroom-study for a couple of hours to go over his colleagues' "dicta" and to ferret out Groucho's "contradicta." He'd sit in the easy chair at the foot of his bed, and I'd plop on the floor before him, taking notes. It wasn't any conscious obeisance on my part to sit at the master's feet. It was just a natural posture, and if Groucho took it for more than that, he silently accepted it as his due.

As a lagniappe, he would relate anecdotes—many of them unusable for the project at hand—about his days in vaudeville and films, of the famous people of his time, of life in general. It was apparent that, after having written five previous books and now working on his sixth, there was still a seventh in Groucho—particularly since the Groucho Marx Collection being donated to the Smithsonian Institution after his death contained rare photographs never before seen by the public. *The GrouchoPhile* would be the result.

Meanwhile I began collating the reminiscences of show personnel and contestants for the book, and inserting Groucho's reactions to their observations. I presumed to supplement some of Groucho's witticisms with my own. When the first draft was completed, I dropped it off with him. For several days there was no reaction.

Finally, one morning he called me to his room, where he was sitting reading the daily newspaper. One of the great comic writers of his time looked at me and gently said, "You shouldn't try to write funny." In so many words, I was being instructed to stick to what I did best and leave the hard stuff for those who can do it better. I shouldn't try to write funny. They've become words to live by.

Hanging in a place of honor in the screening room at Groucho's house is the original of a William Hamilton cartoon which appeared in *The New Yorker*. A group of oh-so-sophisticates are sitting around a table. One of them is saying, "The tautology of their symbolism thus begins to achieve mythic proportions in *A Day at the Races*, *Duck Soup* and *A Night at the Opera*."

Though Groucho refuses to intellectualize about his art, and finds considerable amusement in the convoluted logic of the film cultists, a lot of heady talk persists about these three, sometimes four, brothers who, when they left school to help support the family, were as unemployable as they were unwashed.

Minnie's Boys.

In the beginning, they were five brothers (a sixth had died in infancy), the sons of a lovable, forceful, well-upholstered German lady and her handsome, diffident, French-born husband.

Both Sam and Minnie Marx were Jewish mothers. Minnie was the most famous stage mother of them all, and the least typical. There were no hard edges to her. She was round and plump and flirtatious and manipulative and intrusive; she possessed untapped layers of charm. She looked after her boys and their careers with the ferocity of a mother lion.

"I can still hear her voice," Groucho often says. "She was talking to a friend about us. 'Sam can cough all night and I never hear him,' she said. 'But if one of my boys coughs just once, I'm wide awake.' "

Frenchy—as Sam was called—looked after the family's creature comforts with a sweetness and a gentleness which he passed on to his son Harpo. He was a chef without parallel, making ambrosia out of potato peels. His magic as a tailor, Frenchy's actual calling, was considerably more mundane.

It was a topsy-turvy family. Minnie traveled with the boys while Frenchy stayed home banking the fires, if not any great amount of money. You could say she wore the pants, though Minnie was too much a product of her time and her femininity to do so literally.

Theoreticians today claim that the middle child is usually the one to give parents the most trouble. This should have been Groucho, the third of the surviving five sons. In actuality, it was Chico, the eldest, who was the biggest headache, who was as irresponsible as he was naturally charming. (Right after the Marxes became Broadway stars, a feature article in Collier's dismissed him with a phrase: "Chico played truant, and the piano." And this in a time when a boy with books overdue at the library was considered a juvenile delinquent.)

It wasn't in Harpo's peaceful nature to take up the cudgels, so he passed. Groucho, the serious one, with his head always buried in a book, who much as he loved his family never seemed to be at home at home, took up the leadership by default.

It was he who led the brothers into show business, influenced and impressed by the success in vaudeville of their uncle Al Shean, Minnie's brother. Only after Groucho had achieved a modicum of success on his own did Minnie decide that the act should be expanded to include one, then two, then three other brothers, with supporting players along the way, which occasionally included Aunt Hannah, with her lyrical soprano voice, and Minnie herself.

At the theaters they played, one sign backstage invariably read, DON'T SEND OUT YOUR LAUNDRY TILL THE MANAGER SEES YOUR ACT. Another warned, ANYONE SAYING HELL OR DAMN DURING A PERFORMANCE WILL BE IMMEDIATELY FIRED.

The Marxes didn't need to resort to sex and profanity. They were developing solid talents on which to fall back, and it was Chico who urged them onward and upward whenever their resolve faltered. They were, as a reviewer of the time put it, "clean and crude."

These were the days when most of the smaller variety theaters were called the Bijou, and the mention of Yonkers on a vaudeville stage was always good for a laugh, and every burlesque show had an Irish and a Jewish comedian, as well

as a rich widow. Margaret Dumont didn't spring up full blown. There was tradition to her type of character, just as there was to the characters played by the brothers themselves. They may have thought their *Fun in Hi Skule* routine was a steal from the current "Boys and Girls" act put together by Gus Edwards, but what evolved had roots going back to the origins of theater itself. The Groucho character was perhaps the most evocative.

Aristophanes was the first to combine beauty and wit and bawdry when his first play was produced in 425 B.C. He introduced the concept of Parabasis, where the chorus, in the midst of the proceedings, would wheel around and make a direct address to the audience. On the other side of the world, in China and Japan, the stage manager or property man was performing the same function. He would hand small properties to the actors during the performance, occasionally with spoken asides, or attend to their costumes. His presence, like Groucho's greasepaint mustache, indicated at once that realism was unnecessary. He was testimony to the imaginative quality of the whole production.

The art of mime, beginning in Sicily in the fifth century B.C., may have been more the birthright of Chico, the Italian brother, than of Harpo, the Irishman—Harpo, after all, *did* start off his career as Patsy Brannigan.

It wasn't until the 1600s, with the advent of *commedia dell' arte,* that we can see the four classic Marx characters roughly approximated. There was no written text, and the way the brothers improvised many a stage performance, they didn't need one either. This was comedy of the profession and of the streets, geared to a broadly popular audience, instead of the more exclusive *commedia erudita,* which was the amateur play of the court.

In *commedia dell 'arte,* four comic characters carried, and often dropped, the ball. One was a strangely dressed humpback wearing a dark half-mask with a sharply curved nose and a wrinkled receding brow. The second was an even more grotesque type with a long drooping nose and exaggeratedly large spectacles. His dress consisted of jacket, flapping trousers, short cloak and a beret with a large, curving feather. (The beret is Groucho's vestigial and unconscious homage to the tradition from which he sprang.) The third character was bespectacled and largely nondescript, and the fourth was older and ridiculously pompous.

The four players would go through scenes of great fear. The more the crowd laughed, the more absurd would become their gestures. With the tumult over, they would sit down to talk about their misadventures, and the thought of food would come to their minds.

Silvana the shepherdess would later be introduced in the proceedings. All four comic characters would fall in love with her. She would agree to marry the best sleeper. (There wasn't much difference in that regard to the skimpy plot of the brothers' first Broadway hit, *I'll Say She Is!* where the leading lady agreed to marry the one who would give her the biggest thrill.)

The characters Groucho created of Captain Jeffrey T. Spaulding, Professor Quincy Adams Wagstaff, Rufus T. Firefly, Otis B. Driftwood, and Dr. Hugo Z. Hackenbush embodied the term "anti-Establishment" years before it became fashionable. Groucho is the symbol of rebellion, and yet I wonder if in his real life he protested too much.

Groucho takes considerable pride in his honors: the Oscar, the Emmy, the French Commandeur des Arts et Lettres, which he is the only native-born American to receive. This pride is tempered by an extreme insecurity which he denies possessing. But it's a quality found in the greatest comedians, and is the common thread running throughout his fabled life.

In 1967, when Simon and Schuster published *The Groucho Letters*, a compendium of witty and literary correspondence written to and by Groucho, several letters were already part of the American folklore, such as the one he wrote on his resignation from the Friars Club of Beverly Hills. He had some misgivings about the quality of the members, doubts which were verified a few years later when an infamous card-cheating scandal erupted there. When he decided to drop out of the group, he wrote: "Gentlemen: Please accept my resignation. I don't care to belong to any social organization that will accept me as a member."

Previously, in the early 1950s, when *Confidential* magazine was raising havoc among the burghers of the movie colony, Groucho had been the target of some stories which implied that when it came to the fair sex, Groucho was the Jewish Errol Flynn. "If you continue to publish slanderous pieces about me," he wrote, "I shall feel compelled to cancel my subscription."

Then when an exclusive beach club blackballed him from membership because he was Jewish, Groucho plaintively asked, "Since my daughter is only half Jewish, could she go in the water up to her knees?"

These are whimpers more often associated with a Woody Allen, and not the Groucho of films who walks across tables and all over people to get his way. Yet, throughout Groucho's life, he's opted to press his nose to the window outside.

When it came to the ladies, he was tongue-tied and still mustering up courage to ask for a date long after Chico had tucked the lady in bed. Groucho, of course, had his moments, and I find it impossible to believe that he was the type of guy who, when getting a phone call from a married lady telling him the coast was clear, would plan to spend a day at the beach. The women he fell in love with, and still carries the torch for, were not the cupcakes who wound up as his wives, but the classy ladies he aspired to but couldn't win.

But Groucho has been the outsider all his life. Was it always a matter of choice?

When, in 1924, the Marx Brothers burst on the Broadway scene, it wasn't Groucho who was taken up by the literary Algonquin Round Table. Harpo the mime was the one fawned over by the likes of Woollcott and Benchley. He never had Groucho's literary aspirations, but Harpo never drew to an inside straight and was considerably more expansive than Groucho has ever been. It must have seemed odd to Groucho that, friendly as he was with the Algonquinites, he was largely relegated to the house at Great Neck with his first wife and children, while Harpo, the near illiterate, became the darling of the intelligentsia.

Coming to Hollywood, Harpo was taken up by the Hearst circle. Even Chico was on a higher social level, becoming a card-playing crony of Irving Thalberg and other studio moguls, and just incidentally making movie deals for the team. Groucho was delighted to spend time at the writers' table at the studio commissary with such comers as Norman Krasna, Nat Perrin, and Irving Brecher. Siberia time again. The irony that is Hollywood found Groucho now lunching regularly with the expatriates from New York who'd come west for the money, Benchley and Ben Hecht and Charles MacArthur.

During his first two marriages, Groucho lived in the very respectable flats of Beverly Hills. With his marriage to Eden Hartford must have come the realization that the type of social acceptance that came so easily to Bob Hope and Jack Benny did not come as readily to him. Why should it? He's punched holes in inflated balloons all his life. The decision of the Marxes to build a new home in Trousdale, that haven for the nouveau riche, replete with sunken bathtubs and circular bedrooms, was Groucho's emphasis that a life in society was not what he was all about. It was far better to be loved by the people.

He remained a major star at a time when Harpo and Chico were reduced to playing county fairs. Groucho had the foresight to age before the public eye. He became the not so dirty old man, while his brothers, now in their seventies, were still playing Puck and the Rapscallion, characterizations they'd created fifty years previously. They looked and acted tired, and though they were still loved, they weren't nearly as lovable.

The time came when Groucho's career slowed down. It coincided with our first meeting. He was divorced and alone. It was a melancholy time.

That he bounced back to become an epic figure is testament to the discernment of the public and the efforts of Erin Fleming. She came into his life and motivated him into trying. In doing so, she became a controversial figure, for she took on the fight for Groucho, and occasionally the fight *with* Groucho. Erin is not a shadow boxer. She delivers solid punches, especially when she feels that the magnitude of the man is not being given its proper due. She refused to allow Groucho to feel sorry for himself. Before long he was making a comeback on the concert circuit.

Socially, he was out in public again. He bought a new wardrobe, and redecorated his house. Groucho's been a frugal man all his life, and if he agreed to spend tens of thousands of dollars to renovate his place of residence, you can be assured he's staying around to enjoy it for a while.

During one of his recent illnesses, a fan sent him a card with a quotation from Emerson inside: "Give me health and a day, and I will make ridiculous the pomp of emperors."

Health stays with him, and so does that vital mind. Groucho has found as big a softie in me as I find in him. It must have taken me all of three seconds to become his abject admirer. Whenever he adjourns to the living room after one of his dinner parties to entertain his guests with a few songs, I get a lump in my throat to see him up there still trying. At times like that, I could live forever. I have no doubt that Groucho will.

After a lifetime of veneration, could there be any suppressed desires and unfulfilled ambitions left in him? Without overly delving into family matters that aren't the public's business, I can state that Groucho, who's been a devoted family man all his life, must regret the geographical and/or emotional separation from his three children, if not his grandchildren, who remain the staunchest of Groucho's fans. It must have been extremely difficult for his children to walk in his tall shadow. He doesn't verbalize these feelings, but they are obviously there. One Sunday, I went with Groucho and Erin to the Academy of Motion Picture Arts and Sciences to see a film documentary on the life of Charlie Chaplin. At the picture's end, Chaplin at eighty-six is seen gamboling on a vast expanse of lawn with his children and grandchildren. When the lights came up, Erin and I discovered Groucho in inexplicable tears. Was he moved by the great happiness being experienced by his old friend Chaplin, or was he regretting that his own couldn't take the same form? I didn't presume to ask.

What I do ask is why a man who has spoken so eloquently to the young across the span of four generations, who became a college of one and taught himself to become a cultured and educated man, has never received an honorary degree from any college or university. In 1975, a poll of incoming college freshmen revealed that after Jesus Christ and Albert Schweitzer, Groucho Marx was the man they most admired. That same year, a poll of students showed that after Henry Kissinger, Groucho was the most sought after college lecturer. Yet, at this writing, no degree has been awarded him. It's an irony and an injustice that he should be so ignored, when he is one of a handful of men in the world who truly needs no Introduction.

No one is more aware of that fact than myself. In my frustration, reaching for words which at best will be considered adequate, considering the uniqueness of the man, I've considered throwing one of Groucho's lines back at him: "Do you suppose I could buy back my Introduction to you?"

It's a conceit of mine, though I have no indications to that effect, that Groucho would answer, "It's not for sale."

Hector Arce
Beverly Hills
August 1976

Prologue
Groucho Singing at Home

No one has a better time at my house than I do. On any given evening, after dinner with congenial and receptive company, we gather in the living room. An accomplished piano player is always among the invited guests, so that I can commandeer my captive audience and raise my voice in song. Some nights, happily, Bill Marx isn't busy and he'll come over. It's fitting that Harpo's eldest son should be sitting at the piano, playing those songs I sang centuries ago with his father and uncles, and that Erin Fleming, who is so much a part of my todays, should fill in as the chorus:

¹ *Way down by the sad seaside*
Sat two lovers side by side.

² *First he sighed and then she sighed*
And then they both sighed side by side.

³ *Peasie Weasie, that's his name.*
Peasie Weasie, Peasie Weasie, what's his game?

⁴ *He will catch you if he can,*

⁵ *Peasie Weasie, Peasie Weasie is a bold, bad man.*

The song ends, the guests applaud, and I'm pleasantly trapped with my memories. Other times and other songs:

1

2

2

3

[6] *With the table between us,*
She looked exactly like Venus.
Ach Gott! How that woman could cook!

That's a song written by Gus and Grace Kahn. We shared the world of vaudeville together. Gus wrote the music for one of the Marx Brothers shows in 1919. I like to sing their songs because I share so much more with the Kahns: two grandsons named Steve and Andy Marx. Memories—some happy, others not—are evoked. I suppose, to use a line from one of our pictures, I'm just a sentimental old fluff.

6

5

4

3

Early Childhood

In the beginning came the secret word—but I digress. The word actually was no secret. It was laughter, and I learned it at my mother's knee. Her name was Minnie Schoenberg. A beauty. She'd come over from Germany with her parents, who'd operated a traveling theatrical troupe. Minnie had seen the world of entertainment, and found it to her liking. She also liked a clothing cutter, with pretensions to being a tailor, named Simon Marx. So, at the age of nineteen, in 1884, three years after this picture was taken, she married her Frenchy from Alsace-Lorraine. He was dapper and handsome and thirty. Simon changed his name to Sam. He must have been the original Sam who made the pants too long, but if he had failings as a tailor, he more than made up for them as a chef. Ach Gott! How that fellow could cook! Times were rough for these first-generation Americans. You know the adage: the rich get richer and the poor get children.

7

8

8 I was Sam and Minnie's fourth son. The oldest, Manfred, died of old age. He was three at the time. Leonard and Adolph were the second and third sons. You know them as Chico and Harpo respectively—if not respectably. Milton (Gummo) and Herbert (Zeppo) would come later. We were all delivered by Doctor Berrgheim. I remember him well, for I was ten, going on eleven, when Zeppo, the baby of the family, was born. The doctor made house calls in a horse-drawn surrey, and, in his silk hat and frock coat, he dazzled me. Because of him I had boyhood dreams of becoming a doctor with a beard, a little black bag and a bedside manner that would charm the most frigid female. Fortunately, someone wiser than myself was instrumental in talking me out of this ambition. This was a stroke of good fortune not only for myself, but for the medical profession as well. I must confess that over the years my bedside manner has been remarkably unimpressive.

9 This, to my knowledge, is the first picture ever taken of me. Now that I've said it, out of the musty files will come the collections of the cultists, showing eight thousand baby pictures from the ages of one to five. Nevertheless, I *think* this was the first picture. It was taken, I presume, with a German camera, for the picture itself was taken in Germany. When I was five, I went with Mother and Chico to her native town of Dornum, Germany. Minnie's cousin, *the* Wolfenstein who owned a prominent men's furnishings store in New York, gave her the money to visit her homeland. I'm holding my hand in front of my face, cousin Hattie Wolfenstein holds her hand in her lap, Chico holds a soulful pose, and Cousin Edna holds a violin.

10 At home, Uncle Al was starting his career in vaudeville. He changed his name from Schoenberg to Shean and his profession from pants presser to comedian. The name of the first group was the Manhattan Comedy Four. They were Sam Curtis, tenor; Arthur Williams, bass; Al Shean, the comic; and Ed Mack, the baritone. Later, Uncle Al would appear in a show called *Crovadis Upside Down*. It was Shakespeare with a different dialogue. The straight man would say to Uncle Al, "Yonder in the distance an island lays." He would reply, "Lays what—eggs?" They would go on like that until the audience left the theater. Although he didn't appear so on stage, Uncle Al was a dandy and a bon vivant. He would visit us, reeking of bay rum and good cheer. Soon, he'd also be reeking of the limburger cheese he'd send us out to buy for him. He may have been the first man I ever saw wearing spats. At the end of the visit, each nephew would get a quarter. The kids in the neighborhood would be waiting outside, for Uncle Al made a ritual of taking one hundred pennies out of a bag and throwing them in the air. The boys would scramble for them. I longed to be like Uncle Al. He made $200 a week. He had style. And a pretty wife, Aunt Joanna:

Until I was four I couldn't tell the difference between the sexes. I was going to say "the two sexes," but today there are so many variations that if one says "the two sexes" your friends are apt to regard you as a withered anachronism and wonder what rock you've been residing under for the past three decades.

My first realization that a fancier world existed dawned upon me one day when the only aunt I had who possessed both money and sophistication came to visit my mother. She was the wife of a successful vaudeville actor and, although still a young woman, had been to Chicago, St. Louis, and once had even spent the night in Denver. She had red hair, high heels, and a nice, tight shape that bulged where all desirable shapes were supposed to bulge. (I know that the word "shape" dates me, and I'm only sorry I wasn't old enough to date her.)

When she sailed into our flat, the whole area began to take on a tantalizing, exotic fragrance that later in life I recognized as the standard odor of a bordello. Of course, at the time I had no idea what I was inhaling. For all I knew, it might have been embalming fluid. But whatever it was, it was exciting, and certainly far removed from anything I had ever smelled before.

In our moth-eaten flat I was accustomed to the combined odors of four generally unwashed brothers, bean soup, and a kerosene stove that smoked. Now, here I was, breathing the heady perfume of the ages: a fragrance that made strong men tremble with desire and weak men whimper in despair.

My aunt was exceedingly pretty, and when she looked at me she smiled admiringly. Turning to my mother, she said, "You know, Minnie, Julius has the loveliest big brown eyes I've ever seen."

Until that moment I had never given my eyes a thought. Oh, I knew I was nearsighted, but it never occurred to me that my eyes were anything out of the ordinary. Conscious now of my new-found charms, I lifted my eyebrows as high as I could and stared at her. She didn't look at me again, but I continued to stare, hoping that if my eyes continued to bulge she would pay me another compliment. But no, she was busily gossiping with my mother and apparently had forgotten all about me. I kept walking up and down in front of her, hoping she would again say something flattering about my big brown eyes.

9

10

8

After some time my eyeballs began to ache from the unaccustomed strain, and her scent was making me dizzier and dizzier. I still couldn't seem to attract her attention, but, desperate for another eulogy to my peepers, I began coughing. Not a dainty little cough, but a steady, tuberculous, deep-throated blast, somewhat reminiscent of a lesbian playing Camille. As a result of this continuous coughing, my head began to ache, but despite my constant attempts to squeeze another compliment out of her, she never noticed me again.

I finally realized that my case was hopeless, and, reeling from my various ailments, I staggered from the room puzzled and feverish, but happy at the first compliment I had ever received from a woman—even if it was only a casual remark from an aunt.

It wasn't until much later that I looked into a mirror and discovered that my eyes are gray.

From *Memoirs of a Mangy Lover*

11 In 1898, my mother's parents celebrated their golden wedding anniversary. My grandfather, whom we called Opie, had been a juggler. Our grandmother, Omie, played the harp. They toured the German countryside in their theater wagon, along with their eleven children, putting on shows wherever they could collect an audience. Through them, Minnie and Uncle Al were hooked on the world of show business, as was, to a lesser extent, Aunt Hannah, who had a beautiful soprano voice. Omie died soon after this picture was taken. I remember we were having a pillow fight in our room when she died. The brothers all slept in a double bed, two at each end. Opie would live to the age of 101, dying in 1919. He was still ice skating in Central Park at the age of eighty. Sam's side of the family also had some long livers. (Their kidneys were of the conventional shape.) His aunts, Fratschie and Frietschie, were the oldest twins in Alsace-Lorraine, and they died on the same day at the age of 102.

Going back to my bedside manner, I just remembered something—when I learned my limitations in regard to the so-called weaker sex. I was eight. Across the street from us lived a seven-and-a-half-year-old confection named Rosie Block. She wouldn't give me the time of day. Naturally, I was in love with her. One summer she went off to Europe. For weeks I awaited her return, wearing a red rose in my buttonhole which I planned to whip off and give to her as a welcome-home gesture. I imagined that we would have these extensive conversations, comparing notes about our travels. You'll re-member I'd been to Europe at the age of five. Finally, Rosie returned to her house on 93rd Street. Through great maneuvering on my part, I just happened to be walking by her front door when she came out. I took the rose from my lapel. Rosie, as expected, *did* give me the time of day. "If you don't get off my sidewalk by ten-thirty—which is two minutes from now—I'm going to call the police." Perhaps it was just as well. Here she'd been on the Grand Tour, visiting all the great European capitals, I'd been told, and my sole layover had been the not-so-cosmopolitan town of Dornum. (You could call that the Minnie-tour.)

12 I was nine years old and Harpo almost eleven when this picture (p. 4) was taken on the stoop of our apartment house on East 93rd Street. On the other side of the street were more imposing single-family buildings. Rosie Block lived in one of them. Next to her lived a man named Erich Weiss. He was in show business, and went by the stage name of Harry Houdini. Marie Wagner, a champion tennis player, lived in another house. It was a melting-pot neighborhood of Italians and Germans, not like the ghettoes of the Lower East Side where Mother worked trimming straw hats. All around me was a better world: Uncle Al and his fabulous life, the well-off people across the street, the characters in the books I read. Chico, who would soon be working as a lifeguard at Far Rockaway, would bring home dime novels every week, and I'd voraciously read them. I'd read the same Horatio Alger story every week, though the hero always had a different name. He would rescue the rich man's daughter, and be given a job that would start him on the road to fame and riches. I particularly empathized with Julius, the Street Sweeper. In school, I'd already started reading about the great Disraeli, and if he could become a Jewish Prime Minister, what was to stop me from becoming the first Jewish President?

I had to leave school in the seventh grade—nobody, after all, should stay in school after the age of twenty-two—but I would regard Yale as my alma mater. As a youngster I feverishly followed the career of Frank Merriwell, the dime-novel hero, at Yale. In these stories he was pictured as a combination of Jim Thorpe, Paul Bunyan and Hercules. Intellectually, he was a bust. The only Homer he ever heard of was the victorious one he inevitably hit

10

11

14

13

in the ninth inning, usually with the bases loaded. He was a one-man football team. No matter what the game—hockey, rowing, track—it made no difference; he always emerged victorious. Oddly enough, he never emerged from Yale. I followed the Frank Merriwell stories for many years. Scholastically, he never seemed to make progress. Other students graduated and went on to become lawyers, scientists, doctors of philosophy, even college presidents. Merriwell apparently was a borderline idiot. For all I know, this cretin is still up at New Haven, at the age of ninety-eight, batting out homers, running the length of the field.

13 This was Minnie, around the turn of the century. Through her and Uncle Al, I was in turn developing a love for the stage. I'd go see Uncle Al when he was on the bill at Proctor's. On rare occasions, I would save enough money to go to the Hippodrome, with its big ice shows. The Palace Theatre, of course, was the ultimate. It was the big time, and yet the audience was the most common. They would throw programs at the inferior acts. (Who could afford to throw tomatoes?) I had crushes on all the actresses. One I remember was Kitty Gordon, who had the most famous back in show business. She would sing songs or do dramatic readings. Sometimes the audience would fall asleep. Then she'd wake them up by showing them her naked back. Once while she was reciting a poem, even she fell asleep.

However, there wasn't enough money to see many of the great stars of the day. The first money I ever made was at school. There was a handsome teacher, a tall Irishman named O'Reagan, and all the girls were crazy about him. He said that if I'd get his lunch for him every day, he would give me a lump sum at the end of the school year. So every day I delivered his lunch to him. I was hoping to get ten dollars, but it was a much smaller lump than I'd expected—one dollar. The coffeepot at home leaked, so I bought Minnie a new one with the money.

The first real job I ever got was on Coney Island. I sang a song on a beer keg and made a dollar. Later I sang in a Protestant church choir—until they found out what was wrong with it. For that I got a dollar every Sunday. Before long I had to get a full-time job and leave school. There wasn't enough money to feed five brothers, parents, grandparents, Cousin Polly, Aunt Hannah and Uncle Julius. That's when I got into the big money, making $3.50 a week at the Hepner Wig Company. I lugged the big cans in which the wigs were washed. I'd been promised that someday, after I'd worked my way up, I'd be able to comb the wigs and put them on some famous actress's head. On my way home after my first day at work, the smells of the three breweries in our neighborhood melding into one, I knew this wasn't the High Life I was looking for.

14 I would say the fellow on the left is Harpo, but I'd be lying. I don't remember who it is, but I do recall the day of my bar mitzvah. Opie had paid five dollars for the speech I recited. The same speech had been handed down from Chico and Harpo. So had the suit. They were pretty words:

My dear parents, for thirteen long years you have labored for my happiness; from the time I first saw the light of day you have watched over me . . .

That's all I can remember of the speech now.

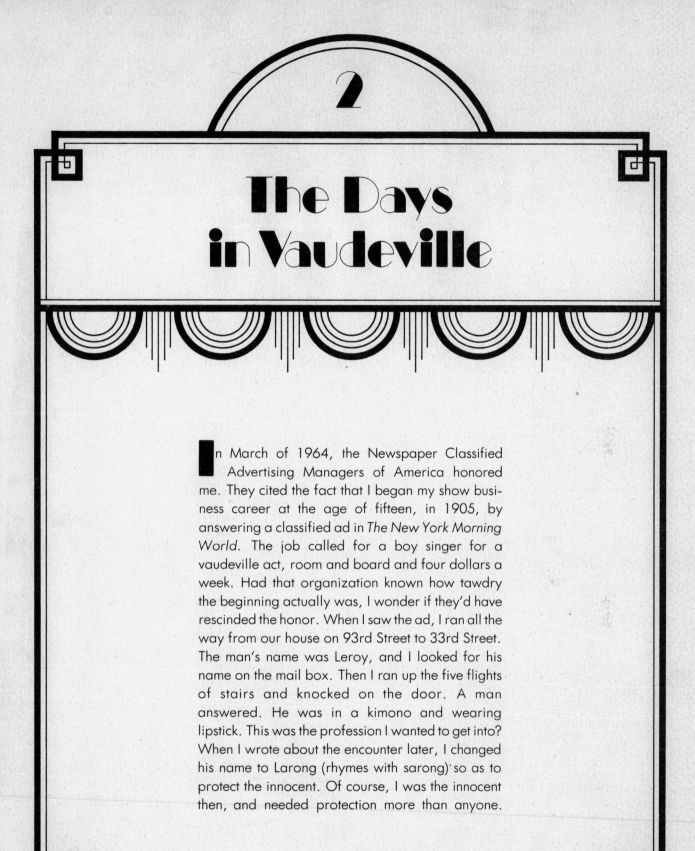

2

The Days in Vaudeville

In March of 1964, the Newspaper Classified Advertising Managers of America honored me. They cited the fact that I began my show business career at the age of fifteen, in 1905, by answering a classified ad in *The New York Morning World*. The job called for a boy singer for a vaudeville act, room and board and four dollars a week. Had that organization known how tawdry the beginning actually was, I wonder if they'd have rescinded the honor. When I saw the ad, I ran all the way from our house on 93rd Street to 33rd Street. The man's name was Leroy, and I looked for his name on the mail box. Then I ran up the five flights of stairs and knocked on the door. A man answered. He was in a kimono and wearing lipstick. This was the profession I wanted to get into? When I wrote about the encounter later, I changed his name to Larong (rhymes with sarong) so as to protect the innocent. Of course, I was the innocent then, and needed protection more than anyone.

Robin Larong (for that was the name of the gent in the weather-beaten kimono) finally appeared. In a voice considerably higher than that of the average man, he announced that he had signed up for a distinguished vaudeville tour and needed a good boy singer and a boy who could dance. Luckily, there were only three singers in the crowd. The rest were hoofers of varying ability. From the dancers he picked a tough East Side kid named Johnny Morton. After I sang "Love Me and the World Is Mine," he smiled toward me, and pointing an imperious finger at the rest, he shrilled, "Get out!"

I was fifteen at the time, and knew as much about the world as the average retarded eight year old. I asked, "Where are we going, Mr. Larong? And when do we start?" He replied that we would open in Grand Rapids and then go on to Denver. He didn't mention any other cities, and I didn't question him. He had said he had a distinguished vaudeville tour lined up, and as far as I was aware, two weeks constituted a tour. All I knew was, I was in show business! The theatre was calling me, and I was ready to listen.

I was a little nervous as to how the announcement of my departure would be received at home. I had visualized a family group, bent with sorrow, or if not quite bent, at least saddened by the thought of my leaving them. Not only was there no sorrow or recriminations, but my announcement seemed to galvanize them into a state of joy that I wasn't to witness again until some years later on Armistice Day. Had they been in the street, I'm sure there would have been dancing and hat throwing. A gay carnival spirit seemed to come over the whole family, and all they wanted to know was how soon I was clearing out. Furthermore, they implied that if I didn't come back, that was all right, too.

We rehearsed about two weeks. Since the boss, Larong, lived in one room of this tenement, we did our rehearsing on the roof. In the August sun, the tin roof under our feet felt like a red-hot stove, but we were young, enthusiastic and hungry, and, for the theatre, ready to endure anything.

When I said goodbye, my mother cried a little, but the rest of the family seemed able to contain themselves without too much effort. As a parting gesture, just as I was leaving, the dog bit me.

My luggage consisted of a paper suitcase and a shoe box filled with pumpernickel, bananas and hard-boiled eggs. Eggs must have been cheap that year, for I never saw so many in one box. Though I was only going as far as Grand Rapids, I had enough eggs to carry me all the way to Frisco.

From *Groucho and Me*

15 Here I am, the budding star, at fifteen, ready to go on the road with The Leroy Trio. I wore a fake celluloid collar, a fake tie and a fake carnation. The hair, however, was my own. Johnny Morris (not Morton) was the buck dancer in the troupe. Buck dancers are known as tap dancers today. We took the train to Grand Rapids. "Where do I sleep?" I asked Leroy. "You sleep where you're sitting," he said. It was a day coach. The show opened with four colored performers dressed as Chinamen,

which he called the Whangdoodle Four. I wore a sweater that said The Leroy Trio. Later I wore a fake altar boy's outfit as I sang a song called "The Palms" . . . "la-la-la Jerusalem . . . Jerusalem . . . lift up your gates and sing to the highest of the high." Then Leroy would come out dressed in a short skirt and high-heeled shoes and sing, "I wonder what's the matter with the mail, it never was so late before . . . I've been up since seven bells and nothing's slipped under my door." Finally, Morris did a tap dance.

When we opened in Grand Rapids, Morris was doing his tap dance, and one of his shoes flew off and hit somebody in the audience. Instead of getting sixty dollars for the act, the management fined us twenty dollars and all we got was forty dollars. We moved on to Cripple Creek. I should have noticed that Leroy and Johnny Morris were getting pretty thick, but I didn't. Shortly after we arrived in Colorado, Leroy eloped with Morris, leaving me stranded. Luckily, I'd put my eight dollars in savings in a grouch bag under my pillow, so I'd have money to tide me over until I got money from home. (A grouch bag was made of chamois with a leather drawstring, and most actors of the time carried them. Contrary to opinions in some quarters, that's not how I got my name. If such were the case, there'd be ten thousand Grouchos instead of the one, the only.) The money was gone. I had to get a job delivering groceries on a wagon from Cripple Creek to Victor.

16 Beautiful downtown Victor.

FAREWELL KILLARNEY

EDWARD MADDEN WROTE "BLUE BELL" "I'VE A FEELING FOR YOU" "COLLEEN BAWN" ETC.

GUS EDWARDS WROTE "SCHOOL DAYS" "SUNBONNET SUE" "TAMMANY" "IF A GIRL LIKE YOU LOVED A BOY LIKE ME" "I'LL DO ANYTHING IN THE WORLD FOR YOU" "I JUST CAN'T MAKE MY EYES BEHAVE" AND A 100 OTHERS.

LYRIC BY EDWARD MADDEN

MUSIC BY GUS EDWARDS

PUBLISHED BY GUS EDWARDS MUSIC PUB. CO.

¹⁷ Back in New York, I then got a job with the Gus
Edwards show, *Boys and Girls.* My picture was on
the sheet music for "Farewell, Killarney." Edwards,
a clever man, thought my present sixteen years
weren't callow enough, so he put a picture of me
when I was ten or eleven on the sheet music. Working for Edwards was a great experience. There
would be some very famous men coming out of his
later troupes: Walter Winchell, George Jessel,
Eddie Cantor, Harry Ruby. Edwards wrote "School
Days" and "I'll Do Anything in the World for You."
His brother Leo, who was a very fat man, accompanied the troupe on the piano. The highlight of my
stay with Edwards was the benefit at the Metropoli-
tan Opera for the victims of the San Francisco
earthquake. I went on the stage with a seventy-piece
orchestra and sang "Somebody's Sweetheart I
Want to Be." There were several people getting
their starts in show business in those days. A fat
blonde girl, billed as "The Refined Coon Singer,"
was building a reputation. Her name was Sophie
Tucker. Dancing in a touring musical burlesque
show was a funny kid named Fanny Brice. A young
fellow I'd seen around town was getting established
in the vaudeville team of Whipple and Huston.
Within a few years, he would be known the world
over as one of America's most distinguished
actors—Walter Huston. A mistrial had been declared that year in Harry K. Thaw's murder trial,
and Evelyn Nesbit, the woman whose honor had
been sullied by Stanford White, the murdered man,
went into vaudeville, doing a ragtime act with a
partner. We appeared on the same bill. A New
York newspaper commented, "Miss Nesbit protested her husband's innocence by kicking over her
dancing partner's head."

¹⁸ Much had happened by the time the Four Nightin-
gales came into existence. Here I am at top, with
Harpo, Gummo and Lou Levy in descending order.
After my run with Gus Edwards, I went on tour with
a dramatic troupe, eight weeks on the Interstate
Circuit from Norfolk to New Orleans. I was left
stranded in New Orleans when the leading lady
who'd hired me, Lily Seville, as beautiful as she was
untalented, eloped with an animal trainer in the
show. Again my money was stolen. I was determined then and there that the next elopement I
financed would be my own. I then joined a traveling

musical show in Philadelphia, working days as a song plugger. Minnie was upset when she discovered the "traveling musical show" was actually burlesque, but I assured her that despite the ladies in tights, burlesque was a legitimate medium. It became dirty, however, right before my eyes. During one show, a dancer came on with an American flag tied around her waist. The comedian leered and said, "There's been many a battle fought under that flag."

Home again, Minnie decided we brothers should stage our own act. Chico was successfully employed as a piano salesman at Shapiro and Bernstein. Harpo was working at a nickelodeon, a job he'd inherited from Chico. (He only knew two tunes: "Waltz Me Around Again, Willie" and "Love Me and the World Is Mine." These he would play at varying tempos to accompany the action on the screen.) Consequently, Gummo and I formed the basis of the act, with Lou Levy and Mabel O'Donnell being hired to fill out the complement of four. When Mabel left the act, Harpo stepped in. The Four Nightingales toured the country from 1907 to 1910. Because we were a kid act, we traveled at half-fare, despite the fact that we were all around twenty. Minnie insisted we were thirteen. "That kid of yours is in the dining car smoking a cigar," the conductor told her. "And another one is in the washroom shaving." Minnie shook her head sadly. "They grow so fast."

It was around this time that Minnie decided we should move to Chicago, which was more central to the small-time vaudeville circuits we were working. We bought a three-story brownstone house at 4512 Grand Boulevard. Opie moved West with us. We hired a colored cook, and Opie, then in his nineties, was constantly after her. He never caught her. We'd bought the house from a neighbor named Greenbaum, and Opie would watch as a chauffeur took Greenbaum's father out for afternoon drives. He hated the older Greenbaum. On the road, whenever we'd start cutting up on stage, Minnie would stage-whisper a warning from the wings: "Green-a-baum!" We knew what that meant: mortgage payments that had to be met. So we'd cut out the monkey business and go back to the prepared material.

19 Each of us had a motor scooter. Here I am on my Indian. We would travel from town to town, usually with a girl straddling the back. Harpo had a Harley-Davidson, and one day we had a race. We hit a mule. It didn't help the mule any. It was while we were touring that our singing act became intentionally funny. Harpo said in his autobiography that this happened in Ada, Oklahoma. I insist it was in Nacogdoches, Texas. Who's right? I am; I'm still living. Another mule disrupted the show, which was being held in an outdoor theater. We lost most of the audience, and when some of them straggled back, they heard some smart-ass remarks that they took to be funny. We thought we were talking over their heads, but the audience laughed, and a new era began for the Marx Brothers plus Lou.

20 While in New Orleans working on the Orpheum Circuit, I was looking for a girl—any girl. The cigar was a permanent adjunct by now. I started smoking as soon as I went on the stage. I'd made cigars out of the Morning World when I was a kid. Eventually I smoked Havanas. A cigar makers' organization once said that I was the most famous cigar smoker in the world. I don't know if that's true, but once while visiting Havana, I went to a cigar factory. There were four hundred people there rolling cigars, and when they saw me, they all stood up and applauded.

21 Gummo, me, Harpo and Uncle Julius, whom we called "The General" (p. 12). He was well over four feet. Uncle Julius was our manager for a while. I was his namesake, and his sole heir when he died. Sam and Minnie thought he had money, but his estate, when probated, consisted of a nine ball stolen from a poolroom, a box of liver pills and a celluloid dickey.

22 Schoolroom routines were very popular around 1910, and Gus Edwards certainly must have been an influence on them, as he was on us. Fun in Hi Skule was the name of our show. I played Mr. Green, the German schoolteacher. (That's me in the center.) The frock coat was borrowed from Uncle Julius, and the German accent—the most readily accessible—was borrowed from Opie. Gummo (top left) played a young Hebrew boy; Paul Yale (top center) played the nance; and Harpo played Patsy Brannigan, a standard character of the time. Lucille Textrude is the girl in the second row, at left. I

9

don't remember the girl on the right. That's Aunt Hannah on the floor. Once, when she and Minnie were part of our previous act, The Six Mascots, both of them sat on the same chair. The chair collapsed.

We Marx Brothers never denied our Jewishness. We simply didn't use it. We could have safely fallen back on the Yiddish theater, making secure careers for ourselves. But our act was designed from the start to have a broad appeal. If, because of Chico, a segment of the audience thought we were Italian, let them. Then they could admire my proficiency with a German accent, and wonder how the map of Ireland could be printed on the face of the boy with the red wig who played Patsy Brannigan. Later, of course, Harpo would use a blond wig in pictures. Red wigs photographed dark in black and white films.

For this show, we bought our first piece of special material, a song called "Peasie Weasie," for which we paid twenty-seven dollars. A standard device in vaudeville and burlesque was the singing of doggerel verses that allowed the performers to milk the audiences for laughs. Charlie Van, partner with Fannie Van in a vaudeville team of the time, wrote the song.

Verse:
My mother called Sister downstairs the other day.
"I'm taking a bath," my sister did say.
"Well, slip on something quick; here comes Mr. Brown."
She slipped on the top step and then came down.

Chorus:
Peasie Weasie, that's his name.
Peasie Weasie, Peasie Weasie, what's his game?
He will catch you if he can,
Peasie Weasie, Peasie Weasie is a bold, bad man.

Verse:
A humpback went to see a football game,
The game was called on account of the rain.
The humpback asked the halfback for his quarter back,
And the fullback kicked the hump off the humpback's back.

Additional Verse:
Went fishing last Sunday and caught a smelt.
Put him in the fire and the fire he felt.
Of all the smelts I ever smelt,
I never smelt a smelt like that smelt smelt.

25

24

24 A scene from *Fun in Hi Skule*. The girl standing at center is Dorothy, Paul Yale's wife. I was twenty-one, but as Mr. Green, I was made up to look like seventy. Chico had joined the act by this time; he stands at back by the blackboard. The Harris Brothers, tap dancers, sit at rear right. Pointing his finger in ridicule is Harpo. Seated at far right are Paul Yale and Gummo.

25 This is perhaps the first picture of Harpo throwing the "Gookie." The expression is one he copied from a cigar roller on Lexington Avenue, whose name, appropriately enough, was Gookie. Harpo was to use that expression at least once in every show. In the usual order are Chico, myself and Gummo. Gummo, by the way, sang a song, "Yiddle on Your Fiddle, Play Some Ragtime." With material like that, I don't understand why he didn't stay in show business.

26 *Fun in Hi Skule* had played the provinces and back by the time the whole family was able to get together again. Harpo, Chico, Sam, Zeppo, Minnie, Gummo and myself. Zeppo was about thirteen years old at the time.

[29] Myself, Chico, Harpo and Gummo. If we didn't as yet have transcendent talents, we *did* have hair.

[27] When Mother began organizing and booking musical tabloids, she took the name of Minnie Palmer. There was method to her method. There was another Minnie Palmer, a vaudeville star who was as petite as Mother was ample. Perhaps Mother saw herself in the same blonde and lovely light. At any rate, any confusion about the two couldn't hurt. Mother thought borrowing the name would give her own enterprise added prestige.

27

MINNIE PALMER
Chicago's Only Lady Producer Presents
4 MARX BROTHERS & COMPANY
with
GEORGE LEE and PAUL YALE
INCLUDING A CAST OF 19 PEOPLE

This company is breaking all records on the Western Vaudeville Managers Association circuit

MISS PALMER ALSO PRESENTS THE FOLLOWING SUCCESSES
"Six American Beauties," "Golden Gate Girls" and "After Twelve O'clock"

29

28 The real Minnie Palmer.

Home Again

ZEPPO: The garbage man is here.
GROUCHO: Tell him we don't want any.

30

30 In 1914 Uncle Al was on his own, and this might have been the luckiest break for the Marx Brothers. The Manhattan Comedy Four had disbanded in 1900, as did *Crovadis Upside Down* a few years later. In 1910 Uncle Al met and teamed up with Eddie Gallagher. They became huge vaudeville stars in a very short time. But they had a fight and split up, giving Uncle Al the opportunity to write *Home Again* for us. The show evolved from *Mr. Green's Reception*. The musical second half remained, but the schoolroom sequence was replaced by a scene on the docks. Uncle Al discovered that his script gave Harpo only three lines. (Harpo wasn't known for being articulate.) When he realized what he'd done, Uncle Al rationalized it by saying that from now on Harpo should remain silent and perform in pantomime. It was in this show that Harpo first used the silverware-dropping routine, which was done at my suggestion. The way it was first used, Harpo was shaking the detective's hand, obviously innocent, not responsible for the missing silverware. The longer he shook hands, the more silverware dropped from his sleeve. He developed the piece of business until he had tons of knives and forks falling out of his sleeves. They would stop falling, and then I'd say, "I can't understand what's delaying the coffeepot." After a pause, the coffeepot also would tumble down.

31 A double exposure, showing me as my stage character, Mr. Green, and as Julius H. Marx, the man about town.

32 The male cast members of *Home Again*: Paul Yale, Chico, Harpo, myself, Gummo and Moe Lee. Moe was the singer of the group. He had a little piece of business that always got a laugh: he'd stick his chin out. Each of us was getting twenty-five dollars a week; Moe felt he deserved thirty. He didn't get it, and left the act. I don't think he ever worked in show business again.

33

FOUR MARX BROTHERS & CO.
Present
"HOME AGAIN"
Direction of Minnie Palmer
Written and Produced by Al Shean
PROGRAM IN ORDER OF THE APPEARANCE

7

Helen Jones .... Mildred Keefe
Mrs. Jones .... Marguerite La Ponte
Henry Jones .... Julius H. Marx
Harold Jones .... Milton Marx
Soubrette .... Betty Carre
Nondescript .... Arthur Marx

7

Tony Saroni .... Leonard Marx
Policeman .... Edward Metcalfe
Friends of Henry Jones ....
.................................Audrey Pherigo, Gene Maddox, Earle Smith, Mary Orth
1st Act—Scene—Cunard ship line, docks and piers.
2nd Act—Two weeks later. Mr. Henry Jones' villa on the Hudson.
MUSICAL NUMBERS
1st Act—Tenor Solo by Earle Smith and Chorus.
2nd Act—Villa on the Hudson, by Milton Marx and Chorus.
Harp Solo—Arthur Marx.
Dance—Milton Marx, Gene Maddox.
Piano Solo—Leonard Marx.
The Way to Waikiki—Ensemble.
Stage Carpenter, L. W. Burke

8

COMFORT & KING
In Coontown Divorcons
CAST
Alexander Rufus Henry Levy Bluefoot Moore...................Vaughan Comfort
Mr. Salamander Blue ....
Mrs. Salamander Blue ....John King

9

THE BOYARR CO.
Russian Singers and Dancers
"In a Scene at the Kremlin of Moscow"

Orpheum

NEXT WEEK

EMMA CARUS
and
LARRY COMER

Ben—BERNIE & BAKER—Phil
Syncopated Funsters

ADELAIDE BOOTHBY
in
"Novelty Songs and Travesty"
Chas. Everdean (at the piano)

"LOVE THY NEIGHBOR"
("ALTRUISM")
By Benjamin F. Glazer
Direction of Lewis & Gordon Producing Co., Inc.

SELMA BRAATZ
The Renowned Lady Juggler

CLAUDE M. ROODE & ESTELE FRANCE
Something New Upon the Slack Wire

ORPHEUM TRAVEL WEEKLY

ORPHEUM CONCERT ORCHESTRA

STAN STANLEY
The Bouncing Fellow
Assisted by His Relatives

Harris Bros. "SOME DANCERS"

LEONARD MARX, "1914 MODEL" PIANIST.

DEAN CORNWELL. COLONIAL

THE MARX BOYS AT THE COLONIAL—BY CARTOONIST DEAN CORNWELL.

GEORGE LEE, (IGNATZ) SHOWING THE AUDIENCE HIS "DETERMINATION"

ARTHUR MARX and HARP

DEAR TEACHER

MILTON MARX, HIDING FROM THE "PROF."

LL TEACHER

PAUL YALE, OH! TALCUM, RAH! RAH! RAH!

TWO REASONS WHY BOYS GO TO "HI-SCHOOL"

OH! HELLO TED!

THE ONE WITH THE DARK GREEN SASH.

35 For all I know, this is the slow boat to China, but it might have been the Staten Island ferry. In usual order are Harpo; Chico; Saba Shepard, a girl who made a splash singing "My Hero"; May Orth, who was stuck on me; two anonymous types; myself and Paul Yale.

36 The folklore about how the Marx Brothers got their names has more than a kernel of truth. The time was 1914, and we were playing a week in Galesburg, Illinois. We were sitting around backstage playing poker with a monologist named Art Fisher, and talk got around to how "Sherlocko the Monk," a popular comic strip of the time, had infected vaudeville with all sorts of Henpeckos and Tightwados and Nervos. Fisher took the cue. I was the moody one, so he called me Groucho. The harp player would be known as Harpo. The fellow who wore the gumshoes would be known as Gummo. And the one constantly chasing the pretty chicks would be called Chicko. We didn't think much of the idea at first, but it caught on. The "k" in Leonard's new name was accidentally dropped by a typesetter, and it became Chico. Of the four, I was the only one whose name had actually appeared in the strip. Groucho was introduced in this sequence, published on December 22, 1910, and the character continued appearing in the strip until the early 1950s, long after "Sherlocko the Monk" evolved into "Hawkshaw the Detective."

In May of 1915, we were playing Shea's Toronto. Word came that the Lusitania had been sunk by the Germans, and a wave of anti-German feeling swept the Western world. We'd gone into a local restaurant and ordered German-fried potatoes. "Home fried," the waiter corrected. The name of sauerkraut, we also discovered, was now "cut cabbage." Here I was, about to go on doing my German schoolteacher act. And in the show was a German version of "Everybody Works but Father," which I would sing:

Alles schafft aber nicht Vater
Er geht den ganzen Tag herum
Und raucht die verdammte Pfeiffe,
Das Alles geht der Welt rum
Und Mutter "nimmt in washing,"
Und auch die Schwester Ann
Alle arbeiten in unserem Platz
Aber nicht der alte Mann.

Hurried measures had to be taken. Mr. Green suddenly turned Yiddish. Instead of the German song, I sang a tune with a Yiddish intonation:

It's better to run to Toronto,
Than to live in a place you don't want to . . .

The act went over with a dull thud. But that had happened before. One critic in another city had

written, "The Marx Brothers in *Home Again* should be." Percy Hammond, the Chicago critic, wrote, "The Marx Brothers and their various relatives ran around the stage for almost an hour yesterday afternoon. Why, I'll never understand." Nevertheless, we were learning. Call it a trade, call it a craft, and if you're especially kind, call it an art.

There is no formula for comedy. There's only practice, and more practice. My brothers and I worked in vaudeville for many years. We started in Small Time, which meant we performed four shows a day for five days, and five shows a day on Saturday and Sunday. We played split weeks in two cities, which means we moved from one city to another in the middle of the week.

For example, we played three days in Burlington, Iowa, caught the train overnight and played the following four days in Waterloo. This was very hard work: four-a-day for five days equals twenty shows; five-a-day for two days equals ten more shows, for a total of thirty shows per week. In this case we played twelve shows in Burlington and eighteen shows in Waterloo.

Why, outside the necessity of sheer survival, did we do this? We all wanted to be the best, the most perfect, the most flawless, the funniest that we could possibly be. Nobody else could be funny for you. You've got to be funny yourself.

There didn't seem to be the compulsion then for one comic to top the other. We did not want to take from some person or be better than him. Who can possibly be the judge of that? The judgment is the laughter that comes from the audience. We wanted to know we were good, and funny, within ourselves.

We were all constantly striving to improve ourselves, to get more laughs from the audience. We (and by that I mean my brothers, as well as Jack Benny, George Burns, Phil Harris, Frank Fay, and many others who were cohorts in those days) tried to help each other. It was a very good way to live.

There was no television in those days, and only the big cities had silent-movie houses. So, entertainment was live on stage. This is the reason why there were so many shows a day, and why we of that era had a built-in advantage in perfecting our craft, which entertainers of today do not.

We learned the importance of delivery. One cannot pull phrases at random, and sling them together in a sloppy manner with no consideration as to style. The suspenseful building of the structure toward the punch line will, I hope, make the audience respond with laughter. These phrases must be carefully chosen and planned in order to gain the audience's response. It takes many years on the stage, in front of a live audience, to learn this art, to learn how to deliver those carefully chosen words in the most casual, artless way. Finally, if you are dedicated enough, you learn, subconsciously, HOW TO TELL A STORY.

From *The Secret Word Is Groucho*

37-40 A program for the Orpheum Circuit. On the bill was a comic violinist named Ben K. Benny. We'd played with him often in the past. Back in 1909, while playing in Chicago, Minnie tried to recruit the boy, whose real name was Benny Kubelsky, for our act. But he was only sixteen, and his mother felt he was too young to travel. Not too many years later, as Jack Benny, he went very far.

We learned some valuable lessons on those vaudeville circuits. We quickly became aware that Gus Sun of the Sun Circuit would book ten acts and cancel five of them after the opening. We didn't have Actors Equity to protect us then. Shelton Brooks, who was to compose "Some of These Days" and "Darktown Strutters' Ball," didn't have the NAACP in his corner either. He was a handsome, light-colored Negro playing with us in Canton, Ohio. Near the hotel where we were staying was a big lake. Brooks wasn't allowed to use it.

We became friendly with many great stars of the day. Once, while playing the Keith Circuit in Baltimore, we got involved in a sandlot ball game. Will Rogers was playing second base for the opposing team. I'd hit the ball and was on my way to second, thinking I could run my scratch hit into a cheap double. Rogers was standing twenty feet in front of me. He caught the ball that was thrown to him from short left field and spun around. "You're out!" he called to me.

"How can I be out?" I called back. "You have to touch the base, and you're standing twenty feet away."

Rogers answered, "Groucho, when you get to be my age, wherever you stand is second base."

We were on the bill with Fanny Brice, along with Swayne's Rats and Cats. This animal act was quite novel. A miniature race track would be set up on stage. The rats would be dressed in jockey outfits, and ride around the track on the cats' backs. One day, while we were doing our act, a scream came from Fanny's dressing room. When we got there we found her standing on a chair. Swayne came in and saw a rat by the door. This wasn't a rat from his act. It probably had come up from the sewer. The next year, the rat was the star of the show. Fanny, by the way, had great style. She's the only person I ever knew to have three sets of false teeth: one for show, one to eat with, and a spare.

NEWS AND PROGRAM

Published in the interest of our Patrons

Next Week's Novelties

Among Theatrical Families, The Four Marx, who come to the Orpheum next week, are unique, for their's is the only case on record where four brothers have adopted the stage, pooled their talents and are appearing continually together. These four young men are unusually capable performers and have together built a musical comedy which supplies each of them with an excellent vehicle for the exploiting of his particular ability. The name of their offering is "N' Everything" and it tells of a newly rich family who try to break into society and their ludicrous attempts to achieve this ambition furnish great fun. The Marx Brothers introduce a variety of amusements, indeed it is hard to find a theatrical accomplishment they do not excel in that is not incorporated in their performance.

Sarah Padden, whose triumphs in "The Clod" and "The Eternal Barrier" are fresh in the public memory, is always assured of a cordial welcome in this city. She is an artist in the truest sense of the word, who never fails to "hold the mirror up to nature." Her new offering is entitled "Betty Behave," and its author is Tom Barry, who also wrote "The Eternal Barrier." She is supported by a specially selected company.

Ben K. Benny is versatile, talented and amusing. He is really an excellent violinist though he chiefly devotes his attention to popular music. He is also an enjoyable comedian whose monologue is original and highly diverting.

Dan Mahoney and George Auburn will entertain with a novel specialty, which consists of the rapid manipulation of Indian clubs, accompanied by bright and witty "patter."

Basil Lynn and Howland indulge in a racey conversation which is highly amusing. Both men are capital comedians and agreeable contrasts to each other.

Bostock's Riding School and Miss Billie Shaw & Co. in her Dance Drama will also be included in the new bill.

The Alexander Kids are a trio of juveniles who have won success in both America and England. They are indeed prodigies whose natural talents have been carefully developed and there are probably nowhere three more capable children.

FOUR MARX BROTHERS
Next Week at the Orpheum

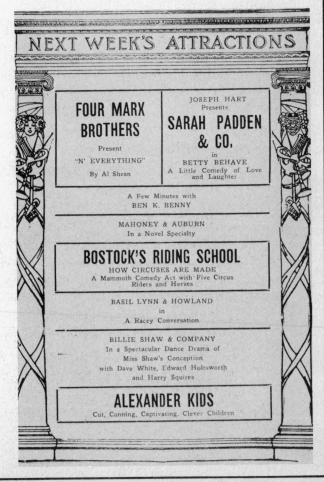

NEXT WEEK'S ATTRACTIONS

FOUR MARX BROTHERS
Present
"N' EVERYTHING"
By Al Shean

JOSEPH HART
Presents
SARAH PADDEN & CO.
in
BETTY BEHAVE
A Little Comedy of Love and Laughter

A Few Minutes with
BEN K. BENNY

MAHONEY & AUBURN
In a Novel Specialty

BOSTOCK'S RIDING SCHOOL
HOW CIRCUSES ARE MADE
A Mammoth Comedy Act with Five Circus
Riders and Horses

BASIL LYNN & HOWLAND
in
A Racey Conversation

BILLIE SHAW & COMPANY
In a Spectacular Dance Drama of
Miss Shaw's Conception
with Dave White, Edward Holtsworth
and Harry Squires

ALEXANDER KIDS
Cut, Cunning, Captivating, Clever Children

41

We met everybody in vaudeville, and we played before everybody too. Once we played for President Coolidge in Washington. He was a tough nut to crack. In fact, he only laughed once. I looked out into the audience and asked, "Where's Senator Borah?"

In Chicago, I even got to know Carl Sandburg, who was then the critic for the *Daily News*. I went to the movies with him. He instructed me to wake him up ten minutes before the movie was over, but I was asleep too. That's how the term "sleeper" was coined to describe some pictures.

41 When the United States entered World War One, we decided to save the country by raising vegetables. We bought a farm in La Grange, twenty miles outside of Chicago. If there was any connection between the war effort and the feeding of crows, we surely did our part. We bought some chickens, but their eggs were eaten by rats. Next door to the farm was a golf course, and the only money we made was for retrieving stray golf balls that landed on our not-so-green acres. We'd sell them back for twenty-five cents. The first morning on the farm, we got up at five. The following morning, we dawdled

in bed until six. By the end of the week we were getting up at noon, which was just enough time for us to get dressed to catch the 1:07 to Wrigley Field, where the Chicago Cubs played. Those carefree times would soon change for Gummo, however: he got drafted. He entered the army and left the act— never to return—to be replaced by Zeppo, who had just finished high school.

42 Frenchy and Minnie, seen here around 1920, had seen their sons develop into the most prominent of vaudevillians. We were a good draw on whatever circuit we appeared on. Performing wasn't as arduous. In Big Time Vaudeville you only played two shows a day. For the first time in our careers, we knew what the good life meant. In an Oklahoma City hotel, we entered the dining room. When the waiter came, Harpo ran his finger down the menu, then said, "And coffee."

We were also doing well backstage. A pretty eighteen-year-old girl named Ruth Johnson was hired as Zeppo's dancing partner. She was blonde and blue-eyed and weighed 118 well-distributed pounds. We were married at Chicago City Hall, and had an overnight honeymoon on the pullman to Des Moines and points West. I was a blushing thirty.

43 The top of the ladder: the Marx Brothers at the Palace. We would go on to hold the record among big-time acts for having played sixty consecutive weeks in first-class vaudeville theaters in New York. We went straight from the Palace to the Fifth Avenue Theatre. One day, getting back late for an evening show, I didn't have time to apply my fake mustache, so I took some greasepaint and smeared it on my upper lip. The theater manager collared me later. "Don't pull those cheap tricks on me," he said. "You wore a regular mustache at the Palace, so you have to wear one here too." When I pointed out to him that the audience laughed just as hard, he consented to let me use the greasepaint mustache. I wore one from then on, no matter where we played.

Once while we were playing the Palace, Sarah Bernhardt was the headliner. It was widely publicized that she insisted on getting $1,000 in cash before each performance. By this time, she only had one leg. Imagine how much she could have made if she'd had two.

44 Gallagher and Shean must have been the original Sunshine Boys. The two hadn't spoken in six years. Finally, Minnie patched things up between them, and they teamed up again to become greater stars than they'd ever been. Their new act was called

"Mr. Gallagher and Mr. Shean in Egypt," and it opened at the Fox Crotona Theatre in Long Island in April of 1920. Within two years they would be starring in the *Ziegfeld Follies*. Bryan Foy wrote the lyrics and Uncle Al wrote the music for a new song in the show. It was the only song Uncle Al ever composed, and the words went like this:

There are two funny men, the best I've ever seen.
One is Mister Gallagher, the other Mister Shean.
When these two cronies meet, it surely is a treat,
The things they say and the things they do,
And the funny way they greet.

"Oh! Mister Gallagher!"
"Oh! Mister Shean!"
"Oh, Mister Gallagher, oh, Mister Gallagher."
"Hello, what's on your mind this morning, Mr. Shean?"
"Everybody's making fun of the way this country's run.
"All the papers say we'll soon live European."
"Why, Mister Shean, why, Mister Shean,
"On the day they took your old canteen
"Cost of living went so high
"That it's cheaper now to die."
"Positively, Mister Gallagher?"
"Absolutely, Mister Shean!"

While Gallagher and Shean were preparing to open in the *Follies*, the Marx Brothers were in England, having mounted, as the ads for the Coliseum Theatre at Charing Cross put it, a "musical revuette" called *On the Balcony*. It was a variation of *On the Mezzanine*, which we'd done at the Palace in New York. The show didn't go over well with the English audience. They started throwing pennies on the stage. "We've come a long way to entertain you," I told them. "The least you could do is throw silver." That brought one of the few laughs of the evening. The reviewers were surprisingly kind. According to an unsigned article in *The London Times*, shortly after we opened in June of 1922:

It is hard to differentiate among the Brothers, but a word of appreciation should be said in passing for the smart and resourceful gentleman who plays the Hebrew part; for the skilful pianist who can extract so much fun from his fingers; and for the speechless partner whose work on the harp is as good as anything of its kind we have yet had at the Coliseum.

In spite of the nice notices, we decided to revert to *Home Again*. The rest of the tour was a great success.

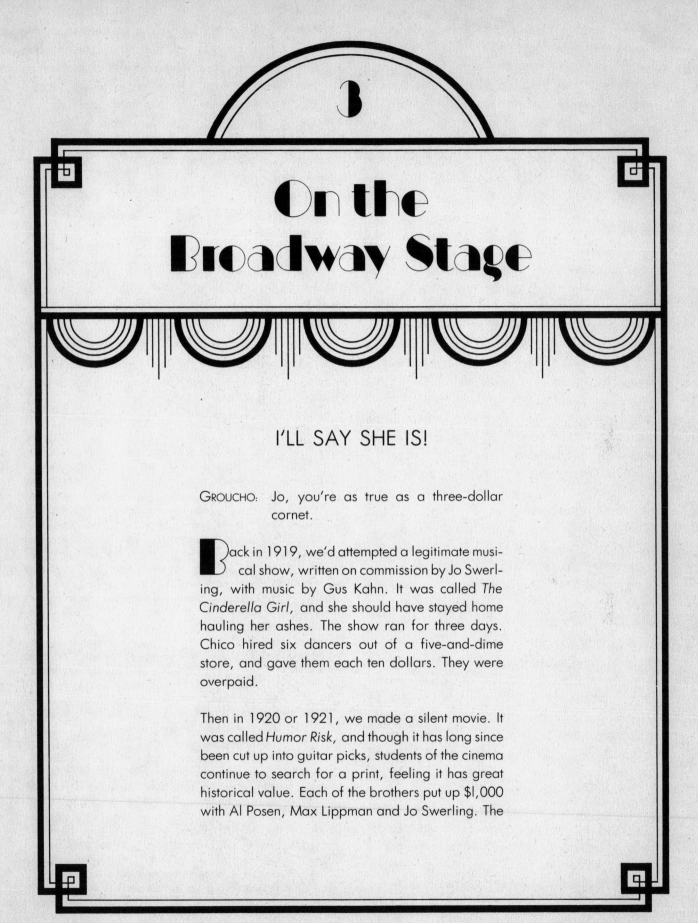

3

On the Broadway Stage

I'LL SAY SHE IS!

GROUCHO: Jo, you're as true as a three-dollar cornet.

Back in 1919, we'd attempted a legitimate musical show, written on commission by Jo Swerling, with music by Gus Kahn. It was called *The Cinderella Girl*, and she should have stayed home hauling her ashes. The show ran for three days. Chico hired six dancers out of a five-and-dime store, and gave them each ten dollars. They were overpaid.

Then in 1920 or 1921, we made a silent movie. It was called *Humor Risk*, and though it has long since been cut up into guitar picks, students of the cinema continue to search for a print, feeling it has great historical value. Each of the brothers put up $1,000 with Al Posen, Max Lippman and Jo Swerling. The movie was shot at Fort Lee, New Jersey, in a vacant lot near the vaudeville theater in which we were playing. Interiors were shot in a Tenth Avenue studio in New York. Harpo played Watson, the love interest. He made his entrance wearing a top hat, sliding down a coal chute into a cellar. Mildred Davis, who later married Harold Lloyd, was the leading lady. I played the villain, and the finale showed me in ball and chain, trudging off into the distance.

The only thing that can be said in our favor about these misadventures is that we were reaching out, trying to find new mediums and avenues of expressions—terms *artistes* know well.

James P. Beury was a coal-mine owner. He had an interest in a chorus girl. Harpo did too. Through some fast-talking on our part, Beury agreed to underwrite a musical revue, planning to play it out of town before bringing it into New York—providing the chorus girl got a featured spot. The show was a conglomeration of old gags and routines. Two productions—*Love for Sale* and *Give Me a Thrill*—were merged and formed the basis for the show. It had a silly plot line about a girl looking for a thrill and promising to marry the man who could supply it—other than the obvious one, that is. New skits were written by Will Johnstone, the cartoonist for *The New York Evening World*. The show was divided into twenty-four scenes. We got the title from a popular exchange of the day. "Isn't she a beauty?" "I'll say she is!"

45 Lotta Miles, who'd predictably starred in many print ads for automobile tires, was the beauty around whom the action revolved. She was not the chorus girl inamorata of Beury and/or Harpo. Surrounding her in a scene from the Napoleon sketch are Harpo, Chico, Zeppo and myself. We opened the show in Philadelphia in the early summer of 1923, and toured with it for almost a year.

46 Groucho, Zeppo, Chico, without makeup.

47 This picture was taken outside the Walnut Street Theatre. It reminds me of the time I bought a car in Philadelphia from a Frenchman. He called it a "stoo-duh-bay-kaire." The car was delivered to me during intermission. I took it out for a spin. The streets were very narrow around the theater, and I got caught in a traffic jam, with streetcars in front and in back of me. The second act would be starting any minute, so I chose to leave the car where it was. I got out of the car and ran to the theater—in my Napoleon suit. People on the street must have thought I was a nut. A cop chased me. When he caught up, I explained the situation. "I'm an actor," I told him.

"That doesn't give you the freedom to leave your car deserted on the street," he said. I gave him a couple of passes to see the show.

President Harding died while we were playing in Philadelphia. Before a hushed audience, rain pelting the tin roof of the theater, I made the announcement. Women in the audience cried. Strong men gasped. On another rainy day, Zeppo lost the sheep dog he'd brought back from our tour in England. The last time I saw Zeppo, he was still looking for him.

. . . a big musical will run into two or three hundred thousand dollars. However, if you know the right costumers and the right warehouse, you can buy an awful lot of stuff for twenty-five grand. We always had fun looking at the names on the back of the scenery that we finally bought for that show. It was a sort of scenic, theatrical Who's Who. There was hardly a show that had been on Broadway in the preceding twenty years that wasn't represented in this assortment of leftovers. There were pieces of scenery from *The Girl of the Golden West, The Squaw Man, Way Down East, Turn to the Right* and many others. If memory doesn't play me false, I'm sure we even had a piece of the river scene from *Uncle Tom's Cabin* where Liza crosses the ice.

The scenery didn't quite fit, and the score was probably the most undistinguished one that ever bruised the eardrums of a Broadway audience. The girls, like all chorus girls, looked pretty good. The rest of the cast was strictly amateur night in Dixie. What we *did* have, however, was something money couldn't buy. We had fifteen years of sure-fire comedy material, tried-and-true scenes that had been certified by vaudeville audiences from coast to coast.

We decided to call the show *I'll Say She Is!* (An expression that was considered pretty hot in those days. That same expression today would be "real cool," which should give you an idea of the progress civilization has made in the last thirty years.)

Unlike most of the big revues, we couldn't afford those tall showgirls dressed in a million dollars' worth of Mainbocher clothes, diamonds and furs. We didn't have that kind of money. This was a poverty-stricken revue, and we cheated all along the line. Boy, did we cut corners! We cut enough corners to build a whole new street. I don't know what they call them now, but in the twenties the little dancers were called "ponies." That's what we had. They were cheaper. They weren't too much on looks and they couldn't sing, but they could *dance*.

. . .The story of my mother on the opening night of *I'll Say She Is!* has been told many times. Having four sons open on Broadway in a successful show was the climax of her career. Like any other woman, she had ordered a new dress for the occasion. When I say "ordered," I don't mean she went to Bergdorf Goodman's. She sent to Brooklyn for her dressmaker. While standing on a chair, being fitted for the gown that was soon to dazzle the first-nighters, she slipped and broke her leg. I believe a disaster of this size would have discouraged most women from going to the theater, but not my mother. If anything, that made the opening night even more exciting. I doubt if anyone ever entered the theater more triumphantly than she did. Smiling and waving gaily to the audience, she was carried in on a stretcher and deposited in a front-row box seat.

This was her personal victory. This was the culmination of twenty years of scheming, starving, cajoling and scrambling. And I'm sure that, to her, that night was worth every minute of it. You'll have to concede that this was a most unusual occasion. Never in the history of the theater had four brothers appeared on Broadway as the stars of their own show, and a little thing like a broken leg was not going to rob her of that supreme moment.

From *Groucho and Me*

Because we were now part of the legitimate theater, we used our real names in the billing. Vaudeville audiences knew who we were. The opening scene of *I'll Say She Is!* had me on the stage with a straight man. It may have been Ed Metcalfe, who later appeared in *The Cocoanuts* and taught me to love Gilbert and Sullivan as much as he did. I said, "I played a part in *Ben Hur* once." He said, "What part did you play, sir?" My answer: "A girl. She played the part of Ben, and I played her." From that opening, each of the brothers went on to do an impersonation of Joe Frisco. The plot weaved through Chinese opium dens, serious ballet acts, a courtroom scene where Harpo was given the opportunity to drop his knives, and the finale, Napoleon and Josephine exchanging farewells before he went into battle. Johnstone and I wrote this scene together, and its reception was so enthusiastic that we became, after twenty years in the business, overnight stars. I played Napoleon; Gaston was played by Harpo; Chico was François; and Zeppo played Alphonse. The script for the sketch has been missing for thirty years. It miraculously turned up only recently—in one of my desk drawers.

Napoleon Scene

FOOTMAN: The Empress! (Empress walks downstairs L., followed by two pages. Everybody bows.) The Emperor! (Groucho bows)

NAPOLEON: As you were. (Everybody bows again) Begone, peasants! Take French leave! (Everybody exits) (Turns to footmen) As for you, take that bib off—we don't eat for an hour yet.

EMPRESS: Napoleon, did you hurt yourself? You told me you would be in Egypt tonight. You promised me the Pyramids and Sphinx.

NAPOLEON: That remains to be seen, but where are my faithful advisers, François, Alphonse and Gaston? Josephine, the whole thing Sphinx.

EMPRESS: Do you wish their advice?

NAPOLEON: Of course I do. They are always wrong. Let me think. (Business of posing with hand in coat and taking snuff) Ah! I love to sniff snuff.

EMPRESS: How often have I asked you not to use that horrible snuff?

NAPOLEON: Josephine, snuff.

FOOTMAN: Alphonse, First Gentleman-in-Waiting. (Passes Napoleon with outstretched arms to Empress)

ALPHONSE: Napoleon!

NAPOLEON: Alphonse!

FOOTMAN: Francois, Second Gentleman-in-Waiting.

FRANÇOIS: Napoleon! (Passes Napoleon with outstretched arms to Empress)

NAPOLEON: This devotion to me is touching, but it's not touching me. I must be quarantined—irritating—fills me with schmerkase.

FOOTMAN: Gaston, Third Gentleman-in-Waiting. (Heads straight for the Empress)

NAPOLEON: Well, they are all taking the detour. Over there, Gas! Emperor of the world, what is there left for me to conquer?

ALPHONSE: Go to the North Pole—Africa.

FRANÇOIS: Go to the end of the world.

NAPOLEON: What, Napoleon in Russia, and leave my Josephine alone with the Court?

EMPRESS: Napoleon, how can you doubt my love? (Business of everybody kissing Empress)

NAPOLEON: There is a lot of heavy lipping going on around here, but somehow or other I got shoved out of it. Forgive me, my Queen. I don't doubt your love. When I look into your big blue eyes, I know that you are true to the Army. I only hope it remains a standing Army. Fortunately France has no Navy, but then every man has qualms, even if they are only steamed qualms. Even an Emperor. (Business with hat)

EMPRESS: Ah! Ah! Napoleon.

NAPOLEON: But I must not tarry. I must be off. Josephine, if I leave you here with these three snakes—chiselers—I must be off. I must be off to make Russia safe for sinus trouble. To make Russia safe for the five-year plan. That's how I bought this furniture.

EMPRESS: Napoleon, when you go, all France is with you.

NAPOLEON: Yes, and the last time I came home all France was with you, and a slice of Italy too.

FRANÇOIS: He means me.

NAPOLEON: Oh, it's you.

EMPRESS: Napoleon, fight as you never fought before. Don't forget your flannels.

NAPOLEON: I shall not fire until I see the whites of their eggs, and you can lay to that. There's a good yolk. Josephine, when one wears flannels, one can't forget. Alphonse . . . François . . . well, it's still breathing. He took a crack at it. I'll leave my Josephine in your arms. My honor is safe.
              (Harpo does baseball slide onto dress)

FRANÇOIS
AND   Safe!
ALPHONSE:

NAPOLEON: If you are going to get on, I'm going to get off. Get me a reservation for tomorrow night. It is like a free lunch counter. Three jolly woodpeckers. Can you play . . . (To Gaston) Hey, wait until I'm through. Hereafter, gentlemen, the line forms on the right. Farewell, my Queen. Beyond the Alps lies more Alps, and the Lord 'Alps those that 'Alps themselves. Vive la France! (Music. Exit L.)

ALPHONSE: Darling, I'll be right back. (Exit L.)

FRANÇOIS: Josie, I'll be hump back or half back. (Exit L.)
              (Harpo business with Empress. Exit L.)

ALPHONSE: Josephine!

EMPRESS: Alphonse!

ALPHONSE: Why are you crying?

EMPRESS: I thought you were never coming.

ALPHONSE: I thought Napoleon was never going.

EMPRESS: Are you sure he has gone?

ALPHONSE: Yes, he just kissed me goodbye.

EMPRESS: Me, too.

ALPHONSE: Josephine! (Knock offstage)

EMPRESS: Alphonse! Hide! Someone is coming.
              (Napoleon peeps in)

NAPOLEON: Ten seconds I've been gone, and she is still vertical, and no one is here. Ah! She loves me. Isn't she beautiful? (Business of dancing)
              (Enter footman)

EMPRESS: Alfred, bring champagne.

NAPOLEON: Get me a bologna sandwich. Never mind the bologna. Never mind the bread. Just bring the check. Get me a wine brick.

EMPRESS: Oh! It's you. I thought you were at the front.

NAPOLEON: I was, but nobody answered the bell, so I came around here.

EMPRESS: Well, what are you looking for?

NAPOLEON: My sword—I lost my sword.

EMPRESS: There it is, dear, just where you left it.

NAPOLEON: How stupid of you. Why didn't you tell me? Look at that point. I wish you wouldn't open sardines with my sword. I am beginning to smell like a delicatessen. My Infantry is beginning to smell like the Cavalry. Farewell, my Queen, farewell. I'm going any minute now, farewell. It's ten cents a dance. I run on the hour and the half hour. Get a load of this footwork. Get me while I'm hot, Josie.

EMPRESS: Napoleon, remember, I expect you to return home victorious.

NAPOLEON: Our just is cause. We cannot lose. I am fighting for France, Liberty, and those three snakes hiding behind the curtain. Farewell, vis-a-vis Fifi D'Orsay. If my laundry comes, send it general delivery, care of Russia, and count it—I was a sock short last week. My brassiere was missing too. The last time I had to use my mashie and you might sew on a button hither and yon. Hither is not bad, but yon is terrible. Farewell, my Queen. Vive la France. (Music cue. Exit L.)

ALPHONSE: Josephine!
              (Knock offstage)

EMPRESS: Alphonse—hide.

FRANÇOIS: Josie, has he gone?

EMPRESS: Who?

FRANÇOIS: Anybody. Ah! Josie, you are so beautiful.

EMPRESS: Remember.

FRANÇOIS: But, Josie, I am just starting.

EMPRESS: But remember, I'm an Empress.

FRANÇOIS: Well, you don't Empress me very much. Why don't you marry me?

EMPRESS: What about Napoleon?

FRANÇOIS: I'll marry him too. He's got money. He's the guy I'm really after.

EMPRESS: Why, that's bigamy.

FRANÇOIS: Yes, and it's bigamy too.

EMPRESS: Please play. I love music.
              (François plays piano)
              (Knock on door—enter Napoleon)
              (François hides)

NAPOLEON: I passed a groundhog coming in here. Farewell, my Queen, farewell.

EMPRESS: Napoleon, now what's wrong?

NAPOLEON: I lost my sword. I had a swell chance to stab one of those Russians. It was right near the gates of Moscow. If I find my sword I Moscow and get him. He promised to wait, but you can't depend on those Greasers. He was a Russian Serf. It Serfs me right. I'm sorry now Lincoln freed the Serfs, if that's the way they're going to act. I am getting disgusted with the whole war. If it rains tomorrow, I think I'll stay in bed. What are your plans, babe? The only thing that keeps me going is your devotion; it keeps me coming back too, I guess. It's women like you that make men like me like women like you. I guess I said something that time. Jo, you're as true as a three-dollar cornet, and believe me, that's nothing to blow about, and if you don't like it, you can trumpet. Where's my sword? Without my sword I'm a second lieutenant—letter carrier. I'm always holding the bag. I'll be an elevator starter by the time you get through with me. Ah! There's my sword. I wish you wouldn't open sardines with my sword. Oh, no, we had that, didn't we? Looks like I'm off again. The Russians are in full retreat, and I'm right in front of them.

EMPRESS: Ah! Darling, when you're away at night, I do nothing but toss and turn.

NAPOLEON: I don't mind the turning, but cut out the tossing. There has been a lot of talk about that lately. Farewell, my Queen. Caesar had his Brutus, Charles the First his Cromwell, and I've got rhythm—last two weeks in August. (Music cue—Exit L.)

EMPRESS: Gaston! I thought you were never coming. Won't you please play for me? (Harpo plays the piano. Knock is heard—Harpo sits on couch—Empress sits on Harpo's lap to hide him—Napoleon enters)

NAPOLEON: Farewell, my Queen, farewell. One last kiss before I go. (Kneels and kisses Harpo's hand which is around Empress's waist)
My left flank has been turned—my rear end has been cut off, but I'll fight it out. Have you been ploughing? Josephine, have you been hanging around a livery stable? I can't figure it out, as great as I am, I can't figure it out. (Business)
One half of you are getting awfully fresh—certainly having a good time. (Harpo puts finger to Empress's nose) Any answer I give you would seem disrespectful.

EMPRESS: Napoleon, dear, I thought you had gone away. (More business with hands on couch)

NAPOLEON: I guess that's what Studebaker means by free feeling. I was detained. My horse overslept. My horse had his valves ground. When a fella needs a friend. I lost my sword and rubbers. I was in the midst of furious fighting. (More business with hands on couch)
You're going to need a lot of money for gloves this winter. You have more hands than a pinochle deck.

EMPRESS: Napoleon, that's a wonderful uniform you are wearing. (More business on couch)

NAPOLEON: Josephine, you haven't got my horse under there, have you? Have you shifted your ballast, or is it my astigmatism? Where's my sword? (Harpo and Empress point)

NAPOLEON: Josephine, were there three swords? There seems to be a difference of opinion. Ah! There's my sword. (More business on couch)
Come on, the whole three of you. Where are my rubbers?

EMPRESS: Here they are. (Harpo puts feet out from under Empress's dress)

NAPOLEON: Are those your feet? Maybe you better go to war and I'll stay here. You're getting an awful pair of gondolas, Josephine. They must have crossed you with an elephant. You are getting an awful pair of dogs, Josie. Oh! You are breaking them in for me? I wish you wouldn't wear them around the house. You know what happened to Empress Catherine of Russia. Well, she was headstrong and footstrong too, and they had to send for the Court physician. (Business of putting on rubbers) Ah! Ah! Not tonight, Josephine. They certainly feel good, all right. I don't know who is wearing them, but they certainly feel good. (Cue for trumpet offstage) Josephine, what are they playing? That old Southern melody—The Marseillaise in the Cold Cold Ground— the Lucky Strike Hour. Vive la France. (Music—Exit L.)

(Napoleon returns)

NAPOLEON: I forgot to forget my sword.

EMPRESS: Oh, dear. I feel so faint. I must have music, sweet music. The harp. (Empress rings bell. Footman enters.) Bring in the harp. (Harpo starts to play and Empress sings. Harpo stops and plays a few chords at the ends of phrases. After song, Harpo plays solo. At the end of solo, knock is heard.)

EMPRESS: Hide! Hide!

NAPOLEON: (From behind couch) Josephine, it's me, the head man.

EMPRESS: Not yet.

NAPOLEON: Not yet, what? Josephine, it's me.

EMPRESS: I can't see you.

NAPOLEON: You never could.

EMPRESS: Don't be so fresh.

NAPOLEON: I can't help it. I'm wrapped in cellophane.

EMPRESS: François, will you keep quiet? Do you want Alphonse to hear you?

NAPOLEON: Women! Don't try to wool the pull over my eyes. Women! Who's been here?

EMPRESS: I have.

NAPOLEON: Alone?

EMPRESS: Alone.

NAPOLEON: Remember, you can feel some of the people all of the time, some of the people all of the time, all of the—oh! the hell with that. I just made that up. Lincoln copped it from me. Someone has been here. Ah! He's a harp.

EMPRESS: 'Tis my harp, and I was practicing.

NAPOLEON: I don't want you practicing with a harp. That's why I built the English Channel. Deep stuff. Don't you think that your perfidiousness is apparent to me? Do you think you can stand there and make a schlemiel out of Napoleon? Do you think it's fun being Napoleon? How would you like to be Napoleon and stand like this for one hundred and fifty years—a hundred and sixty? Someone has been here. I'm going to investigate. I'll smoke out these Siberian jackrabbits. (Napoleon throws snuff)

EMPRESS: I love but you.

(Business of sneezing)

NAPOLEON: They say a man's home is his castle. Mine must be the Pennsylvania Station. Come out, come out, wherever you are.

EMPRESS: Napoleon, no one has been here, no one is here.

NAPOLEON: Why, if I thought there was I'd . . .

(Business of sneezing)

What was that—static?

EMPRESS: No, my hay fever.

(More sneezing)

NAPOLEON: How many statics have you got? Officer of the Guard, remove the swine.

(Business of soldiers pulling Groucho)

Hey! You've got the wrong swine. If it wasn't so muddy, I'd take off. Come out here, I know you. (To Harpo) Take that off. I know you. (Tries to

remove sword from sheath) Oh! I can't beat popular mechanics. (Harpo spits in sword holder) From Emperor to Cuspidor in two generations. So, my good Queen, while the Emperor has been winning victories on foreign fields, he has been losing on the home ground. So this is how you uphold the honor of the Bonapartes? Zounds on you, you Zanie. Zanes on you, you Zounie. Do you know what I'm going to do to you? Company fall in, right about face, forward march! (They exit)

EMPRESS: Napoleon, what are you going to do to them?
NAPOLEON: Look at them down there in the courtyard. The firing squad will soon give you my answer. (Business of Groucho doing a horse laugh)

                   (First shot offstage)
There goes Alphonse.
                 (Second shot offstage)
There goes François.
                 (Third shot offstage)
There goes Gaston.
       (After third shot, two soldiers run across stage in B.V.D.'s followed by Harpo)
       (Harpo fires two more shots onstage at soldiers)
       (Cue for curtain—Music cue)

48 A promotional sign for the show, using a photograph from the Napoleon scene.
49 Minnie was later photographed with us in the same pose.

We settled in for a long run. Over the years, Chico had insisted we were great talents, and that we belonged on Broadway. Many times, the thought sustained us when things looked bad. But now that his predictions had come true, he didn't say I told you so. He was too busy gambling and chasing girls.

When you're a genuine star, not so subtle differences come into play. Now it wasn't as hard as before to get into Franklin P. Adams's column. Harpo coined the title of a book I was reputed to have written (Nashes to Nashes and Stutz to Stutz), and soon it was being mentioned along with my

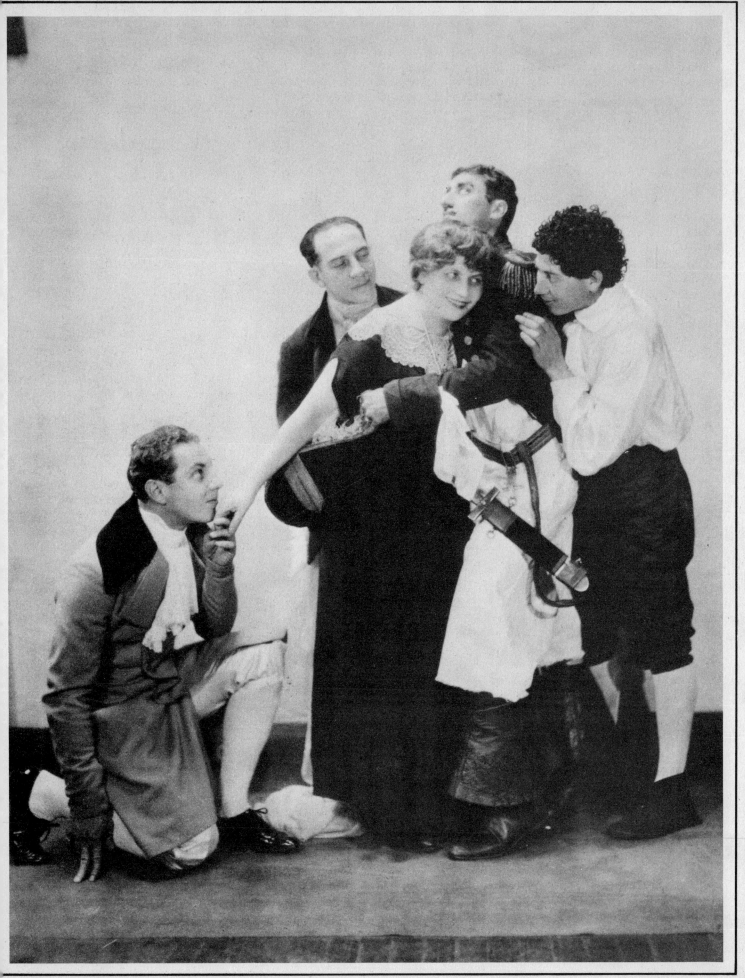

50-58 Overnight we were Broadway stars. The show opened May 19, 1924, at the Casino Theatre, and on May 20, we were the talk of the town.

Not long ago Mr. George S. Kaufman, an author of "Round the Town," complained that I had noted a physical similarity between him and Julius H. Marx, the least beautiful of the Marx brothers. Mr. Marx, an equally sensitive artist, now resents Mr. Kaufman's objections, and makes a few of his own. "Sir," he writes, "while in a subway car this morning I picked up a Herald Tribune off the floor. It might have been thrown there by Samuel Shipman, since it was folded right on your column. At any rate, it had an article by Mr. George S. Kaufman, in which he expressed himself as being greatly annoyed because you said that he looked like me.

"I have never seen Mr. Kaufman in the flesh, or the rough, or whatever they call it. I have seen a number of his plays, and I am not sure whether he has a mustache or not, although some authors find it advisable to wear something on the opening night.

"My make-up is a sort of hit-and-miss proposition, and when I start putting it on I am never sure who or what I will look like when I get through. Some nights I resemble one author, some nights I look like another, and it is purely a coincidence that basically I happen to look like Mr. Kaufman.

"If you can suggest any humorous get-up that wouldn't look like the aforementioned gentleman I would be only too glad to adopt it, but I think you will find that that is impossible."

Return to Town of the Merrymen Marx.

Marx for dollars is good trading at the present rate of exchange in the Rialto: four Marx for three-fifty, which is more than they sold for last season in the Studebaker; but that was before the Dawes plan was put into operation. Another factor in appreciated value is that the boys have since had their show in New York, where, it is stated, the critics took to calling each Marx by his prenomen, so well did they like "I'll Say She Is!" and what takes place therein. George Jean Nathan, who credits himself with knowing far more than there is to know about the Hungarian and Esthonian drama, wrote that the show was worth ten dollars a seat; and it isn't often that he goes into figures.

Whatever it may be worth in money, it is one of the two or three best entertainments housed in the Apollo in the four years since the spacious retreat was opened; and it is so good that the ten weeks of its stay in the Studebaker should be duplicated, at least, for this visit. It is a raffish, rude, and romping thing, more nearly shapeless than anything else called a revue, and yet hung on a plan that holds its parts together after a fashion. As Shakspere says of the judge in the stunt about the Seven Ages, it is a show full of wise fissures and ancient instances. It is bang-up buffoonery, with one of the five best jokes of 1923, having carried through 1924, still successfully asking for honorable mention in the fourth month of 1925: 'tis that wherein Napoleon says of Josephine that she is "as true as a three-dollar cornet."

Later, maybe, Mr. Donaghey will have something to say of all this; but that doesn't imply that you should wait for him before going to see it.
L. I. W.

53

Plays and Players in These Parts

A Dispassionate Inquiry Into the Brains of the Four Marx Brothers.

By ALEXANDER WOOLLCOTT

As this is an appropriate week for talking turkey, it is high time for some official disavowal to be made here of the egregious pen portrait of Harpo Marx which was printed on this page a week ago and which has variously amused or revolted the readers of this journal.

The mailbag has yielded up brief notes on the subject ranging all the way from "Oh, is that so!" to "You dirty logroller, you." The authorship of the anonymous tribute has been evilly attributed to pretty much every one from Mr. Marx himself to the writer of these notes, who at least was innocent.

The story, which bore the caption "HARPO" MARX IS ALSO SILENT OFF THE STAGE, appears in its original form to have issued from an official at the Casino Theater, where the Marx Brothers have been uproariously preoccupied ever since spring in a musical comedy of which I have forgotten the name. In this article the mute brother was pictured as a profound reader and a meditative recluse who spent most of his waking hours in a bookish solitude from which he would emerge only to suggest some new quips or antics for his dependent, awestruck and presumably grateful brothers. He was further described as "the brains of the four." "Most of the time," said this too lightly trusted witness, "he indulges in no diversion except sitting alone in his study and thinking."

Which description is a little difficult to reconcile with the subsequently proffered testimony which has poured in from every direction. On the grounds of newly discovered evidence the case must really be reopened to call attention to the fact that after Harpo Marx has done his regular rounds of golf, has played his almost daily game of mean croquet in Central Park (this dissipation of his can be verified by passersby who keep an eye on the sheep meadow around noon), has attended the Saturday night session of the Thanatopsis Back-to-Back and Violent Emotion Club and has worked in several games of bridge, the amount of time left for thinking could be put in your right eye. Old timers of the two a day are ready to swear that Harpo Marx has not sat alone and thought—has not even sat alone—since the early spring of 1912.

It appears to be true that he has been reading Mr. Pearson's magnificent "Studies in Murder" in his dressing room, but it seems to have taken him eight weeks (including two extra matinees) to get through the first chapter. The stage doorman sends in word to the effect that seeing Harpo Marx skip through a new book is like watching slow motion pictures. Indeed, the whole story seems to have originated with some impressionable soul, struck dumb by the sight of a vaudeville clown deep (sunk, perhaps) in the ravishingly subtle "The Green Hat" of Mr. Arlen. From that startling experience this reporter seems to have suffered a reaction similar to that in the bosom of the chorus girl who kept calling to her grumpy bridegroom only to find him too engrossed in the pages of the Evening Journal to hear her. "My Gawd," she is credibly reported to have said, "and to think I married a bookworm!"

But the most crushing rebuttal has been leveled at the paragraph which said: "Harpo is an accomplished musician—as his audiences realize. But they only know his playing on the harp. He plays the violin as well, and is an expert performer on the flute."

It seems after investigation that Harpo is no musician at all and that he has had no musical education. He holds the big Casino audience breathless every night with his engaging melodies on the instrument from which he took his name, but old masters of that instrument are the first to point out that he does not know how to play it correctly and that he even has it strung and tuned in so mysterious and individual a way that an expert harpist would go mad if he were to touch its strings. Perhaps Harpo says to himself that if they think he cannot play the harp, at least he has fixed it so no one else can play it.

Recently he himself was depressed by a consciousness of his ignorance as a musician and decided, in his middle thirties, to go to school. He reported humbly enough to the master harpist of the town and applied for lessons at the established rate of $10 a lesson. The great Maestro had heard his unorthodox numbers at the Casino and voiced a moody conviction that Harpo would hardly live long enough to unlearn all the bad tricks he had taught himself.

"You do things on the harp I never saw in all my life," said the puzzled Maestro. "Now you take that arpeggio of yours there in 'Mighty Lak a Rose.' How in the name of all that's wonderful do you do that?"

So the abashed pupil showed him how and the Maestro tried it himself a half a dozen times until he could do it too. About ten minutes of this.

"Then there's that trick of yours there where you hold your hand this way," said the still interested Maestro.

And Harpo showed him that one. The Maestro practiced and practiced. About ten minutes of that. Thus ended the first lesson, and the pupil, after paying his $10 down, went away thoughtfully and has not resumed the course.

When they were youngsters together on the sidewalks of New York it was always Chico, the real pianist of the lot, who could have any job he wanted at the keyboard of a movie house. But Harpo, who could not read a note, was always a little behindhand in his mastery of the current tunes and actually could play only two pieces at all well. But since the brothers looked indistinguishably alike, the ingenious Marxes hit upon the plan of having Chico apply for the job, rattle off a dozen melodies, engage to start work next day and then send Harpo to fill the bill. He would sometimes hold in a week until the puzzled management grew sick of his two tunes.

One surprising protest was registered by Will B. Johnstone, official librettist of the Mark Brothers' harlequinade. In the course of his genial but contradictory letter Mr. Johnstone says:

"THE SUN misstates that Harpo 'also plans most of the comedy stunts for the brothers. It was he who evolved the Napoleonic scene of 'I'll Say She Is.'" Since the Napoleonic scene is generally credited with putting the Marx Brothers where they are—on Broadway—it is a great pleasure for me to take an assist in their success and admit that I evolved the Napoleonic scene, which the boys embellished, naturally."

And it really ought to be explained that the "brains of the Four Marx Brothers" is not in the Casino cast at all. She lives in Richmond Hill and is in the ginger ale business.

Josef Rosenblatt to

"I'll Say She Is"

Carlotta Miles—Haven't you ever wanted something you couldn't get?
Julius Marx—Yes, a grape fruit that wouldn't squirt.

"One would think," writes Julius Marx, "that with all the theatrical experience you've had, both as a critic and a musical comedy favorite, that by this time you would have absorbed enough of the chorus girl lingo to make you a howling favorite instead of a leering mute.

"The next time you go out on a wild party, memorize a few of the following gems and you are bound to click. They have all been tried and tested and are guaranteed sure fire.

" 'I'll tell the world.' 'You said it.' 'Ain't it the truth?' 'Butter and egg man.' 'I got what it takes.' 'It's all apple sauce.' 'Ain't you the one dearie?' 'Red hot mama.' 'Sugar papa.' 'Sweet daddy.' 'Runnin' wild.' 'I'm a wow.' 'Hot patootie.'

"If you learn all these and routine them so that they seem spontaneous, you can't miss. Your telephone bell will ring incessantly. Your room will be a bower of flowers. You will be submerged in chicken a la king and all the girls will be calling you Big Boy, Hey Hey."

It is impossible for a scholar with a taste for research not to stumble across something momentous. In, I think, the Vatican Museum is a statue of Harpocrates. Harpocrates was the god of silence. My little readers who have seen the Marx Brothers and wondered why Harpo goes all through the show without saying a word have their answer here, and I am glad to be able to give the first news of this to my newspaper, not a copy of which have I been able to buy in tutta Italia. There is a big future for a New York World circulation manager in Italy. It would take about four months every year, I compute, and if nobody else will take the job, I, in the interests of education and literature, might be broadminded enough to accept same.

By the way, this statue of Harpocrates looks like Harpo Marx. I almost expected a lot of silverware to issue from the image.

It is doubtless true ... and resort to ... times being "I'll Say she is," Casino. This seems to be one of the ways the feeblest comes within our long and affectionate experience, and one of the reasons why the Marx Brothers are to be envied is the fact that they are the only New York family that has never seen the parts of a show which they are not in.

Several marginal notes might be scribbled in the program of any one who has been five times to see this show. One might note, for instance, that they have a new juvenile every week, thus preparing for an almost ... association as large as that of the original "Floradora" sextet. Seemingly there is a high mortality among those who nightly sing "Only You" to the abundant Lottie Miles. They tire. (Automobile joke.)

One might note, too, how fluent and fresh is the humor of Julius Marx, who rewrites his part every night and is as essentially a column conductor as Master Will Rogers.

Your correspondent's enthusiasm for the comic genius of Harpo Marx continues unabated. We are always delighted with the evidence of how much can be said by anyone who deliberately throws away the advantage of speech. The mute Marx can say more with his eyes than many louder if not funnier comedians can communicate by yelling at the top of their lungs. Which recalls our favorite story of how Ned Harrigan, in the season when he was making an actor out of his son, bade him play for four weeks without ever moving his hands.

Fay King Finds Fun Galore In 'I'll Say She Is'

THE MARX BROTHERS

By FAY KING.

There are "easy marks," German marks, dollar marks and laundry marks, but on Broadway, when you mention Marx, you mean the four merry young men who instill so much real comedy and hilarious humor in that exceptionally colorful and charming musical show at the Casino Theatre—"I'll Say She Is."

It might as well be called "I'll Say They Do!" for the Marx Brothers, Julius H., Harbert, Leonard and Arthur, furnish most of the fun!

Arthur Marx, sometimes nicknamed "Harpo," distinguishes himself by playing the entire show from start to finish without saying a single word. He relies entirely upon his red wig and idiotic expression to round up his "mute part." He lets his piano and harp playing speak for him!

It would take a linguist in several languages to say all the nice things that can be said about his playing.

The plot of "I'll Say She Is" is Cinderella backwards. It's about a very rich and beautiful girl who is in search of a thrill. A doctor, lawyer, merchant, chief, poorman, richman, beggarman and thief appear, and each is willing to try and win her by showing her some new adventure that will relieve her from utter boredom.

The thief (Edgar Gardner) takes her to Chinatown and an opium den; and here we see the Chinese Apache dance, and one of her dreams about San Toy and the love boat. But this does not thrill her.

The rich man brings her the wealth of the world.

Japan, the South Sea Islands, Timbuctoo, Brittany, Russia, Zulu and Hindstan each appears and contributes its bit to milady's wardrobe.

And so it goes on throughout the play until love alone wins her!

From start to finish, "I'll Say She Is" unfurls fun and finery. There is no end of beautiful chorus numbers, exquisite art curtains, dancing and song.

"The tragedy of Gambling" is very clever. Out of an enormous stock ticker in the background, comes a little fairy—Mary Melvin—and with her magic wand she brings forth every form of gambling, from the dice and penny and to racing, roulette and Wall St. dime to racing, roulette and Wall St. The costumes in this sketch are virtual objects of art.

The burlesque of Pygmalion and Galatea, "The Awakening of Love," is a scream, and in the Napolean and Josephine number, called Napolean's first Waterloo, the Marx brothers are at their best!

Carlotta Miles, is some looker, and has an excellent voice.

"I'll Say She Is" is a sure fire hit you can enjoy seeing again and again.

THE THEATRE

BY GEORGE JEAN NATHAN

This is the time of the year when the New York stages rid themselves of Shakespeare, Ibsen, Strindberg, Samuel Shipman and the other old masters and go in for the form of entertainment known as the music show. I have just seen five specimens of the latter and have been rewarded for my studious application with the important critical conclusion that a music show is something in which a performer, when he does not know what else to do, turns a somersault. Another equally important deduction that has crowned my diligence is the following: that the talent of the leading lady performers may be assayed in inverse ratio to the size of their feathered head-dresses and their ability to play the violin. And still a third and no less weighty philosophy with which I have been indemnified consists in the finding that almost every other music show producer in town seems intent upon imitating, to a greater or lesser degree, the form and manner of the English Charlot Revue. From the imitations that I have thus far seen, however, it would appear that the producers in point have confined their study of the form and manner of the Charlot Revue entirely to Miss Gertrude Lawrence's limbs, the pleats in the Messrs. Buchanan's and Keys' trousers, and the broad a's of the *tout ensemble*. For aside from a commendable thinning out of erstwhile too sizeable calves, a recherché touch to the men's tailoring and the injection into the proceedings of a somewhat more polished air, I have been able to discern not the slightest similarity to the London article in these counterfeits. Which, for all the circumstance that this London article is an excellent thing of its kind, is potentially perhaps for the best, since when the American music show sticks to its own last and reveals itself at its highest it is as thoroughly fresh, as thoroughly original, as thoroughly amusing—and certainly ten times as beautiful—as the English species.

In this imminent dawning of countless feeble copies of the English revue, with its smooth drawing-room atmosphere and what society leaders in Chicago and headwaiters in New York call tone, there comes as a blessed relief and an equally blessed reminder of the old American music show the exhibit at the Casino Theatre called "I'll Say She Is." If there was ever a poorer music show than "I'll Say She Is," I don't know its name. But if ever there was a poor music show turned into a corking one by its clowns, its name is the name of this one. These clowns are the four Marx Brothers, two of whom, the Mons. Arthur and the Mons. Julius, to wit, are especially proficient in the art of falling down upon their so to speaks and kicking each other in the as it weres and who will therefore doubtless soon be hailed by the Younger Generation as greater geniuses than Michelangelo and Beethoven. There is no greater admirer of the Charlot Revue kind of entertainment than I am, but I would not exchange these Frères Marx for a half dozen such revues that didn't contain a Beatrice Lillie. In such low comedians as they we get again the sweet and fragrant rosemary of the old American burlesque show, beyond a doubt the funniest thing in the music show line that the stage of any nation has ever seen. The Marxes stem directly from Watson, Bickel and Wrothe and the various other comic teams that adorned the burlesque stage thirty years ago when it was at its zenith and before it started on the sharp decline that was to land it, and lose it, in the second-hand costumes and settings of lately deceased Broadway musical comedies. These Marxes are approximately as subtle as so many boiler factories, and as artistic as four pigs knuckles. But they are as comical a quartet, with the emphasis upon two of them, as anything that has come the way of the stage since Al Reeves' checkered suit and ten-pound gold watch chain and Billy Watson's sleeveless red undershirt and three-sheet pantaloons sustained by a single Alice blue suspender first crossed the vision of all connoisseurs of the low, the true, and the beautiful.

The antics of the MM. Marx are a symposium of all the most hilarious didoes of the burlesque bible. The MM. Marx leave out nothing. The floppy Palm Beach suits; the stolen silver spoons that dribble out of the pockets of one of the brothers while the policeman is assuring him that he has never seen a more honest face; the poker game for two in which the dealer gives himself cards from the bottom of the deck, with the other player urging him to give him some from the bottom also, as no one is looking; the red-wigged comedian's wink of the eye at the big blonde prima donna and, on his exit, the nod for her to follow him; the clapping of a miniature derby on the head of the largest comedian—these and a hundred other such genial monkeyshines out of the familiar past are once again brought into play. But never for an instant is their age permitted to impress itself upon the audience. The MM. Marx have a technic of comedy every bit as exact as their memories. With a trick of the voice, a flip of the brogan or a new brand of whimsical moustache they convert these venerable grandpas of comic hokum into what seem to be newborn babes. They are gentlemen of infinite jest. And they turn what is intrinsically a ten-cent show into a masterpiece of knock 'em down and drag 'em out humor.

MARXIAN FUN-MAKING FEATURES "I'LL SAY"

Frequent Laughs, No Mental Strain, in Performance at Jefferson.

By CARLOS F. HURD.

JULIUS MARX, casual creator of compelling comedy, and his brother, Arthur, speechless smile specialist, are the chief entertainers in this week's "musical comedy revue" at the Shubert-Jefferson Theater. There are two other Marxes, not so funny as these, but who may brothers be for a' that.

In the interludes between the Marxian appearances, and supplementing their efforts at times, are dances, starting with an abundance of clothing and getting dow to scanty and narrow sash effects; solo and duo dancing of speed and acrobatic merit; a style show; a rather gorgeous tableau; a King Tut scene; a jazz "sextet" with eight members; Chinatown realism and Wall street symbolism, and much singing, but precious little music.

They call it "I'll Say She Is." As this might mean anything, and in this case means almost nothing, it befits the performance, which means a way of spending an evening with no danger of brain fag.

"Experience" Is Copied.

What it is that "she is," does not appear definitely, but "she" is quite dazzlingly present, being Lotta Miles. Close attention to the stage lines, at certain points, will show that "she" is in search of thrills, and that different members of the cast undertake to supply this demand. This leads to two scenes resembling those in "Experience," one showing an opium den and the other symbolizing the stock market. As a final thrill, she is permitted to imagine herself Josephine, who, it is established after some discussion, was the wife of Napoleon, not of Columbus .

Here Julius Marx, as Napoleon, and his brothers, as the courtiers who entertain the Empress in Napoleon's brief absences, give a very funny piece of comedy, which at the same time may be nearer to historic truth than some serious stage presentations of Josephine have been. Marx is the most un-Napoleonic of Napoleons, as he is one of the most un-comedian-like of comedians. Brother Arthur, who remains inarticulate through the evening, beguiles the lonely Empress with his piano and harp selections, while the Emperor keeps returning from fields of carnage to hunt for his sword and check up on his consort.

A Fairy in Garters.

A courtroom scene, with cubist scenery, gives a comedy lead which is not carried very far. In a Cinderella dialogue, Julius Marx, as the fairy, appears in athletic underwear and garters. The Marxes and others give a laughable tramp ballet, following a pretentious Pygmalion and Galatea dance by others of the cast.

Instead of the usual claims of a long run on Broadway, "I'll Say She Is" has the distinction of having broken records in Kansas City by a three weeks' stay there. It is a Chicago show. Last night's

The Marx Brothers

WE are happy to announce that the laughing apparatus of this department, long suspected of being out-of-date and useless, is in perfect running order and can be heard any evening at the Casino Theatre during those magnificent moments when the Marx Brothers are participating in "I'll Say She Is." Not since sin laid its heavy hand on our spirit have we laughed so loud and so offensively. And as we picked ourself out of the aisle following each convulsion, there rang through our soul the joyful pæan: "Grandpa can laugh again! Grandpa can laugh again!"

"I'll Say She Is" is probably one of the worst revues ever staged, from the point of view of artistic merit and general deportment. And yet when the Marx Brothers appear, it becomes one of the best. Certainly we have never enjoyed one so thoroughly since the lamented Cohan Revues, and we will go before any court and swear that two of the four Marxes are two of the funniest men in the world.

We may be doing them a disservice by boiling over about them like this, but we can't help it if we feel it, can we? Certainly the nifties of Mr. Julius Marx will bear the most captious examination, and even if one in ten is found to be phony, the other nine are worth the slight wince involved at the bad one. It is certainly worth hearing him, as *Napoleon*, refer to the "Marseillaise" as the "Mayonnaise," if the next second he will tell *Josephine* that she is as true as a three-dollar cornet. The cornet line is one of the more rational of the assortment. Many of them are quite mad and consequently much funnier to hear but impossible to retail.

THERE is no wincing possible at the pantomime of Mr. Arthur Marx. It is 110 proof artistry. To watch him during the deluge of knives and forks from his coat-sleeve, or in the poker-game (where he wets one thumb and picks the card off with the other), or—oh, well, at any moment during the show, is to feel a glow at being alive in the same generation. We hate to be like this, for it is inevitable that we are prejudicing readers against the Marx boys by our enthusiasm, but there must be thousands of you who have seen them in vaudeville (where almost everything that is funny on our legitimate stage seems to originate) and who know that we are right.

Oddments and Remainders

By Percy Hammond

NOT long ago Mr. George S. Kaufman, an author of "Round the Town," complained that I had noted a physical similarity between him and Julius H. Marx, the least beautiful of the Marx brothers. Mr. Marx, an equally sensitive artist, now resents Mr. Kaufman's objections, and makes a few of his own. "Sir," he writes, "while in a subway car this morning I picked up a Herald Tribune off the floor. It might have been thrown there by Samuel Shipman, since it was folded right on your column. At any rate, it had an article by Mr. George S. Kaufman, in which he expressed himself as being greatly annoyed because you said that he looked like me.

"I have never seen Mr. Kaufman in the flesh, or the rough, or whatever they call it. I have seen a number of his plays, and I am not sure whether he has a mustache or not, although some authors find it advisable to wear something on the opening night.

"My make-up is a sort of hit-and-miss proposition, and when I start putting it on I am never sure who or what I will look like when I get through. Some nights I resemble one author, some nights I look like another, and it is purely a coincidence that basically I happen to look like Mr. Kaufman.

"If you can suggest any humorous get-up that wouldn't look like the aforementioned gentleman I would be only too glad to adopt it, but I think you will find that that is impossible."

* * *

Plays and Players in These Parts

Monday Meditations on Matters Marked With an M.

By ALEXANDER WOOLLCOTT.

It will be remembered that those three sisters who lived at the bottom of a well were learning to draw and that, as the Dormouse explained to Alice at the Mad Tea Party, they would draw anything beginning with an M—such as mousetrap and the moon and memory and muchness.

Or, as that drowsy raconteur might have added, *Magildis*, Moscow; "The Miracle," the *Madonna*, the Marxes and Miss Miles. Our own meditations on these matters began during the performance of the Reinhardt mystery Saturday afternoon. This was the second visit to the Century within the week, and a dramatic critic who will do that in August for a play that has been running here since midwinter should really be removed from his job. For, in a Puritan country it is against all tradition to suffer a man to continue in a job he obviously enjoys so much.

The *Migildis*, this time was Haroldine Humphreys, Miss Pinchot's alternate in the role of the *Nun*. She is fair to behold. She has a fine physical eloquence. She seems to have brought aptitude with her from Bryn Mawr. And she has a lot of lovely youngness.

Then the role of the *Piper* was superbly played by Lyoff Bulgakoff, a left over when the Moscow Art Players went reluctantly back home. Bulgakoff looks far less like a demon out of a Poe story than does his alternate in the role. There is less malignance and more mischief. He is a gnome, an urchin demon, if you will. A fine actor, Bulgakoff.

Probably every playgoer who returns to "The Miracle" makes mental note of an intention to keep an eye on the waxen *Madonna* to see if she really stands motionless during the long preliminary before the figure comes to life. It is not at all difficult to keep both eyes on so lovely a vision as Elizabeth Schirmer. One wonders if there really is a more trying role in New York than this one, which requires the actress to stand lifeless for forty-five minutes, while the turbulence of the colorful pageant swirls round the base of her pedestal.

The only comparable predicament is that of the ample and good looking and good humored Lotta Miles as the *Empress Josephine*, around whom the riotous Marxes perform their prosperous antics. Miss Miles's real name is as German as that of Frau Schirmer, but she has clung to the trick patronymic devised when she became the model for the advertisements of an automobile tire. At the end of seventy weeks, during which the hilarious brothers have cavorted and gamboled around her, she is still able to listen to the synthetic harp playing of Harpo Marx and the enchanting piano playing of Leo Marx as if she asked no pleasanter lot in life than just the rich privilege of listening to them all her days on earth. The first prize for cooperation and good sportsmanship is hereby awarded to Lotta Miles.

Speaking of the Marxes, as one does from time to time, these comical brothers have lent a much needed village post office atmosphere to Thirty-ninth street. Recently a traveler passing through this city was heavy laden with a message for one of the Marxes and approached the stage door of the Casino with a good deal of that trepidation all laymen feel about going back stage. You are eyed with animosity by the stage doorman, you blunder into the wrong dressing room and stage hands rather make a point of dropping sandbags and portable houses and the like on your bewildered head. But this messenger's trepidation was wasted, for it was a good fifteen minutes before curtain time and all four Marxes were out on the doorstep in their shirt sleeves.

This neighborly art of making a small town of New York is also a jewel in the crown of A. H. Woods who can usually be found in front of his theater in Forty-second street, tilted back in a cane seated chair for all the world like our favorite grocer in Clinton, N. Y. From that homely coign of vantage he can pass remarks about Neighbor Erlanger and Neighbor Ziegfeld as they moter elegantly past on their way to work. It was there that Margaret Mayo found him once long ago when she had been reading a play for him. The play was a fearful piece of theatrical refuse called "The Eternal Magdalene," which Mr. Woods and the elder Selwyn had bought out in Ohio in a moment of emotion. Afterward doubt dawned as to whether the authorities would tolerate it, and the sagacious Miss Mayo was asked for an opinion. The night after she had waded through the four acts of the manuscript she was tripping along Forty-second street, and this colloquy ensued:

"Did you read that play?"

"Yes, last night."

"What did you think of it?"

"Why," ventured Miss Mayo, tentatively, "I didn't think it was so very salacious."

"I guess you're right," Mr. Woods agreed pensively. "I don't think it's much good, either."

To revert to the Marxes, note might be made of the bitter disputes that wage on the hot question as to whether Julius Marx or Harpo is the more diverting comedian. Families are split on this question as they have not been split since Dr. Cook came wreathed from Denmark. During the summer vacation of your correspondent this department came out boldly for Julius Marx, but order has been restored, and until further notice readers of THE SUN will regard Harpo as the shining Marx.

59

name in all the columns. I was also making contributions, such as the following, to those columns:

MAY DAY CAROL
by Groucho Marx
(Author of Nashes to Nashes and Stutz to Stutz)
My wife takes the breast of the chicken;
"The leg is for Junior," she sings.
But listen: I feel just like Eugene O'Neill—
All God's chicken has nothing but wings.

Now in the higher-income brackets, I could afford to buy some beach bungalows, twenty-four of them in all, in partnership with Nate Sachs. Nate was a lawyer and a longtime friend. We had Minnie's advice, Uncle Al's experience, and Nate's taste. Any time we were dubious about using some piece of material, we'd check with Nate. He kept our act clean and classy.

We were stars about town. Harpo was taken up by the Algonquin wits. Chico and Zeppo amused themselves elsewhere. I had it both ways, stardom on stage and anonymity in everyday life. Without the greasepaint mustache, I could have been any suc-

cessful businessman commuting to his house in Great Neck. One night Ruth and I went to the Winter Garden. Our old neighbor from 93rd Street, Harry Houdini, was appearing on the bill. He called for a volunteer from the audience. I got up. He didn't recognize me, either as his former neighbor or as a fellow performer. Houdini had a routine where he would put some needles in his mouth, along with a spool of thread, the result being that he would spit out threaded needles. He turned to me on the stage. "What do you see in there?" he asked, as he opened his mouth. "Pyorrhea," I replied. Then I left the stage.

59 Our house in Great Neck. It was a happy environment in which to raise Arthur and Miriam, who would be born in the next year. We became landed gentry. First thing I did was pay $5,000 to join a fancy golf club. I invited Gummo to join me there one Sunday morning. The first ball he hit broke a window in the club president's car. The second ball went into the clubhouse and almost killed the president.

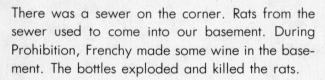

60 Son Arthur at a water pump.

61 With Ruth and Arthur.
62 And Miriam makes four.

There was a sewer on the corner. Rats from the sewer used to come into our basement. During Prohibition, Frenchy made some wine in the basement. The bottles exploded and killed the rats.

George Kaufman used to come play ball with us. During this time, he was the intermittent drama critic for *The New York Times,* and he would take leaves of absence from the job whenever some theater project came up. Morrie Ryskind would be the pitcher and Kaufman would catch. One day Eddie Cantor came to play with us. He arrived in evening clothes and stationed himself in the outfield, his butler beside him. Whenever a ball was hit his way, he'd have the butler catch it for him.

⁶³ A picture of George Gershwin and Irving Berlin, taken sometime in the 1920s. Both were great talents and became good friends of mine. Irving would soon be writing the music for our second Broadway show, *The Cocoanuts*.

THE COCOANUTS

GROUCHO: I'll meet you tonight under the moon. Oh, I can see you now—you and the moon. You wear a necktie so I'll know you.

Despite our great success in *I'll Say She Is!,* we were well aware how pieced together the show actually was. It had been financed for $50,000 tops, and had brought back ten times that in profits to its backers. Sam Harris now stepped into the picture. A wonderful man, Sam was once told by George Jessel, "If you were a woman, I'd marry you." Sam hired a recently widowed socialite to appear with us in the stage version of *The Cocoanuts.* Her name was Margaret Dumont. He also engaged George S. Kaufman to write the play and Irving Berlin to compose the music. In a biography of Kaufman a few years ago, I was quoted as saying George supplied me with my walk and my talk. I'd been in show business for twenty years when *Cocoanuts* opened in 1925, and I'd been walking and talking for at least thirty-three years, so the evolution had gone on for quite some time before I met Kaufman. There is so much more to credit him with. He was the wittiest man I ever knew, and perhaps some of that quality rubbed off on me.

Kaufman didn't appreciate music, finding it an intrusion on the narrative. *Cocoanuts* has the distinction of being the only Broadway show of Berlin's that didn't have a hit song. It might have, however, if Kaufman hadn't insisted on dropping "Always" from the score.

The Marx Brothers were involved in the Florida land boom—that was the story of the show. Frances Williams, the nominal star of the show, was a well-known Charleston dancer who was engaged to supply some kick to the proceedings. When the show opened, I asked Minnie, "Mother, how did you like it?"

"They laughed a lot, Julius," she replied, "they laughed a lot."

65 Harpo. During one scene with Margaret Dumont acting as my straight woman, I heard the sound of a taxicab horn from one side of the stage. Suddenly a blonde ran in front of us, with Harpo chasing after. The scene was funny enough without that bit of business, but now it stopped the show. From then on, Harpo would always chase a blonde across the stage or on screen whenever the proceedings got too tame for his taste.

65

66-67 I have been pictured among bevies of beautiful girls throughout my career, but if anyone should have been so pictured, it was Chico. What I'd try to say by wiggling my eyebrows, he'd verbalize in far more direct fashion. If I'd ever tried that gambit I would have been slapped into the middle of last week. With Chico, the response was usually a smile and a nod, then off they'd go. Because he was my brother, I loved him. Because he was selfish and irresponsible, I had little respect for him. He was the oldest brother, and we should have looked up to him, but he was the biggest headache of us all. Once, while we were touring the Great Lakes area, his gambling debts caught up with him. When he found out some goons were after him, he disappeared. All the time he was gone I had to do the routine with myself. Harpo was around, of course, but he didn't talk. It was up to me to ask the questions and answer them. I had little sympathy for Chico's excuses when he finally did show up. I don't remember ever having a cross word with Harpo, but Chico and I fought constantly.

Two of the Four Marx Brothers—Harpo on the Left and Groucho on the Right—As They Appear in "The Cocoanuts," at the Lyric. Between Them Is Frances Williams, She of the Charleston.

THE STAGE
By Bide Dudley

"The Cocoanuts," at the Lyric

NATURALLY, FOLKS, THESE FEW REMARKS WILL BE TO GIVE ALL THE GOOD MARKS TO THE BROTHERS' MARX —

FIRST OF ALL THERE IS GROUCHO MARX, WHO IS VERY VERY FUNNY —

THEN THERE IS HARPO MARX WHO SAYS NOTHING, YET SPEAKS VOLUMES

THEN THERE IS CHICO MARX WHO PIANOLOGUES PRETTY LIKE,

AND LASTLY ZIPPO, WHO IS JUST THE OTHER QUARTER OF THE MARX FAMILY.

THERE ARE OTHER GOOD THINGS TOO — FRANCES WILLIAMS! BOY, HOW SHE CHARLESTONS!

ONE OF THE LITTLE MONKEY DOODLE DOO'S

AND BASIL RUYSDAEL SINGING ABOUT HIS SHIRT

AND THEN GROUCHO ALL OVER AGAIN

"PENELOPE"

National

W. C. FIELDS

"Not a word to the folks!" had been this veteran comedian's gag for ten years in the *Follies* until one night something popped in *Poppies* and he said it! Who, so well as he can tease oranges away from juggling plates, or shoot an eloquent mustache from a retiring nostril? Any wonder he was "pulled in" to the Movies

(Below)
AL JOLSON

The greatest propagandist for motherhood. Al has also increased the traffic on the trains *Going South*, *Back to Dixie* and *Mammy* to such an extent that the Pennsylvania Railroad now vies with U. S. Steel in market value. What would Broadway be without Al? What would Al be without Broadway?

White

GROUCHO MARX

Take an old gag, a mustache made of stove blacking, a pair of glassless spectacles, and you have Groucho—the elder and leader of the Four Mad Marxes now cavorting hilariously through *The Cocoanuts*

Vandamm

Apeda

Strand

Apeda

FRANK TINNEY

As an explorer this comedian holds a unique place in American history. But as a lecturer who illustrates his story with colored slides Mr. Tinney furnishes the best and funniest reason on earth for the patronage of home products

JAMES BARTON

Wonder where Mr. Ziegfeld's sense of humor was when he named his latest and most gorgeous effort *No Foolin'* and then put Jimmy Barton at the head of the class of principals?

JULIUS TANNEN

If you've ever done anything to get your name or picture in the papers, keep away from the *Vanities*. Julius believes in that intimate touch and turns every performance into an Old Home Week Reunion, with you as a guest of honor

KINGS OF COMEDY
Who have long reigned on Broadway by successfully humoring their subjects

THE STAGE
By Alexander Woollcott

The Plot Sickens

"When we opened at the Lyric Theatre, way back in the winter of 1925," writes the returning Groucho Marx, "the Roxy and Paramount Theatres were still to be built, the joke about the dog in the Manger Hotel was still new, pig women and sash-weights were unheard of, Harry Thaw had been ejected from a Harlem cabaret for the fifth (and what every one hoped was the last) time, and Italy was cowering under the lash of Mussolini.

"This was a memorable and soul-satisfying winter for us. It was the first time we had ever been in a show with a regular plot, and all the critics, even the man on the Wall Street Journal, spoke about it and congratulated us on our legitimacy. We were all so happy. After being known for so many years as hodge-podge comedians, to be suddenly hailed as actors in a regular play was no mean honor. We were thrilled, if you know what I mean. We felt as though we were well on the road to Arthur Hopkins, and maybe, some day, even Otto Kahn.

"A year passed and we left the Lyric for the road. After we had been out a while we noticed that fewer and fewer people mentioned the plot. The out of town experts apparently liked the show, but they either didn't believe we had a plot or they couldn't find it. At any rate, there seldom was any mention of it in the write-ups. Most of them wound up their reviews with the cut and dried bell-ringing. You know the old standby—'The boys entertained with a hodge-podge of tomfoolery that shook the rafters.' It seemed we could never get away from hodge-podging and rafter-shaking. even merry *mélange* would have been better. But invariably it was hodge-podge. It was quite discouraging.

"We now woke up to something that we had suspected ever since we hit the road—and that was that our plot had taken the air. Well, Mr. Woollcott, we were frantic about it, and we decided we would find it or know the reason why. We looked all over for it—in the wardrobe trunks, the girls' dressing rooms, and understudy's suitcase, the lobby. But neither hair nor hide could be found. We found bits of 'Bluffing Bluffers,' remnants of 'The New Yorkers' and a good - sized chunk of 'The Girl in the Spotlight,' but the plot of 'The Cocoanuts' had melted completely away. Once at a never-to-be-forgotten matinee in Newark it raised its ugly head for a moment, but a hoarse and emphatic razzing from the gallery caused it to slink off, and that is the last we ever saw of it.

"Now, Mr. Woollcott, we can't afford to give $500 for the best ladder, I mean letter, as to why our show is doing so much good, but we will give a copy of the Life of David Belasco (with a foreword by Robert Benchley) to the one who sends us to a 200-word article, or less, telling us where we can find our plot. Remember, it is not necessary to see the show to win the prize. In fact, it is better if you don't see the show. Address all communications to Groucho Marx, care of Whatever Has Become of Our Plot Contest, Century Theatre."

* * *

The present engagement of "The Cocoanuts" at the Century is for two weeks. That winds up the season, but the fool show starts off again in the fall and goes bucketty-bucketty across the country, much to the surprise of its father. Speaking of the author of the missing plot, he has had a long-standing wager with this department, over the final outcome of which this department is beginning to get pretty discouraged. It was an even-money $10 bet that "Abie's Irish Rose" would run forever. This pig-headed department took the negative.

* * *

"The Cocoanuts" was preceded at the Century by "Cradle-Snatchers," which also seems to have undergone some kind of change on tour. Concerning the three juveniles in that frisky farce, Amy Leslie, the Chicago critic, so far calmed down as to write thus:

Where they ever found the boys cannot be conjectured, unless the searchers for talent, allied with physical adaptability and youth, went to some fraternity house to pick their men. The boys are delightful actors, but they are prettier boys and nicer fellows than could be found or trained out of ordinary actor factories to-day. Humphrey Bogart created a furor as one of the hired lovers. Here is a youth handsome as Valentino, as dexterous in elegant comedy as E. H. Sothern and as easy and graceful as any of our best romantic actors.

At that, Miss Leslie's critical goings-on do vaguely recall the utterances of some of our own reviewers when commenting on any new actress under fifty who hasn't a hare-lip.

It Seems to Me
By Heywood Broun

"It was a great shock to my brothers and myself," writes Groucho Marx, "to learn that you were addicted to pajamas. It was a little discouraging too. We have always told every one that you wore nightgowns. It was just a natural inference on our part. Why, we never dreamed that you were such a flossy dresser. Pajamas we had always thought of in connection with slick stacomb sheiks, slim-hipped, spatted devils.

"You, we always looked upon as a sort of ascetic. Whenever we spoke of you (which was often) we always fancied you lumbering around a bare unadorned bedroom in nightgown, sleeping cap and woolen slippers, prim and austere, maybe even a candle in your right hand. In my family Broun and nightgown were practically synonymous. It was just like Weber and Fields, Mellon and aluminum, bacon and eggs.

"I don't know whether you have ever worn a nightgown, but some day you will. They all do. For freedom, grace, comfort and ventilation, yes, and even looks, they are far superior to those boudoir prince alberts.

"I will concede that a nightgown wearer looks awkward crawling out of, or even into, bed, but this can easily be overcome by wearing pajamas underneath. Yours for flowing robes."

But I won't wear a nightgown. Freedom, liberalism, laissez-faire—yes. But no nightgown. Each man must have some one thing to which he clings. Pajamas are my principle.

      ♫   ♫   ♫

Groucho and the other Marxes have no right to talk about me, often or infrequently, if they are simply disseminating fallacies. Why don't they brush up on the subject of Broun? Lumbering indeed! I am now within five pounds of what the books say you should weigh at this height. Yesterday I ran three miles and beat the course record. And the mark won't stand forever at twenty-seven minutes either. Nurmi could do better, but he'd lose time, too, at the bathroom corner where the athlete must come to a full stop and turn before beginning on another lap. Part of the way I carried eight pounds in dumbbells and I'll challenge any Marx at two miles and up around this circuit.

      ♫   ♫   ♫

And I don't crawl out of bed. I'm up with a bound (never much later than noon) and start the day right by punching the bag.

      ♫   ♫   ♫

I'm not at all certain that I shall keep the regime up indefinitely. Now that I've got my insurance I might ease up into loose and lazy living just to make suckers of the examining doctors.

      ♫   ♫   ♫

Insurance doctors have no tact. There was not one of all those who came to chat who did not drop in on a morning which followed a farewell party to some one or other. For twenty-four hours I would train most rigorously and after such a preparation nobody ever showed up. To bring an insurance doctor all I ever had to do was to stay out till 6 A. M. and then without fail there'd be one round by 10 to eavesdrop on my internal mechanism.

      ♫   ♫   ♫

[71] This page from *Theatre Magazine* is a good representation of the leading comic lights on Broadway in 1926, though putting Jolson in that category stretches the point a bit. Some remain household words today. Frank Tinney (in lower left-hand corner) isn't one of them. He's remembered in *my* household. There's something crazy and wonderful about a man who would pull his Shetland pony onto a crowded street, hail a taxi and send the pony for a ride in the cab.

The Forward Pass

By Groucho Marx

POLICE reserves were rushed from the West 47th Street Station to the Lyric Theatre yesterday afternoon to quell a crowd that threatened to tear the theatre into tasty little bits and take home pieces of the lobby as souvenirs.

The front of the theatre, usually a fairly busy place, looked like a combination of Edgemere's fake boom last summer, Boyle's Thirty Acres and a man hunt through the lower east side. What was the reason for this terrific jam? Why was the lobby of the Lyric so congested and the lobby of the New Amsterdam across the street comparatively empty? (Cries of "No, No!" and "I object!" from Mr. Dillingham.) Had the prices been slashed from five-fifty to ten, twenty and thirty? Had Mr. Harris put a bathtub scene in the show?

"The Cocoanuts" was a good show and undoubtedly a hit. But still with five-fifty and a little influence it was usually possible to buy a ticket, and with eleven dollars one could even buy two tickets.

Well, it's a long story (I think they wanted about 700 words), and I may as well begin at the beginning. Sam Harris when he contracted to star the Marx Brothers promised them among other things a box during the hot months. Not one of the downstairs boxes—these are usually sold years in advance and occupied by high-hatted, lorgnetted people—but one of the upper boxes, plenty good enough for newspaper men, automobile salesmen and relatives.

June Days

As soon as June 1 rolled around, the date when the boys were to take over the box officially, things began to hum at the Lyric. Each one of the brothers sent out for a dozen sharp pencils, a gross of scratch pads and a telephone book. Rolling up their sleeves and throwing back their hair they tore loose and went to it. The noise backstage began to resemble a munition factory with a war order. The sound of pencil meeting paper and the feverish rustling of telephone and address books could be heard over the land.

That night as soon as the show was over each one went his own way. Chico, the first one out, went to his bridge club where he got rid of enough Annie Oakleys to fill the Hippodrome and a couple of stadiums. Harpo naturally first went to the Algonquin and then made a tour of all the hotels he had ever stopped at, this bringing him as far north as Yonkers. Zeppo gave his to all the policemen, firemen, insurance agents, newsboys, conductors,

apple women and girls he knew or thought he knew. Groucho, who had just bought a home in Great Neck, felt pretty good about the whole thing.

The only ones he gave passes to were the fellow who built his house, the plasterer, the plumber, the landscape artist, the gas and electric man, the fellow who installed the screens, the fellows who took them out and any one else in Great Neck that looked as if he had enough fare to ride to New York and pay the war tax.

The first performance after the pass act had been enacted was a Wednesday matinee. It was warm outside, the sun was shining and it looked like a dull business afternoon. The boxes on the right hand side were empty, in the orchestra there were rows of seats that had not even been put down by the ushers and even in the balcony, which is usually sold out. Splendid seats could be had for the asking and two dollars. But when the eye traveled around and met the upper left hand box you could see that business was good. It was better than good. It was tremendous! There were thousands of people in that box. They were hanging over the rail ten deep, they were perched on the chandeliers, they were squatting on the floor. It couldn't last.

The Avalanche

The performance was a great success. The audience just roared at the antics of those four funny fellows (advertisement). That is every one but those gate crashers in the upper left hand cavity. This was afterward explained by Chico, who said: "They would have laughed but there wasn't room in the box." As soon as the performance was over and the vast horde had trooped out the management noticed that there was a peculiar list to the left side of the theatre. It drooped a little on one side like a man who was just about to attach himself to a kidney plaster.

Reaction

A conference was held by the Fire, Police and Building Departments and they unanimously agreed that another performance under the same conditions would be fatal to the structure, to say nothing of the Harris and Oppenheimer bankrolls. So it came to pass that the Marx Brothers were shorn of their passing privilege. They had been big men for twenty-four hours, spreading their favors with a lavish hand, but it couldn't go on. They knew too many people. So they have become actors again, buying their tickets just like other Equity members, and as summer wears on and business sags the upper left hand box grows dusty and empty and damp, and occasionally you can hear it sighing for that memorable day in June when it was the most popular box in the whole world.

Vaudeville Talk

VA: Where's that girl I always used to see you with?

VI: I don't go around with her any more.

VA: What's the trouble; did she throw you down?

VI: No, I married her.

VA: Well, well, well, is this the first time you have ever been married?

VI: No, it's the last time.

VA: No, no, didn't you have a wife the last time I saw you?

VI: Yes, but her husband asked me to give her up.

VA: And did you do it?

VI: Sure. You see it was Lent, and I wanted to give up something.

VA: What do you think of marriage as an institution?

VI: It's all right if you like institutions, the only difference between warden and wife is in the spelling.

VA: Oh, you just like to talk. Where would you be to-day if it wasn't for your wife?

VI: I'm not sure. I've got three or four good telephone numbers.

VA: Ah, it's a wonderful feeling to go home at night and have the little woman waiting for you.

VI: You bet it is, if it's a little woman, but if it's a big woman, it's dangerous.—*Julius H. Marx*

76

74 My byline was beginning to appear more frequently, sometimes as "Groucho" and sometimes as "Julius."

75-76 The Cocoanuts ran 377 performances on Broadway. Then we took the show on the road. From various stops along the tour I sent back some "Vaudeville Talk" columns that The New Yorker printed.

Traveling by train was a boring proposition. I took lots of reading along, and Harpo and Chico would rustle up some card players. When I ran out of reading matter and no poker players could be found, the mischief started. Once, on a lark, we invaded Margaret Dumont's stateroom and took off all her clothes. She screamed louder than the train engine.

Vaudeville Talk

VAUDE: How far is the post office from here?

VIll: Do you want to mail a letter or a postal?

Va: A letter.

Vi: Well, it's a half a mile.

Va: Suppose I wanted to mail a postal?

Vi: You couldn't, the post office burnt down this morning.

Va: You're a pretty fresh fellow, aren't you?

Vi: Oh, I get my share of women.

Va: How many shares do you hold?

Vi: Just one share at at a time.

Va: What is your opinion of the women of this generation?

Vi: I don't know. All those I have been out with have been of the last generation.

Va: You don't seem to get me.

Vi: I don't want you, I don't even want your opinion.

Va: Well, why did you ask me for my opinion?

Vi: Well, I didn't think you had one.

Va: Is there any other post office around here except the one that burnt down?

Vi: Yes, there's one about a mile up the other way.

Va: Is it open now?

Vi: I don't think so; you see they tore it down when they built the one that burnt down to-day.—*Julius H. Marx*

75

[77] Los Angeles, where we arrived on February 8, 1928, was the last stop of our two-year tour. *The Los Angeles Times* identified the lineup as "Harpo, Zeppo, Mrs. Zeppo, Mrs. Chico, Mrs. Groucho, Groucho and Chico."

[78] When the show opened at the Biltmore Theatre in Los Angeles—where this picture was taken—there, sitting in the front row, were Douglas Fairbanks, Mary Pickford and Greta Garbo. All of them were holding cigars and wearing false mustaches.

[79] Somewhere along the way, Chico came up with the idea of "shooting the keys." He'd play a well-recognized tune, then pause before the final note of the bar, point his finger, and strike the key. It became almost as big a rage among piano players as "Nola."

ANIMAL CRACKERS

GROUCHO: One morning I shot an elephant in my
pajamas. How he got in my pajamas,
I'll never know.

While George Kaufman and Morrie Ryskind were writing *Animal Crackers* for us, we went off to Europe on holiday. Sam Harris was again producing. We opened at the 44th Street Theatre and went on for 191 performances.

80 The immortal Captain Spaulding. I'm told this is the last existing solo picture of me from the show. You'll notice the pith helmet, the jodhpurs, the knee-high boots, the bow tie, and the wide-lapelled coat. Soon, all your everyday African explorers were dressing this way.

81 Among the great supporting acts in the history of the theater.

82 The Napoleon scene from *I'll Say She Is!* was adapted into the Du Barry scene: a costume party, a play within a play, with Margaret Dumont playing the pivotal role.

83 Harpo, Chico and friends.

84 Harry Ruby and Bert Kalmar wrote "The Musketeers" as a finish for the Du Barry sketch.

Unless we tell you who we are, you'll never guess;
We're not Napoleon or da Vinci.
A lot of people think we are, but none the less,
We're not Napoleon or da Vinci.
We're not even Washington or Lincoln,
Jefferson or Alexander Carr;
You'd be wrong whoever you begin on
So we'll let you in on who we are.
So stand by, unseen listeners. (Bugle call)

Chorus:
We're four of the three musketeers.
We've been together for years.
Eenie, meenie, minee, (horn),
Four of the three musketeers.
We live by the sword, by the sea, by the way,
And we fight day and night,
And we sleep night and day,
My country 'tis of thee,
Land of the light wines and beers.
We're cheered from Cologne to Algiers.
Each time our motto appears,
It's one for all and two for five.
We're four of the three musketeers.

Patter:
When the Queen needs recreation and she strolls along the path,
Where are we? Right by her side.
When she's filled with jubilation or consumed with raging wrath,
Where are we? Right by her side.
We've sworn that we'd shield and protect her.
We're her guardsmen, true and tried.
When she gets up in the morning and she slips into her bath,
Where are we?—Far from the old folks at home.

Second Chorus:
We're four of the three musketeers.
We've been together for years.
Athos, Pathos, Mathos, (horn),
Four of the three musketeers.
We fight for the King, for the Queen, for the Jack,
And we're first at the front
When the front's at the back.
Three cheers for Richelieu,
Here's how we give him the cheers. (Business)
The foe trembles each time it hears
This motto ring in its ears.
It's one for all and two for five.
We're four of the three musketeers.

Though Kaufman and Ryskind wrote the bulk of the show, I wrote a segment too. A few minutes were needed for a scene change, so I wrote some words that I recited in the show, one foot planted on the stage and the other on an ordinary kitchen chair:

Did you ever sit and ponder as you walk along the strand,
That life's a bitter battle at the best;
And if you only knew it and would lend a helping hand,
Then every man can meet the final test.
The world is but a stage, my friend,
And life is but a game;
And how you play is all that matters in the end.
For whether a man is right or wrong,
A woman gets the blame;
And your mother is your dog's best friend.
Then up came mighty Casey and strode up to the bat,
And Sheridan was fifty miles away.
For it takes a heap of loving to make a home like that,
On the road where the flying fishes play.

81

68

82

83

84

69

Here I'd take my foot off the chair, and drag it—the chair—slowly off the stage as I sang:

So be a real-life Pagliacc' and laugh, clown, laugh.

The first four weeks I recited the poem, the audience would scream. These were the sophisticates, the professional audiences, I suppose. After four weeks, the out-of-towners started coming in. They applauded respectfully. To them my recitation was a great piece of philosophy.

⁸⁵ Harpo always urned his way.

⁸⁷ This sketch was delivered to me backstage one day. It was quite a thrill receiving it. Bruce Bairnsfather was a great celebrity of the day, the Bill Mauldin of World War One. He was an Englishman, a captain in the Royal Warwicks, whose cartoons became a worldwide symbol of the war. They were published in book form under the title *Fragments from France*. A stage play, *The Better 'Ole*, was inspired by his drawings, and it was as famous a World War One play on both sides of the Atlantic as the later *What Price Glory?*

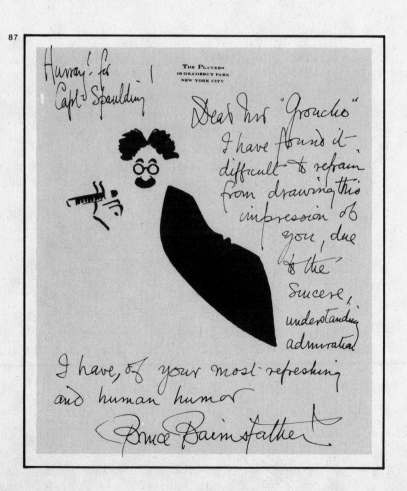

4

Early Movies

THE COCOANUTS

GROUCHO: Now, uh, in arranging these lots, of course we use blueprints. You know what a blueprint is, huh?

CHICO: Yes, oysters.

GROUCHO: How is it you never got double pneumonia?

CHICO: I go around by myself.

GROUCHO: You know what a lot is?

CHICO: Yeah, it's-a too much.

. . . I was called into conference and informed that I would have to discard the black painted mustache. When I asked why, they explained, "Well, nobody's ever worn a black painted mustache on the screen. The audience isn't accustomed to anything as phony as that and just won't believe it."

"The audience doesn't believe us, anyhow," I answered. "All they do is laugh at us, and after all, isn't that what we're getting paid for?"

Talk about sticklers for tradition! We finally had to compromise with them. We agreed to shoot an experimental scene with the painted mustache and run it at a local theater. The reaction was the same as it had been at the Fifth Avenue Theatre in our vaudeville days. The audience didn't seem to care what kind of mustache I wore so long as the jokes were funny.

On the stage I frequently stepped out of character and spoke directly to the audience. After the first day's shooting on *Cocoanuts*, the producer (who has since retired from the movies, for the good of the industry) said, "Groucho, you can't step out of character and talk to the audience."

Like all people who are glued to tradition, he was wrong. I spoke to them in every picture I appeared in. (Sometimes they answered back. This I found rather disconcerting.)

From *Groucho and Me*

During the spring of 1929, we were appearing in *Animal Crackers* on the stage at night and filming during the day. Paramount Pictures, which had signed us to a contract, had outfitted a studio in Long Island for sound recording. In just a couple of years, Tallulah Bankhead would be filming her first pictures at the same Astoria studio. *Cocoanuts*, produced by Sam Harris, was virtually a filmed version of the play. Getting top billing were, not the Marx Brothers, but the exciting new love team of Oscar Shaw and Mary Eaton. Mary was lovely, Shaw was strictly no-talent. Through some brilliant piece of logic, Paramount assigned Robert Florey, a Frenchman, to direct. What came up, in some ways, was Greek to me.

95

Somewhere among the palm trees is a microphone. Harpo's shushing motion isn't altogether a gag. The microphone picked up all extraneous noises, and we weren't allowed to supply any—not even some well-needed ad libs. If this movie is more static than most of ours, it's because our movements were hampered. We couldn't just spout our speeches any old place. For the first time, I had to toe the mark.

95

We'd been reaping the huzzahs from theatrical critics for the last few years. Movie reviewing was a new art form, if you can call it that, and the vocabulary was still being worked out. Mordaunt Hall, in his May 25, 1929, review in *The New York Times*, put it—mordauntly:

Fun puts melody in the shade in the audible pictorial transcription of the musical comedy *The Cocoanuts*, in which that incongruous quartet, the Marx Brothers, made their screen debut at the Rialto on Thursday night. Groucho Marx, equipped with George S. Kaufman's crisp lines, rather monopolizes things, allowing but scant time for the fair Mary Eaton and her partner, Oscar Shaw, to rhapsodize on love to the music composed by Irving Berlin. Although the comedy aroused considerable merriment among the first-night gallery, it is of the robust variety livened here and there by witty words.

As the talking pictures are still in their puppyhood, it is justifiable to comment on the registering of the voices and the incidental sounds. Groucho's flow of repartee comes out clearly and naturally. He and the microphone get along well. Chico and Zeppo also succeed in their utterances, and, so far as the fourth Marx is concerned, it matters little to him whether pictures talk or not, for he is the illustrious Harpo, who is content with a silence that is golden. True, in this film he shines, as he did before the footlights, in playing the harp and the piano.

Hall went on to single out "the dainty dances photographed with the camera looking directly down on them. This sequence proved so engaging that it elicited plaudits from many in the jammed theater." (The musical numbers, predating Busby Berkeley, were staged by co-director Joe Santley.) If movies had a long way to go, so did movie criticism. Had the words been more stilted, they would have been delivered by the same stork that delivers us all.

No hit songs came out of *The Cocoanuts*, and this was one of them.

**THE
4 Marx Brothers**
in **"The Cocoanuts"**

PARAMOUNT'S
ALL TALKING
SINGING
DANCING
MUSICAL
COMEDY

FOX ALEXANDER
4 Days Starting
Monday, August 5th

WHEN MY DREAMS COME TRUE
by IRVING BERLIN
The Love Song
in
"The Cocoanuts"
Sung by
MARY EATON
and
OSCAR SHAW
with
THE
MARX BROTHERS
in
"The Cocoanuts"
A Paramount
TALKING & SINGING
PRODUCTION
MADE IN U.S.A.
ORDER CODE "MYDREAMS"
Irving Berlin, Inc.
MUSIC PUBLISHERS
1607 Broadway New York

Two weeks after this picture was taken at Lou Shean's house, Minnie died. Shown here are Uncle Lou and his wife Jessie, Minnie and Aunt Hannah. I don't recall the young girl sitting in front. Aleck Woollcott accompanied the family to Woodlawn Jewish Cemetery. On a nearby tombstone was the name of Tom O'Flaherty. "There's a spy in this cemetery," he told me. A few days later, Aleck's written eulogy appeared in *The New Yorker:*

A short history of the magician's daughter who was the managing mother of the Four Marx Brothers. . . . Last week the Marx Brothers buried their mother. On the preceding Friday night, more from gregariousness than from appetite, she had eaten two dinners instead of the conventional one, and, after finishing off with a brief, hilarious game of Ping-Pong, was homeward bound across the Queensboro Bridge when paralysis seized her. Within an hour she was dead in her Harpo's arms. Of the people I have met, I would name her as among the few of whom it could be said they had greatness. She had done more than bear her sons, bring them up and turn them into play actors. She had *invented* them. They were just comics she imagined for her own amusement. They

amused no one more, and their reward was her ravishing smile.

She herself was doing sweatshop lace-work when she married a tailor named Sam Marx. But for fifty years her father was a roving magician in Hanover, and as a child she had known the excitement of their barnstorming cart rides from one German town to another.

Her trouble was that her boys had got to Broadway. They had arrived. Thereafter, I think she took less interest in their professional lives. When someone paid them a king's ransom to make their first talkie, she only yawned. What she sighed for was the zest of beginnings. Why, I hear that last year she was caught hauling her embarrassed chauffeur off to dancing school, with the idea of putting *him* on the stage. In her boredom she took to poker, her game being marked by so incurable a weakness for inside straights that, as often as not, her rings were missing and her bureau drawer littered with sheepish pawntickets. On the night *Animal Crackers* opened, she was so absorbed that she almost forgot to go at all. But at the last moment she sent her husband for her best wig, dispatched her chauffeur to fetch her new teeth, and, assembling herself on the way downtown, reached the theatre in time to greet the audience. Pretty as a picture she was, as she met us in the aisle. "We have a big success," she said.

Minnie Marx was a wise, tolerant, generous, gallant matriarch. In the passing of such a one, a woman full of years, with her work done, and children and grandchildren to hug her memory all their days, you have no more of a sense of death than you have when the Hudson—sunlit, steady, all-conquering—leaves you behind on the shore on its way to the fathomless sea.

She was in this world sixty-five years and *lived* all sixty-five of them. She died during rehearsals, in the one week of the year when her boys would be around her—back from their summer roamings, that is, but not yet gone forth on tour. Had she foreseen this—I'm not sure she didn't—she would have chuckled, and, combining a sly wink with her beautiful smile, she would have asked, "How's that for perfect timing?"

My first book—and what a thrill it was—was published just as the country was knocked over by the Depression. Instead of buying my book, *Beds,* most people took to their own.

A reader in Clinton, Iowa, wants to know the origin of that expression, "You've made your bed, now lie in it." Well, that's a long story, but like the Boston Braves I'm not going anyplace. After all, I've seen every movie in town but *Animal Crackers,* and I am getting pretty tired of those Marx Brothers, especially the one with the black mustache who talks so much. But it's about time we were doing something to please the Iowa trade.

The whole thing happened seventeen years ago, come Mickleberry, when Brooklyn Bridge was still a wheat field, and Persia had just merged with Arabia (they later took over the Chase National, and became the second largest company in the world, but that's a story that can wait). At any rate, there was a young Arabian named Coffee. She was beautiful in a wild sort of way, with streaming walnut hair, and a white gown that left no doubt as to her sex (it later developed that she was a female). These Bedouins were kurrazey for her, and she was pretty hot for the Bedouins herself. Everything would have been all right except for Coffee's mother, a hag whose map had been lifted so often that you needed a stepladder to talk to her (one fellow who climbed the stepladder said it wasn't worth it). In loud and lewd moans she deplored the conduct of the alluring Coffee, who was rapidly copping off all the Bedouins who meant anything. The fair Coffee would mount her silvery steed and race across the desert, hotly pursued by feverish sheiks, who were in no mood to be toyed with. Round and round the hot sands they would spin, with the wild Coffee always a lap in front of them, and the Arabs getting hotter and hotter. Hour on hour they kept up this dizzy whirl, stopping for neither meat nor drink, until finally the Bedouins' horses would drop in their tracks, and the riders would fall from their saddles, panting and exhausted. As it happened (it probably wouldn't happen that way again in your lifetime or mine), all the sheiks fell right in front of the tent occupied by Coffee's mother. When the old dame heard the falling bodies, she rushed out and took a look at the weary

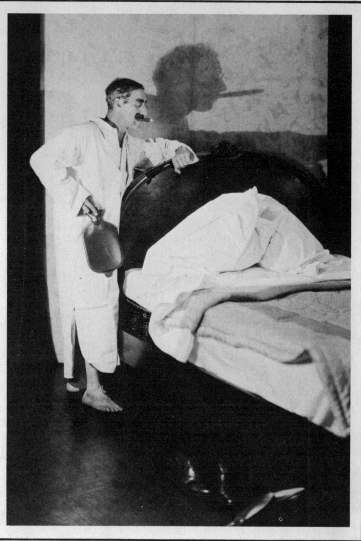

101

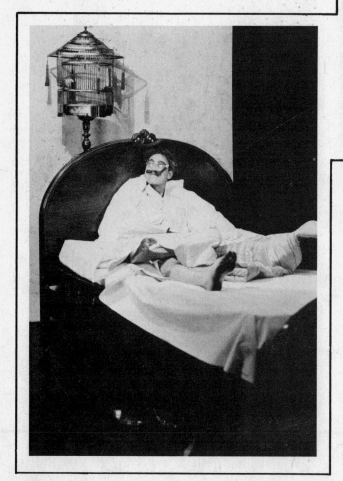

102

riders, huddled in a group; then she turned to her daughter and said, "Never come into my tent again. You made your Bedouins, now lie in them."

From *Beds*

103 Captain Spaulding as movie star.
104 Signor Emanuel Ravelli, Horatio Jamison, Captain Spaulding and The Professor.

104

105

ANIMAL CRACKERS

GROUCHO:	Are we all going to get married?
MARGARET IRVING:	All of us?
GROUCHO:	All of us!
IRVING:	But that's bigamy!
GROUCHO:	Yes, and it's bigamy, too.

That exchange, originally used in the Napoleon sketch from *I'll Say She Is!*, proves that the Marx Brothers were pioneers in ecology. What other comedians would dare to recycle their words, to be used again another day? Our second Paramount picture was again shot at Astoria, the same year that Claudette Colbert, Fredric March and Miriam Hopkins were also leaving the theater for films. There was no doubt this time that the Marx Brothers were *the* stars of the picture and that Lillian Roth and Hal Thompson would be secondary, playing the love interests. That's the way it was to remain for the rest of the Marx Brothers' pictures.

The Depression had taken a heavy toll on us all, and we needed the distraction of work. Sam Harris had tried to lend me some money after I'd lost $250,000 on the stock market, but he wasn't in a much better financial position himself. We had to work harder. We were soon to discover that talking pictures were the coming thing, and none of them could lose money. The shiftover from stage to film came at a time when the Theater—the Fabulous Invalid, as they still call her—was having one of her periodic relapses. Switching to films, the Marx Brothers, in very short order, were better than ever and better-off than ever.

When the picture was released, our old friend Mordaunt Hall of *The New York Times* again dissected our appeal. His review of August 29, 1930, read in part:

The Marx Brothers are to be seen at the Rialto in a further sample of amusing nonsense, this time the audible film of *Animal Crackers*. This mad affair suits the principals, and its absurdities brought forth gales of laughter yesterday afternoon. It is, however, the sort of thing that will only appeal to those who revel in the work of these four brothers.

Hall didn't need to point out that our audience wasn't necessarily universal. He didn't like my type. The feeling was mutual. I couldn't imagine anyone not liking Harpo, however, and in his name I take umbrage—every day before breakfast.

106 The movie entrance. The Music Masters played the Nubians, and lost, 6-0.

107 Harpo makes a gookie on film.

108 Margaret Dumont, Margaret Irving, Harpo and Chico.

109 With Lou Sorin. When I was in New York in 1974, I tried to look him up. Unfortunately he'd just died. I never got a chance to tell him what a great straight man he was. In the picture, Lou's character was patterned after Otto Kahn, the great financier and philanthropist. Woollcott once told me a story about Kahn. He was walking down the street with a close friend, Marshall Wilder. Wilder was a hunchback, and a well-known comedian. Walking up Fifth Avenue, they passed a synagogue. Kahn smiled. "I used to be a Jew," he told Wilder. "Really?" Wilder replied. "And I used to be a hunchback."

110 With Ruth on the same Art Deco set as the scene shot with Lou.

111 Chico, Lou Sorin, Hal Thompson, Lillian Roth. The studio's caption reads:

Arabella Rittenhouse, who has persuaded Signor Ravelli to substitute a painting by her fiancé for a masterpiece, is overjoyed when art connoisseur Roscoe Chandler recognizes it to be a work of genius.

Frankly, *I* found the painting quite derivative, and from an old-fashioned school—P.S. 37.

112 Hal Thompson, Lillian Roth and Chico.

113 They rarely laughed when Harpo sat down to play. He held the instrument all wrong, and he got sounds out of the harp that professionals didn't know existed. Years before in vaudeville, I confided to Harpo that I was worried about the ending to an upcoming scene. "Don't worry," he said, referring to the glissandos with which he invariably concluded his performances, "I'll give them the shit finish."

114 Mrs. Rittenhouse and Captain Spaulding. We got the name Rittenhouse from a hotel in Philadelphia. The Marx Brothers called Margaret Dumont Mrs. Rittenhouse from then on, no matter what part she was playing. Contrary to popular mythology, Captain Spaulding's name wasn't taken from that of a Hollywood dope peddler. The name was concocted by two New Yorkers who'd spent little time in California: Kaufman and Ryskind.

116 Prior to moving to California as part of our Paramount contract, we went to London to star in Charles B. Cochran's *1931 Varieties*. This picture was taken at the Savoy Hotel. Chico shoots the keys while his wife Betty, my son Arthur, Zeppo's wife Marian, Zeppo, my daughter Miriam, and Ruth and I look on.

117 This separate picture was taken of Harpo at about the same time, without makeup. He was in his early forties.

Margaret Dumont was with us in London, and we extracted the choicest bits from *Cocoanuts* and *Animal Crackers* into one forty-minute turn, as part of the first variety bill to play the Palace Theatre in almost twenty years. We were a smash.

The Marx Brothers Stock Company—that's what we were. In various combinations we made thirteen pictures together, some of them brilliant, others embarrassing. But they all had a common thread, for better or worse: our famous public personalities. We were characters, in both senses of the word. This is the way I remember them:

118 GROUCHO—Obnoxious, irreverent, egomaniacal. He was the first one to bring the theatrical convention, the spoken aside, to the film medium. He also brought the greasepaint. In all the pictures he was, in a way, the synopsis of the story—no matter how silly the story. The actor playing him in all his incarnations—Captain Jeffrey T. Spaulding, Professor Quincy Adams Wagstaff, Rufus T. Firefly, Otis B. Driftwood, and Dr. Hugo Z. Hackenbush among them—didn't have as good a time working in films as he seemed to be having.

118

119 HARPO—Sweet, innocent, disarming. "Puck in a fright wig, Till Eulenspiegel on the burlesque circuit." That's how *Time* magazine described him. They also said he was the warmest and most wonderful of the brothers, to which I also agree. The dames he chased were in no danger. He didn't know what to do with them once he caught them. In real life, however, he did.

120 CHICO—Italian, dumb like a fox, a born gambler, a great straight man. His character lacked depth and soul. The actor behind him brought the least preparation to his work, and it irritated me that he got away with it, which may prove that his was a more natural talent than mine.

121 ZEPPO—Handsome, wooden, slightly obtuse. The fill-in. His character brought logic to a basically illogical story, and he was often an intrusion. In real life, the wittiest of men, and a scrapper.

122 MARGARET DUMONT—Lovely, dignified, put upon. The Establishment. Sweet and agreeable. Of another planet. She could never quite understand what was going on. She never understood any of the jokes. A great straight woman.

119

123

123 The movie was *Monkey Business,* and here I stand with the writers who put it all together: Sol Violinsky, S. J. Perelman, Will Johnstone and Arthur Sheekman. The producer was Herman Mankiewicz. Students of the cinema see in him a great auteur, and some of them claim his was the sole genius behind *Citizen Kane.* He must have grown considerably as an artist in the interim. I found him an irritating drunk who didn't give a hang about the movie project.

124 Before we got too far into the shooting, we went on holiday to Mexico (I'm the figure cut in half at left) with William Perlberg and Arthur Sheekman. We had nothing to do, so we set fire to the mayor's sweater.

125

124

MONKEY BUSINESS

GROUCHO: I know. I know. You're a woman who's been getting nothing but dirty breaks. Well, we can clean and tighten your brakes, but you'll have to stay in the garage all night.

Hollywood was a sleepy little town when we moved to California. There'd been a time, years previously, when Hollywood was a hot spot, a den of iniquity. (I'm sorry I wasn't there at the time, if only to find out what "iniquity" means.) These were the silent days and the roaring nights. All the equipment necessary to become a movie star was a little luck, a good profile, and some hair on the chest. I am, of course, referring to the male actor.

We piled aboard the Santa Fe and set off to stake a tentative claim in movieland. The year was 1931. When we stepped off the train at Los Angeles the air was sweet with a heavy blend of orange and lemon blossoms. The rush to California had not yet begun, and Hollywood still had that quiet, pastoral air about it.

The talkies had just intruded on the movie industry and scared the hell out of most of its members. Gilbert, Garbo, Charlie Ray, Tom Mix, William S. Hart, Fairbanks and Pickford and a few others comprised the movie royalty. Taxes were still nominal, and Hollywood's queens and kings lived far more luxuriously than most of the reigning families in Europe. Most of them tossed their money around as though they manufactured it themselves in the cellar. They went in for solid gold bathtubs, chauffeur-driven Rolls Royces, champagne for breakfast and caviar every fifteen minutes. It was the kind of world that today only exists in the pages of movie magazines and for the sons of a few Latin American dictators.

There was plenty of talent in the top twenty, but the rest got by mostly on their faces and their figures. Some of the girls knew the producers much better than their wives did. In time, many of them became the wives and the ex-wives became agents or sold real estate.

This was Never Never Land that hadn't been parallelled since the red-hot days of Rome. The parties were lush, and so were most of the guests. No party was considered a success unless a number of the survivors were tossed into the swimming pool in their evening clothes, and I don't mean pajamas.

From Groucho and Me

It was very easy to become acclimated to California. We all felt five years younger. (That's how many years the studio took off our ages in publicity stories.) Harpo immediately took up with the crowd at San Simeon. Though I was often invited to parties given by Charlie Lederer, who was related to Marion Davies, I never went to William Randolph Hearst's ranch because I disapproved of his political philosophy. Chico soon became a card-playing crony of some of the most powerful men in town, among them Irving Thalberg. I was content to spend the bulk of my leisure time with my family. California in the early 1930s was a wonderful place in which to raise children.

From New York, George Kaufman wrote that he was thinking of combining the title of one previous show with the song hit from another: *Let 'Em Eat Cake* and "Mine." The new production would be called *Let 'Em Eat Mine*. A few years later, after the Mary Astor scandal, George would be very careful what he put down on paper and mailed to California. I'd already learned some of the bizarre habits of the lotus eaters out West when, in 1929, we were touring in *Animal Crackers* and played the Pantages Theatre in Los Angeles. Alexander Pantages was accused of raping an actress in his office at the theater. He was dumfounded. Like so many others in the business, he had always thought that was what actresses were for.

The Groucho Marx family settled on North Hillcrest Road in Beverly Hills, a thirteen-room, seven-bath spread which I bought in 1933 for $44,000. I sold it ten years later for $200,000, and now it's worth half a million. The house is now owned by Lalo Schifrin, the composer-musician.

127 With Miriam and Ruth at Paramount Studios in Hollywood.
128 Macko is director Norman McLeod; Echo is assistant director Charles Barton.

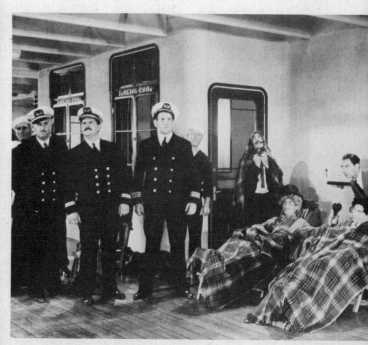

131 A view from the sidelines. McLeod (in white shirt and knickers) was inexperienced, but he'd been a good boxer, so he whipped us into shape.

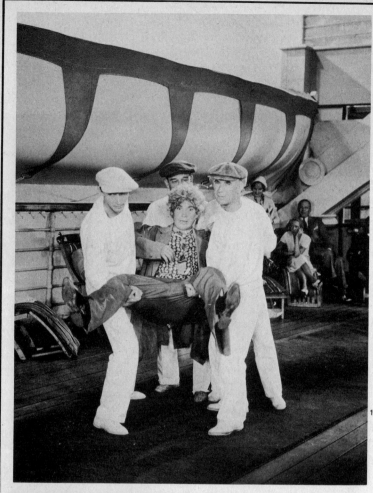

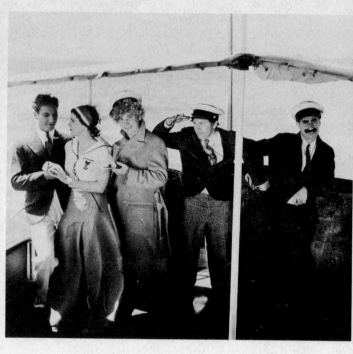

136 For the first time Zeppo was actually given something to do. He was the love interest.

139 In a scene cut from the picture, Harpo dresses in nurse's drag and carries Billy Barty. This is the same Billy Barty who later appeared with me on a Bob Hope comedy special in 1976. (Picture 679.)

141 Standing behind us, the figure in the white hat, is Frenchy. In the movie he's seen standing on the ship as a passenger and on the dock as a visitor. He got twice the normal extra's pay.

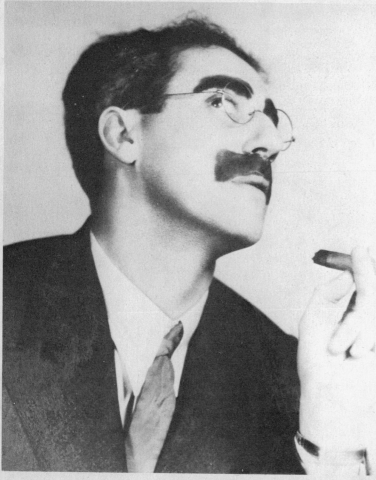

143
-45 With Thelma Todd. A couple of years later, when Thelma was found murdered in the garage of her Pacific Palisades house one morning, a line from the picture was quoted to show the long arm of coincidence: "Well, we can clean and tighten your brakes, but you'll have to stay in the garage all night." She was a beautiful, reckless girl. In one scene she was required to jump out of a rowboat and swim to shore. Only after she'd dived in did she inform us that she couldn't swim. Stagehands had to fish her out of the water.

146

152

153 The last picture of the brothers taken with our father, Frenchy. He died two years later. Minnie's personality was so vivid that Frenchy often seemed to fade into insignificance. He was anything but insignificant. There was a lot of Frenchy's personality in Harpo. Our father was a gentle man, and I was crazy about him. Whenever Minnie went on tour with us, Frenchy kept the home fires burning. It must have seemed odd for those days, but it worked for them.

Monkey Business was released the same time as Charlie Chaplin's City Lights, which was acclaimed as an instant classic. Our picture was described by "Sid" in Variety of October 13, 1931, as "the usual Marx madhouse with plenty of laughs sprawling from a plot structure resembling one of those California bungalows which spring up overnight."

HORSE FEATHERS

GROUCHO: I'd horsewhip you if I had a horse.

To some critics, *Horse Feathers* was a lesser Marx Brothers effort. It had important elements of our previous picture, including director Norman McLeod and writers Sid Perelman and Will Johnstone. We even had those old hands from *Animal Crackers*—Bert Kalmar and Harry Ruby—mixing up the brew. It was a good picture. Perhaps the audience was used to us by now and our brand of lunacy was predictably unpredictable. No one made the point better than "Abel," in his *Variety* review of August 16, 1932. Speaking about Thelma Todd's contributions, he wrote, "She's a luscious eyeful and a swell foil for the Marxian boudoir manhandling, which is getting to be a trade-marked comedy routine."

158 The secret word is swordfish.
162 An apple for the teacher.

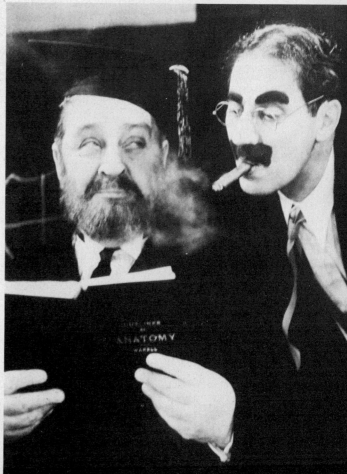

163 Arthur and Ruth visit the set.

164 With the luscious eyeful.

169 While we were filming the football game at Occidental College, a pretty little girl with golden curls stood watching from the sidelines. She was three or four years old, and Harpo fell in love with her. He turned to the little girl's parents and offered them $50,000 for her. The couple told him that their daughter was not for sale. The little girl was Shirley Temple.

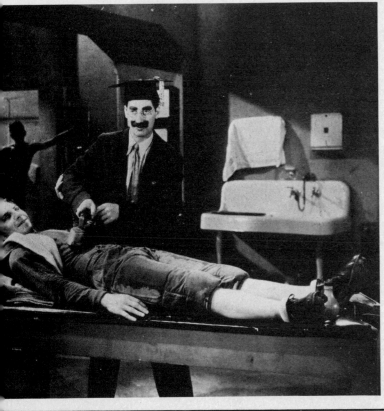

171 We had fully arrived as film stars when, in conjunction with the release of *Horse Feathers*, the Marx Brothers made the cover of *Time* on August 13, 1932. By the time the article appeared, Harpo was doing a concert tour in Russia, working on the original Borscht circuit.

174 A ritual that cemented our foothold in Hollywood, at Grauman's Chinese Theater. Sid Grauman stands in back. There was no need to inform us of the protocol involved. We were from Chicago, and knew all about cement.

TIME
The Weekly Newsmagazine

THE BROTHERS MARX

Volume XX — Number 7

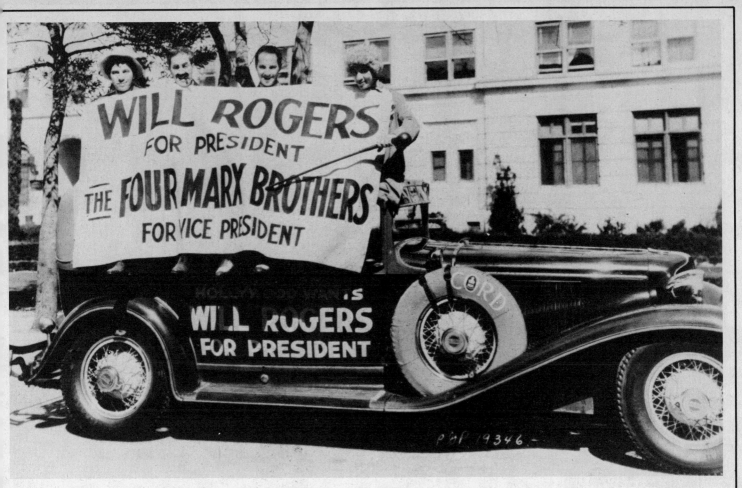

Confesses He Ruined Party by His Singing

Lavish in His Praise of Producer Who Celebrated 20 Years in Pictures

By WILL ROGERS.

It was a grand party, the biggest thing I ever saw. It would take me three columns to tell you who all was there. The list read like one of those "Who's delinquent in their income tax." Out by one of the orchestras I run onto Groucho Marx. I say one of the orchestras, for there was orchestras for you to get out of your car by, another for you to check your hat by, and another one to dance by.

Why every coupie had their own orchestra. Well this one I am talking about was Hawaiian and was playing "The Last Roundup." Groucho suggested that a cowboy tenor voice would be just about what was lacking in this whole musical set up, so I joined in.

Now here is a funny thing about those Marxes, Groucho can play as good on the guitar as Harpo can on the harp, or Chico on the piano, but he never does. He is really what I call an ideal musician. He can play but don't.

In New York when I was playing with Miss Dorothy Stone in "Three Cheers" he even tried to teach me to play the guitar. He would come over to my dressing room before our two shows started, and he would play, and we would sing these old songs, and so this thing was really nothing new we was pulling, but it was new to the gang.

"The Last Roundup," instead of us dying off, why that just give us encouragement, and for a half hour we totally ruined (musically) Mr. Roach's party. Course lots of folks joined us, to try and drown us out, but not us.

The next night Mrs. Rogers and I had dinner over at Groucho's and we took up right where we had left off, only he played the piano that night.

I love to sing old songs, and any time anybody will start one I am the loudest, and if they won't start 'em, I will myself.

But we did have a good time at Hal's party, and I believe everybody did and when he is in pictures forty years, I am going to go to another one for him. Roach says he will hire Groucho and me the next time. But the songs we sing now will never become old songs. No one will ever remember 'em that long.

There was even talk of our running for political office. Will Rogers would run for President and the four brothers would be his running mates for vice president.

Among my famous correspondents over the years was Booth Tarkington, surely one of our better American writers. His political philosophy was as rock-ribbed and far right as the coast of Maine, where he chose to settle in his final years.

November 16th, 1932

Dear Mr. Marx:-

I appreciate your thoughtfulness in describing to me, in one phrase of lightning-like clarity, the most intelligent man in the United States.

If he will send me either or both of the books you mention I shall do myself the honor of inscribing them.

Congratulating you warmly upon having such a friend and hoping that you and all of your relatives are happy and well, I am

Faithfully yours

Booth Tarkington

176 Radio, in 1933, was quickly becoming a national medium when Chico and I went back to New York to do the NBC series *Flywheel, Shyster & Flywheel*. I played Waldorf T. Flywheel, senior partner in an ambulance-chasing law firm, and Chico was my assistant.

177 A portrait taken of me at the time, without mustache, glasses and cigar—incognito.

178 We were still in New York when Marlene Dietrich arrived from Europe in October of 1933, on her way to Hollywood to do her next picture, *The Scarlet Empress*. Since we were both Paramount stars, the studio thought we should be photographed together. Marlene and I had something else in common. She was our next-door neighbor in Beverly Hills, shortly after the Marxes moved to California. The year before, we'd all spent sleepless nights following the Lindbergh kidnapping. Marlene had a small daughter, and Ruth and I had Arthur and Miriam. One night, a black limousine pulled up in front of our house. When I looked out, there was no one about. The car idled in the driveway for hours. I called Marlene next door, and we decided to hide the children. The next morning, the car had vanished. Two years later, I was dancing at a party with a famous actress whose name I don't remember—shows how famous she was. Somebody tapped me on the shoulder; it was Lorenz Hart. "Did you ever find out who put the car in front of your house?" he asked. I said no. "It was me," he replied. That was Larry's idea of a joke. Lucky for him that he chose to become a lyricist.

DUCK SOUP

GROUCHO:	I suppose you'll think me a sentimental old fluff, but, uh, would you mind giving me a lock of your hair?
MARGARET DUMONT:	A lock of my hair? Why, I had no idea!
GROUCHO:	I'm letting you off easy. I was going to ask for the whole wig.

For the first time in our film career, we were working with a superior director, Leo McCarey, a nice man and a good drunk. Margaret Dumont, after an absence of two pictures, was back with us. Was it that daring to be antiwar in those days? This was our only picture with a totally mythical background, the country of Freedonia, and yet its message was real enough to be banned in Italy by Mussolini.

Duck Soup wasn't one of our biggest box-office hits, though it's clearly one of the best pictures we ever made. Kalmar and Ruby wrote the screenplay, with additional dialogue by Nat Perrin and Arthur Sheekman. I'd met Sheekman while on tour. He'd been a newspaper columnist in Chicago, and during an interview I volunteered to write his column. Then, I hired him to come to Hollywood to work on the Marx Brothers' films.

Duck Soup has some of my favorite lines: "But there must be a war. I've paid a month's rent on the battlefield" . . . "Clear? Huh! Why a four-year-old child could understand this report. Run out and find a four-year-old child. I can't make head or tail of it" . . . "Remember, we're fighting for this woman's honor, which is probably more than she ever did."

By this time, we were well established in films, and our characters were well embedded in the public's mind. Roger Manwell, in his book *Film,* offers an overview of our appeal:

In a world of pomp and circumstance, the Marx Brothers burst like a wind of relief. They represent all the things that one was brought up not to do. They take the place to pieces with steady glee. They dress like nothing on earth except that their clothes are recognizable in bits and pieces. Groucho moves with the assured insolence of a ballet dancer who cannot stop dancing offstage. . . . He is the great charlatan who, when he goes, takes the door with him. Straight from music hall to film, the Marx Brothers do not care a dime about the camera. They treat it like Margaret Dumont, though they know they cannot do without it.

So much conjecture had been offered about Zeppo's contributions to the act that the studio felt compelled to issue a statement—of sorts:

Zeppo, despite his straight character, is a most important part of the team. He's an expert gag man and is so splendid at imitating any one of the brothers, that should an illness stop one from making an appearance, Zeppo can immediately take his place. Clearing up *that* mystery.

Once, while playing in Chicago, I'd had an emergency appendectomy. Zeppo took over my part. He got such huge laughs that, out of self-protection, I got out of the hospital as fast as I could.

The opening scene of the picture.

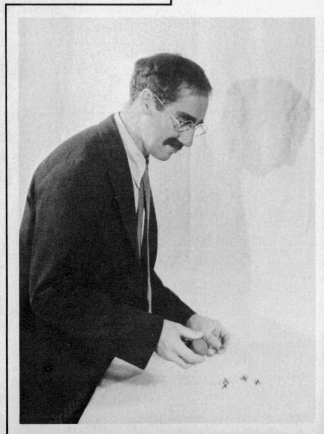

183 Harpo and Edgar Kennedy.

187 Chico, Harpo, Louis Calhern.

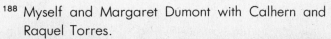

188 Myself and Margaret Dumont with Calhern and Raquel Torres.

189 "To war!"

190

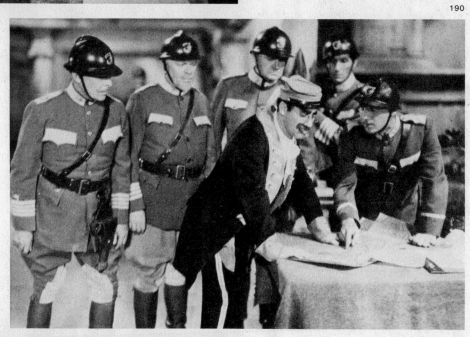

194

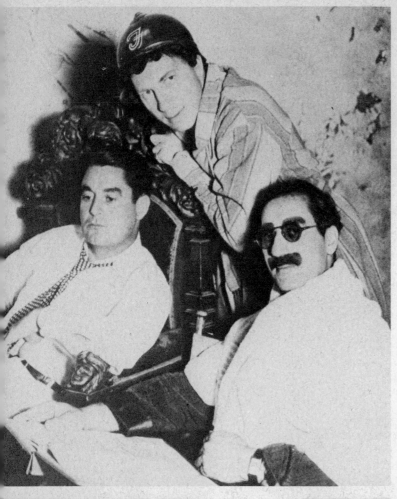

192 With director Leo McCarey. One of the most memorable sequences of the picture was the mirror scene, which was McCarey's inspiration. It had first been used in vaudeville. Max Linder, the great French comedian, did a similar sequence in one of his films, but it wasn't as intricately timed and well developed as McCarey's version. We shot the whole mirror scene on a Saturday morning. It took perhaps two hours. Harpo was a brilliant mime and he simply copied whatever movements I made. Very few setups and minimal takes were required.

193 With Arthur on the set.

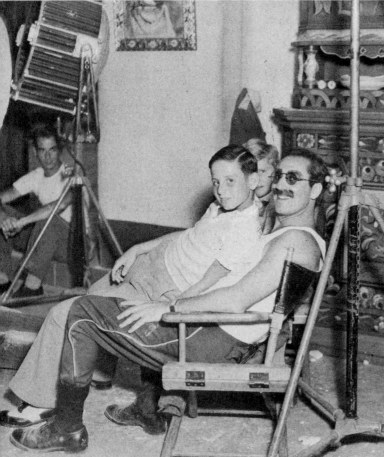

To Groucho From his loving brother Zeppo

195

WORLD-TELEGRAM   MARCH 29.

So This Is Broadway

Four Marx Brothers' Combination May Shrink to a Trio, Zeppo Stepping Out.

By GEORGE ROSS

IT may not be the foremost item of the day, and it is possible that it will not rock the entertainment world to its soft-clay foundation, but there is a report about that the Four Marx Brothers are about to become a trio. The comical quartet (?), it would appear, have just had one (1) lay-off. It seems that the Brethren Four may dispense with the services of Zeppo, their straight man—or vice versa.

At any rate, such an action would not only add to the already weighty problem of unemployment, but deprive the wags of their stock, mischievous commentaries. How may one inquire hereafter. "Have yuh seen the three Four Marx Brothers?" and so on almost any provocation. That jest, if the foursome becomes a threesome, is over.

As for their whereabouts, Zeppo is in Hollywood at the moment, breaking in on a new, off-stage occupation. He has set out to be an actors' representative and agent, merchandising talent. His three brothers, when last seen and heard from, were in Manhattan. Another of the fraternal clan is still engaged in the manufacture of feminine apparel. Meanwhile Moss Hart and Robert Sherwood are contemplating a show for the Marx Brothers (three), which Irving Berlin will set to music and which Sam H. Harris will put on next season.

On and Off Broadway.

IT has been a long time since Lee Shubert has taken his Broadway attractions to London. He will leave for the British metropolis tonight, to arrange for the production of two of them. He will present "No More Ladies" in association with Gilbert Miller, somewhere in the vicinity of Piccadilly Circus. He also will arrange for a presentation of the "Ziegfeld Follies."

An English cast will be engaged for "No More Ladies," which will be put on early in the summer, so as not to interfere with the New York run of the comedy. The Ziegfeld Follies' showing, to be made at a later date, will include all the principals of the Broadway company. Mr. Shubert also plans to look around in the English playhouses and inspect a few exhibits, for possible American importation. Mr. Shubert probably will run into Ferdinand Bruckner aboard the Olympic. Mr. Bruckner is to sail tonight, too. He is the author of "Races," the play about Nazi Germany which the Theatre Guild has decided to cancel. He is going to rejoin his family in Paris. He may come back in the fall if the Guild gets his play out of the closet again.

At Random.

MAYBE it is a note on the trend of irreverence, but business has been better in the playhouses this Holy Week than showmen had anticipated. Yesterday's matinees did a brisk trade. . . . That play called "Brain Sweat," with the all-Negro cast, will arrive at the Longacre on April 4. . . . James Montgomery, who wrote "Irene," "Nothing But the Truth" and a couple of other popular successes, is producing it together with Henry B. Stern, reformed playwright. . . . The installation of "Brain Sweat" at the Longacre will send Arthur Beckhard's show, "Wife Insurance," scurrying elsewhere. It's possible that it will be postponed for a week or so. . . . Charles Hopkins, who's had some tough luck this season, bought a play yesterday for production in the fall. It is entitled "These Have I Loved," and Lewis Beach is the author. . . . Herman Shumlin, who still visits his office daily, hasn't found the play he wants to do yet. Step in at any hour and you'll find him reading one script or another. Will he do Molnar's "Riviera" together with Lawrence Weber? Mr. Shumlin blames that query on old Dame Rumor.

John Golden, back from his Florida vacation, goes to his offices atop the Lincoln every day and contemplates the future. He doesn't intend to start any production until July at the very earliest. And he may be looking for (or writing) a play for Mady Christians.

Cornell Finds Stages Few in Pennsylvania

Only four cities in Pennsylvania are open to the spoken drama, according to Katharine Cornell, who is making a tour of the United States and wishes to act in as many cities as will provide a stage. Philadelphia and Pittsburgh have theatres devoted to the legitimate stage, but of the smaller cities only Reading and Williamsport are available to touring companies. Towns such as Allentown, Lancaster, Altoona, Johnstown, Harrisburg, Scranton and Wilkes-Barre are closed to the actress, though these places in other years furnished large audiences for traveling organizations.

Miss Cornell will appear in Princeton, N. J., and Wilmington, Del., and then in Reading and Williamsport, where she will present "The Barretts of Wimpole Street," which holds the record for spoken drama in Philadelphia and Pittsburgh.

95-196   *Duck Soup* was Zeppo's final course; he decided he didn't want to be a performing Marx Brother any longer. His roles were thankless, and much of the time all he was required to do was show up. It's not that he didn't have the talent; he simply had three older brothers ahead of him. Zeppo decided to become an agent instead. He was a fighter, and he went out to build one of the largest talent agencies in the business. Once, several of us were in a nightclub in Hollywood. My friend Norman Krasna, whom Zeppo was trying to bring over to his agency, was in the group. Norman was playing deaf to Zeppo's hard sell. An obnoxious drunk came to our table and started pestering Krasna. Finally, Zeppo hauled off and hit the drunk on the chin. He turned to Krasna and asked, "Does the other agency give you *that* kind of service?"

197 A night out with Ruth. She was a lovely girl who enjoyed good times.

198 In July of 1933, Gummo gave up the dress manufacturing business in New York to move to California. The plan was that he would manage our affairs, which he proceeded to do as a partner in Zeppo's agency. Local newspapers had Chico and his toy piano meeting Gummo at the plane, one of the proud birds of the Western Air Express-United Airlines fleet.

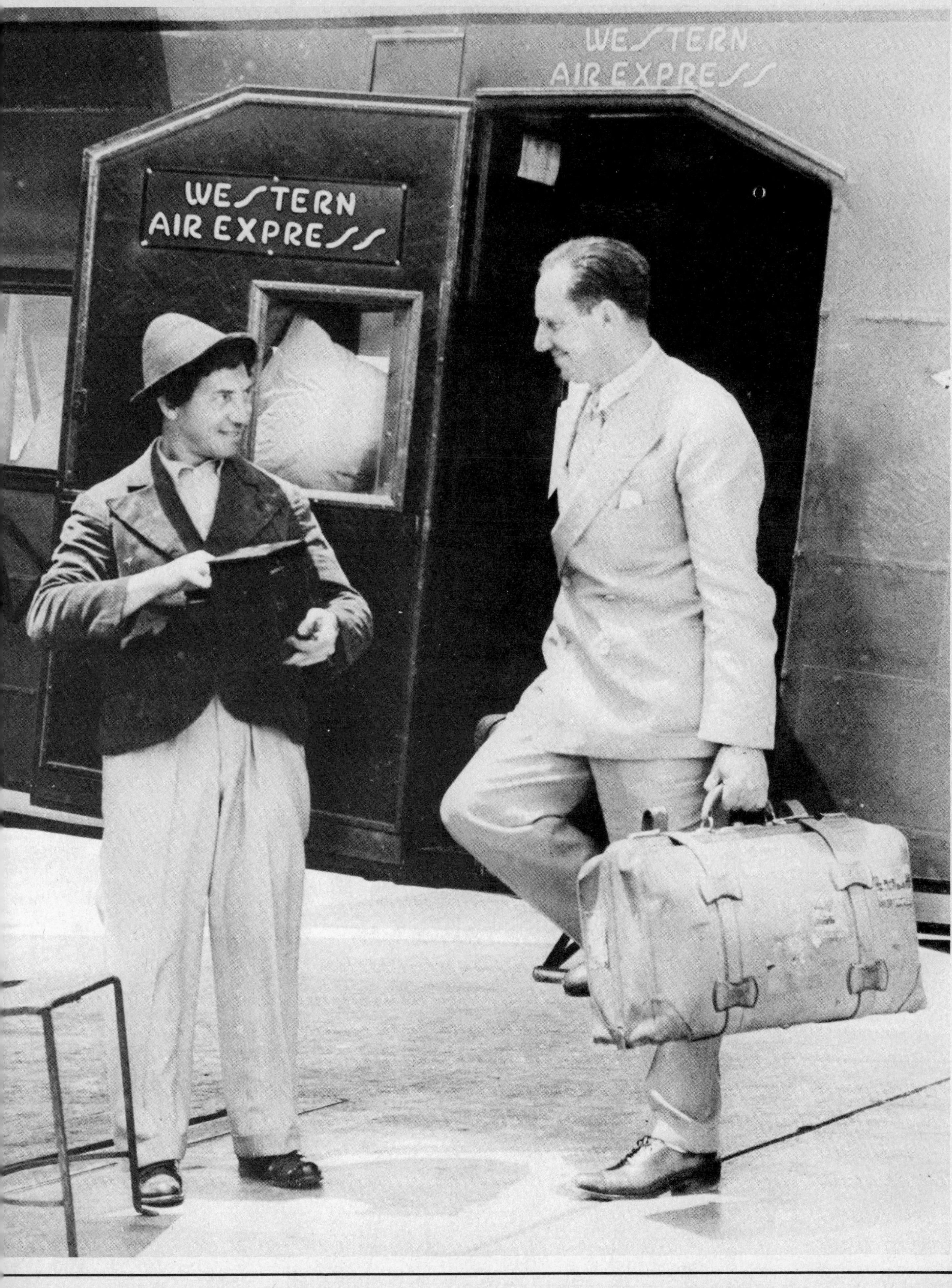
WESTERN
AIR EXPRESS
WESTERN
AIR EXPRESS

¹⁹⁹ Here you have Ulysses H. Drivvle, eagle-eyed news hound, and his assistant, the doughty Penelli. We were again in New York, doing a weekly radio series offering different slants on the news of the world—*That Was The Week That Was*, if you will. Freddy Martin and his orchestra were also on the show, which ran twenty-six weeks.

204 A serious portrait, sans mustache. I wasn't a bad-looking fellow.

Groucho Marx Plays
Without a Mustache
And Misses a Tumble

(Special to The News)

Skowhegan, Me., Aug. 14.—A bit of slap stick brought down the final curtain on Groucho Marx's dramatic debut last night with the Lakewood players. It was not however, either Groucho's own doing or desire.

Groucho Marx

In the closing scene of "Twentieth Century," where Marx, as Jaffe, the theatrical producer, was being wheeled from the station to the theatre, the wheel chair guided by Louis Jean Heydt as Jaffe's press agent, went over the edge of the movable set toward the footlights. Marx jumped up and Leona Maricle playing the Lily Garland role, was bounced around on the arm of the chair. The incident was met with a gale of laughter.

Aside from that there were no unpleasant moments connected with Groucho's opening night. The theatre was filled nearly to capacity. The production, difficult to stage because of the many changes of scene, went as smoothly as could be expected with a single week's rehearsing.

The comedian accepted his venture as an actor with deadly seriousness and knew all the lines.

At the close of the play he was mobbed by autograph seekers from a nearby girls' camp. He received many telegrams during the day, some protesting his discarding of his famous comedy mustache.

Today Groucho relaxed from the tension of his opening night. He faced however, something of an ordeal Wednesday night. His brother Harpo Marx and Alexander Woollcott have made reservations for that performance.

* * *

205 While in the East, I decided to try out something new—the playing of a straight part for a summer run in Maine. *Twentieth Century* was based on producer Jed Harris, though I don't think he was as flamboyant as the character I portrayed. But then, perhaps, neither was I.

207 There was no more conclusive evidence that Zeppo was now a civilian than the neat doctoring job of a Los Angeles tabloid. Zeppo was cut out of one of the pictures of our ritual in concrete at Grauman's, and the background was shadowed in. Now we were three.

That Marx Guy, Again

Aug. 23, 1934.

Editor VARIETY:

There are only two things that ever make the front page in Maine papers. One is a forest fire and the other is when a New Yorker shoots a moose instead of the game warden. Last week, however, they not only had a story that made the front page, but overlapped right into the sporting section.

The story was that Groucho Marx had entered the legitimate, and sans moustache, black eyebrows, and insults to a dowager, had stepped into the Oscar Jaffe role in 'Twentieth Century,' and created a furore that hadn't been equalled since Mansfield played 'King Lear' in Portland.

When VARIETY arrived at the grocery store in Skowhegan, I quickly snatched it out of the grocer's hand (he was looking through the routes for the address of a fan dancer who had promised him one of her fans as soon as the season was over) and hastily thumbed it for the review. Well sir, you could have knocked me over with a copy of Harrison's Reports. There wasn't a line about it. To be sure there were many items of interest. There was a little gem that someone was optimistic and would try burlesque in Pittsburgh, there was a piece about a girl trapeze artist that had sprained her elbow in Kansas City, and a back page telling the world that Joan Blondell always uses Lux after she has removed her cosmetic. But the important fact that I was keeping the drama alive in the Maine woods wasn't even in the obit column.

I realize that you boys are busy making book, but if you want to keep the theatre breathing it might be advisable for you to occasionally get up out of those barber chairs and inject some theatrical news into that so called trade paper of yours.

Don't forget, gentlemen, Groucho Marx in the legit is an important theatrical event and certainly rates as much space as the review you gave to the opening of a cafeteria in Cedar Rapids.

In conclusion I want to say that on my opening night in 'Twentieth Century' the audience cheered for 20 minutes at the end of the first act, but for some reason or other never returned for the next two acts.

Respectfully Yours,
Groucho Marx.

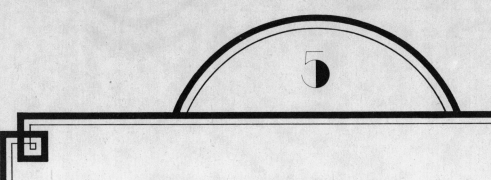

The MGM Years

A NIGHT AT THE OPERA

MARGARET DUMONT: Are you sure you have everything, Otis?
GROUCHO: I've never had any complaints
yet.

Midst flourish and fanfare, we signed a contract with Irving Thalberg at Metro-
Goldwyn-Mayer. He was planning to go into business for himself, and promised to make huge stars
out of us. We thought our pictures had been pretty
good, but Thalberg pointed out that we were often
unsympathetic. Making us warm and nice, sort of,
and giving our films more production values would,
he thought, do the trick.

²¹⁰ Moss Hart, George S. Kaufman and Harpo. This picture must have been taken at Kaufman's farm in Pennsylvania. Kaufman would be writing *A Night at the Opera*, our first feature for MGM, with Morrie Ryskind, and Kitty Carlisle, Hart's future wife, would be the romantic lead. One of Thalberg's brainstorms was the idea that we should "audition" the script on the road, to see how audiences would react. The director could time the laughs and edit the film accordingly. It worked brilliantly.

²⁰⁸⁻²⁰⁹ We wouldn't have been Marx Brothers if we hadn't made a shambles of the contract-signing ceremony. Thalberg was unflappable. So, later, I loaned him my Norfolk jacket.

When we played San Francisco, Thalberg traveled north to see how the script had been refined. We weren't aware he was in the audience until he came backstage. Thalberg, by the way, must have been on quite a culture kick that year. In addition to producing *A Night at the Opera*, he was simultaneously producing *Romeo and Juliet*.

²¹¹ During the tour, we met up with Lou Gehrig in Cleveland and did a gag routine with him at a local stadium. Abbott and Costello were on first, and the Marx Brothers were on second.

Irving Thalberg was a difficult man to see. He would arrive at the studio at noon and leave around midnight. Most everyone in his employ was afraid of him. Perhaps afraid is too strong a word; let's say deeply respectful. But we had been successful in vaudeville too long to be impressed by this cathedral atmosphere, and in his presence we deliberately behaved like the Katzenjammer Kids. He wasn't accustomed to this rowdy familiarity from his hirelings, and I believe that was why he was fond of us. We amused him.

The social side of Hollywood didn't interest Thalberg. He never had time for croquet or polo, and except for an occasional game of bridge, his burning interest was the movies. He never allowed his name to be used on the screen. He didn't care anything about that kind of publicity. He said, "If the picture is good they'll know who produced it. If it's bad, no one cares."

We once asked him why he didn't want his name up there. He said, "I don't want my name on the screen because credit is something that should be given to others. If you are in a position to give credit to yourself, then you don't need it."

He always had three or four story conferences going at the same time in adjoining offices. He would pop in and out, lending a hand here, offering a suggestion there.

We had just started discussing a comedy scene one afternoon in his office when he said, "Hold it, boys. I'll be back in a minute." The minute stretched to two hours. A few days later he repeated this trick. The third time, we got angry. We rolled all the steel filing cabinets against the two doors and wouldn't allow him back in his office until he promised he wouldn't walk out on us again.

Two days passed. We had just begun another conference when he again excused himself. We weren't fooled. We knew he was walking out to attend some other story meeting. In his absence we lit logs in the fireplace and sent to the studio commissary for baking potatoes. When Thalberg returned he found us all sitting naked in front of a roaring fire, busily roasting mickeys over the flames. He laughed and said, "Wait a minute, boys!" He then phoned the commissary and asked them to send up some butter for the potatoes. He never walked out on us again.

From *Groucho and Me*

125

214

212 This MGM sketch was used in the press kits sent out for *A Night at the Opera*.
213-214 Our first studio portraits as a trio.
215 I saw actress Frances MacInerney first, but Chico and Harpo demanded a three-way split.

212

126

217

216 Kitty Carlisle and Harpo.
217 With Kitty Carlisle. Kitty is a supremely talented singer, but she lost interest in her career after marrying Hart. She was a very nice woman when I first met her, and she remains just as nice today.

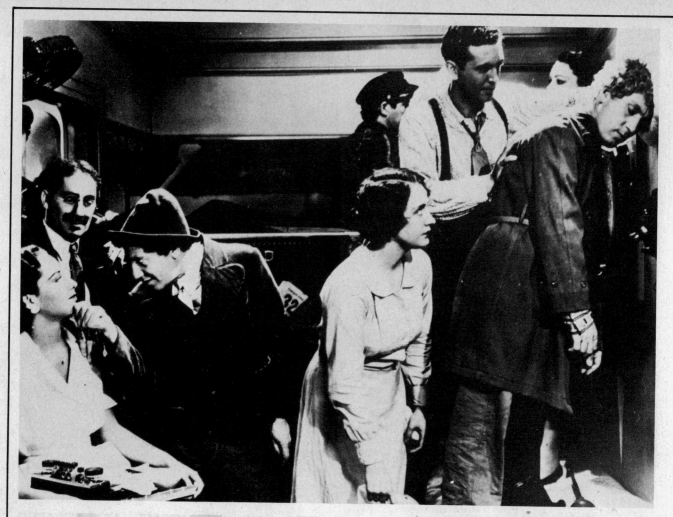

220 The stateroom scene, which today's critics say is one of the highlights of the 1976 Metro-Goldwyn-Mayer picture *That's Entertainment, Part 2.*

221 At the MGM commissary with Al Boasberg. Thalberg proved that the producer was the creative genius on his pictures, and the directors were there merely to do his bidding, almost glorified secretaries. Sam Wood didn't show me otherwise. There was no way I could warm up to him. He was a rigid, humorless man. Our biggest break was getting Boasberg to write for us. He was a comic genius. Curiously, he and Morrie Ryskind didn't get along, though their work meshed very well. Boasberg was a character. We used to match coins every day to see who would pay for lunch. One day he lost. Boasberg paid the twenty-dollar tab, but he never ate with us again; after that, he ate by himself at a lunch wagon across the street. At the time he was getting $1,000 a week to write for Jack Benny, and $1,500 from us to supply jokes for our script. Yet he was a generous man. Every Christmas he would throw a party for broken-down actors and give them clothes and shoes. For many, it would be their entire wardrobe for the coming year.

222 With Kitty Carlisle and Walter King.

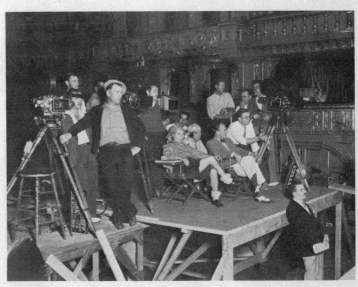

224 On the set with Wood, Kaufman (head in his hands) and Boasberg (at the far right).

225 Wood behind the camera prepares to shoot the scene.

226 And this is the scene: the Marx Brothers with Allan Jones. Zeppo had dropped out of pictures because he felt like a fifth wheel. He was apparently more needed than he thought, because there would always be a Zeppo-like substitute in our future pictures.

227 While we were filming, we welcomed a distinguished visitor: Kakutaro Suzuki, Secretary of the Financial Commission of the Imperial Japanese Government. We discussed taking our act to Tokyo for $10,000 a week. Batteries weren't included.

228 With the great character actor, Siegfried Rumann. Over the years, we were blessed with several great straight men, and Rumann was one of them.

229 Seated are Harpo, Chico, Wood and Boasberg, surrounded by the crew from the film.

235

237

236

238

136

235 The talk looks serious, but actually Wood was discussing with the cameraman the fact that Harpo had put sand in his camera and Chico had stolen his box lunch.

236

237 Harpo tries to measure up to Chico's standards, whatever they were.

238 Chico's daughter Maxine visited us on the *Opera* set. She was planning to attend a New York dramatic school. Maxine is now a talented pianist in her own right, though her forte is classical music instead of the tricky plinkings of her old man. Maxine later went on to become one of New York's top casting directors.

239 Allan Jones's five-year-old son, Theodore Allan Jones, visited us on the set in August 1935.

240 Thalberg insisted we should have musical sequences in our pictures. Finally, a Marx Brothers film had a hit song. "Alone" has become a standard.

Working at MGM was a great satisfaction for Chico, Harpo and me. It was simply the best movie studio—period. We didn't have much to do with Louis B. Mayer. I didn't like him. Since we were under Thalberg's charge, we avoided Mayer as much as possible. Nevertheless, there was a great flurry of activity going on that we couldn't help but notice, with great stars creating their finest roles.

I was standing in the elevator of the Thalberg building one day when Greta Garbo entered. She was then at the peak of her career, acknowledged by all as the greatest movie star of the day.

Miss Garbo was wearing a hat approximately the size of a large manhole cover. The rest of her was encased in slacks and a mannish-type coat. I was standing behind her and, being in a playful mood, I gently lifted the back of her hat.

Thinking back on the incident, I can see that the result of lifting the back of a woman's hat is inevitable: the front of the hat slides down over her face. At the time, however, I had not thoroughly worked out this problem in physics.

Miss Garbo turned on me in a rage, angrily pulling up the hat and revealing the classic features that are still admired by millions. "How *dare* you?" she exclaimed in icy tones.

"Oh, I beg your pardon," I replied. "I thought you were a fellow I knew from Kansas City."

No further words were exchanged. But it is pretty obvious to any student of the cinema that this is the real explanation of why Greta Garbo never appeared in any of the Marx Brothers' pictures.

From Groucho and Me

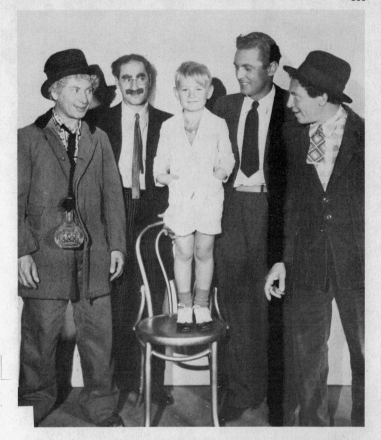

A DAY AT THE RACES

ESTHER MUIR: Oh! Hold me closer! Closer! Closer!
GROUCHO: If I hold you any closer I'll be in back of
             you!

243

[242] I polished the script as we went from town to town. No matter how skillful the writer, there is a very personal rhythm to everyone's speech, and no one knows better what it is than the actor himself.

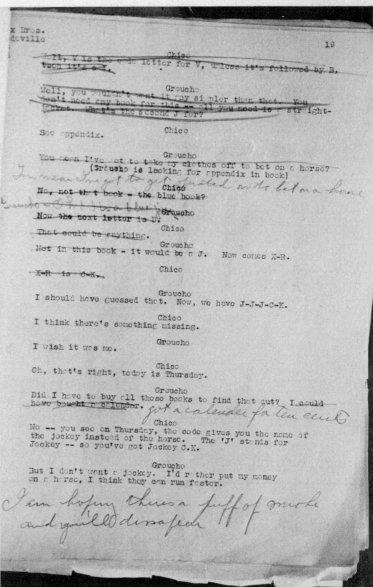

[241] We again went on tour prior to filming *A Day at the Races*, which was written by Robert Pirosh, George Seaton, George Oppenheimer and Al Boasberg. We used real horses in the vaudeville production. While playing in Duluth, one of the horses fell into the orchestra pit. That horse must have known where the horse players were. They had to use a block and tackle to get him out of there.

244

242

247

246

248

249 With Maureen O'Sullivan and Frank Morgan at a studio function.
250 With Maureen. I was crazy about her—but we were both married at the time.

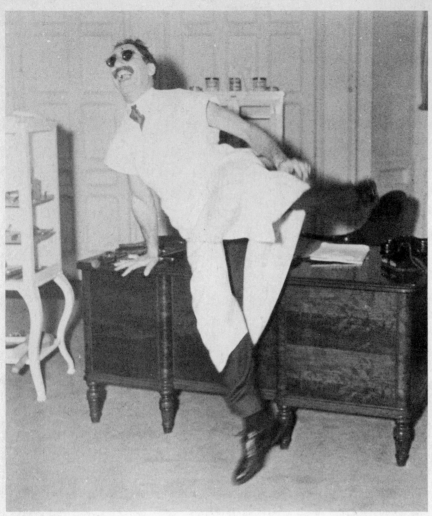

253 Sam Wood was again directing.

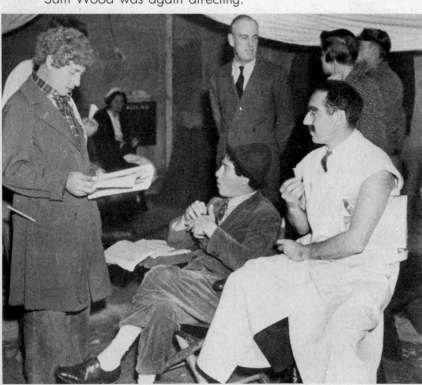

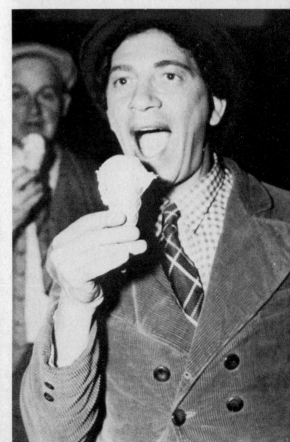

255 Gus Kahn was engaged to compose the music for the picture. This was several years before his daughter Irene married my son Arthur.

256 On the set: Harpo, Allan Jones, unidentified, myself, and Chico at far right.

258 Every picture of the period had to have a Busby Berkeley–type dance sequence. This was ours.

259 With Esther Muir.

260 Esther struck oil while running her fingers through my hair. She retired from films as a result.

261 Because so much paste was being scattered by
-62 Harpo and Chico while I made love to Esther, the scene could only be shot once. Four cameras were used to get all the angles.

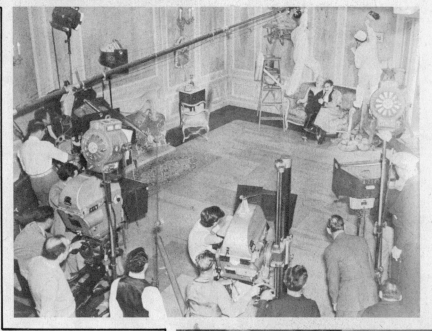

261

With the script clerk, Boasberg, cameraman Joe Ruttenberg, Wood, assistant director Al Shenberg, Chico and Harpo.

266 Harpo with Miriam. All the Marx daughters have first names that start with the letter "M." In addition to Miriam, I have Melinda; Harpo had Minnie; and Chico had Maxine. Shooting days would often last late into the night, but I always insisted on being home early on at least one night. Every Friday over the dinner table, we'd discuss the movies Arthur and Miriam had seen during the week. On one such evening Miriam exclaimed, "I just saw the Ritz Brothers! They're *really* funny!"

268 Now that we were full-fledged stars, we were bombarded with thousands of scripts. Salvador Dali wrote a surrealist movie for us. He approached me one day at the studio. "Hello, Dali," I said. "Groucho," he went on, "have I got a script for you." No, he didn't—it wouldn't play. Neither did the surrealist harp that Dali presented to Harpo, as seen here. It was strung with barbed wire and decorated with dozens of spoons and forks nailed to the frame. Missing is the auto horn.

268

269 Dali's sketch of me as The Shiva of Big Business, as it appeared in *Theatre Arts*.
270 His impression of Harpo.

Ernst Lubitsch, a great director, also had a concept for us. His film would open by following a man climbing some stairs, going into a room where his wife was lying in bed, and opening a closet door. He would discover me standing inside. "Believe it or not," I would say, "I'm waiting for a streetcar." Then a streetcar would come by and I'd jump on, leaving the man open-mouthed as I rode out. The streetcar ran downhill after that; so did the script. The movie wasn't shot.

270

We were in the midst of shooting when Thalberg, who'd always been frail, suddenly died. It was a great blow, both personally and professionally. Max Siegel took over his duties.

274 The horse race.

275 During the time I was filming *A Night at the Opera*, a young writer named Norman Krasna would visit me on the set. We decided to write a screenplay together. *The King and the Chorus Girl* was the result, and any similarity between our story and the love affair between the King of England and Mrs. Simpson was intentional. The picture was produced and directed by Mervyn Le Roy at Warner Brothers in 1937, and it starred Fernand Gravet, Joan Blondell, and Edward Everett Horton. Gravet, a French actor who'd changed his name from Graavey so as not to be mistaken for "the well-known national dish," was cast because of his resemblance to the King. Joan Blondell was cast because of her resemblance to Joan Blondell. Connie Bennett's car was cast as Gravet's car. It had played Mae West's car in a previous picture. Critics raved. *Life* magazine, in its issue of March 29, 1937, called it "easily the season's silliest movie."

276 Ruth and I were now confirmed Californians. By this time there were serious problems in our marriage, but we were making efforts to iron them out, as when we took a vacation without the children at the Brockway Hotel in the Lake Tahoe area.

277 At the Beverly Hills Tennis Club with Harpo, Helen Vinson, Fred Perry, Barbara Stanwyck, and Gloria Sheekman. A moment before this picture was taken, I was telling Barbara an anecdote: A student at Harvard established a world's record that year—1937—by downing seventy-nine live goldfish in two hours. This, I added, was the only athletic event Harvard won that year.

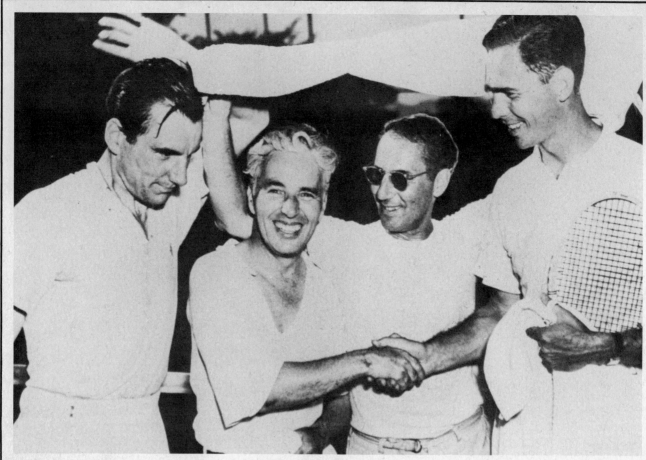

²⁸⁰ Billiards with Arthur.

²⁷⁸ With Fred Perry, Charlie Chaplin and Ellsworth Vines. The occasion was the dedicating of a new clubhouse, and a match between the Americans and the English was set up, Marx and Vines versus Chaplin and Perry. Charlie took his tennis seriously, which I wasn't about to do when I noticed the newsreel photographers setting up. I'd come prepared, lugging twelve tennis rackets and a large suitcase onto center court. The British got off to an early lead, winning the first two games. At that point, I opened the suitcase, took out my lunch, and began to eat it. I offered Charlie a spot of tea, but he declined. Finally, he threw his hands up and let Perry and Vines fight it out.

²⁷⁹ The Marxes were a tennis-playing family. In 1939 Arthur was the Intercollegiate Singles Champion of Southern California. He would go on to become a nationally ranked amateur.

Ruth, unfortunately, would go on to the bar at the club. It was a painful time for us all. Ruth and I had joked about smuggling in whiskey from Canada during Prohibition, but what it led to was no laughing matter. My wife's drinking was now out of control, and the whole town knew about it. Perhaps she couldn't cope with the pressures of being married to a famous comedian. Perhaps the life of a Beverly Hills matron left her with too much free time. No one, however, turned Ruth into an alcoholic but herself.

281

282

154

281 Ruth and I took another vacation in Hawaii, and here I'm seen with Duke Kahanamoku. After this vacation together, we both knew that divorce was just a matter of time.

282 In September 1937, after my return from Hawaii, Chico and I had to appear in Los Angeles Federal Court on charges of violating the copyright law. We were accused of using someone else's skit on our radio series in 1934. At first we were fined $1,000 for our alleged transgression. The decision was appealed, and, like so many other suits of this kind, the matter was inconclusively settled. It seemed to evaporate into thin air, but not before we received some unfavorable publicity.

283 Playing pool at my house with Chico (at left) and Harpo (at right).

286

287

ROOM SERVICE

GROUCHO: You have no fireside? How do you listen
to the President's speeches?

No one at MGM had our interests so obviously at heart as Thalberg had. The love and care he'd put into the two films he produced for us would never be repeated anywhere else. There certainly wasn't anyone left at MGM who could do it. We went on loan-out to RKO to film Morrie Ryskind's adaptation of the play by John Murray and Allen Boretz. Zeppo represented us as agent on *Room Service*, the only picture on which he performed that service for us. Pandro Berman, who'd made a name for himself with the Ginger Rogers–Fred Astaire pictures, was the producer. Doing the film version of a stage play, particularly when it wasn't written for us, was a risk. But it turned out to be a good picture, considering.

284 -85 The Marxes with Lucille Ball and Ann Miller.

284

285

289 Harpo raising cane.

290 With Ann Miller. Years later the NBC radio show *Monitor* did a tribute to me on my birthday. Annie came on to thank me for protecting her secret: that she was only fourteen years old when she made *Room Service* with us in 1938. I don't recall any such secret, though I don't doubt Annie's word. What I do recall is that her mother stuck so close to Annie you couldn't get a word in edgewise—among other things.

291

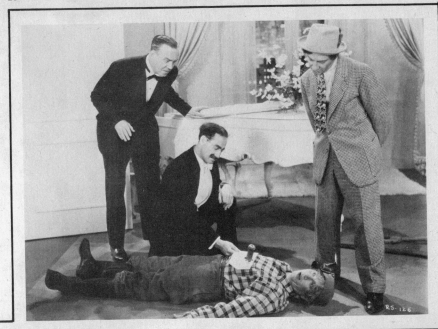

292

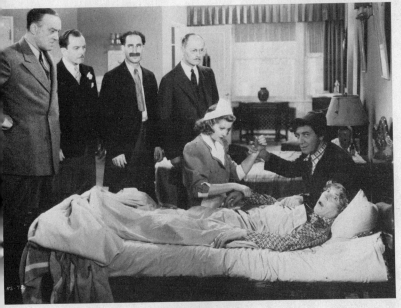

294

293

159

295 Ann Miller, Frank Albertson, and me.

296 Adding a footnote.

297

298

299

300

"MOTHER GOOSE
GOES HOLLYWOOD"
COPYRIGHT 1938
WALT DISNEY
PRODUCTIONS LTD.

301
-02 *Mother Goose Goes Hollywood* was one of three
Walt Disney animated cartoons in which the Marx
Brothers "appeared." The first, released in 1936,
was *Mickey's Polo Team,* which also featured cari-
catures of Shirley Temple, Laurel and Hardy,
W. C. Fields, Charlie Chaplin, Mae West, and
Clark Gable. *Mother Goose* was released in 1938,
and was nominated for an Academy Award. *The
Autograph Hound,* released in 1939, was the third
cartoon.

MICKEY MOUSE
Presents a
WALT DISNEY
SILLY SYMPHONY
MOTHER
GOOSE
GOES
HOLLYWOOD

R.K.O. RADIO PICTURE *in* TECHNICOLOR

303

307

164

305

AT THE CIRCUS

MARGARET DUMONT: Judge Chanock will sit on my
left hand and you will sit on my
right hand.

GROUCHO: How will you eat—through a
tube?

As a director, Eddie Buzzell made a good song-and-dance man—which, in fact, he had been. We'd played on the same bill many times. The Marx Brothers were back at MGM, and Mervyn Le Roy came over from Warner's to produce the picture. Irving Brecher, a young writer who was to become one of my closest friends, wrote the screenplay. The whole movie missed, and, to me, the only positive thing that came out of it—other than my friendship with Irv—was one of my favorite songs, by Yip Harburg and Harold Arlen:

Lydia, oh Lydia, oh have you met Lydia,
Lydia the tattooed lady.
She has eyes that men adore so,
And a torso even more so . . .

In the midst of shooting, the gorilla quit. It's a long story:

. . . Since we had neither the time nor the equipment to capture and train a live gorilla, we were obliged to engage an actor who specialized in playing these roles. Show business is the only profession extant where a man can earn a moderate fortune merely by standing inside a gorilla skin.

The complications were many. It seems the actor we had engaged to play the gorilla had an agent, but he had no gorilla skin. We then discovered that the gorilla pelt also had an agent. The day the scene was to be shot, both agents were on the set to protect their interests and also to make sure they collected their commissions. It was an extremely hot day, and the intense lights on the set helped to make it even hotter. Mother Nature, with her customary slipshod design, had neglected to equip the gorilla with a window or any other form of ventilation. If she had, the gent inside the skin would have been able to survive indefinitely. But since he had no means of getting fresh air—or any other kind—he took the easy way out and solved his problem by fainting.

From Groucho and Me

What followed was a donnybrook between the actor and his agent, the actor refusing to get back into the skin unless some means of ventilation was devised. The matter was at a standstill when the actor excused himself, and made a roundabout trip to the gorilla skin, stopping off at the commissary for an icepick, which he proceeded to use on the skin. Shooting resumed after lunch, the actor staying in the skin for well over three hours before the agent for the pelt determined there was something wrong. No actor had ever stayed in the gorilla skin for more than two hours without fainting. When it was discovered that the actor had cut holes in the pelt, the fireworks really started. The gorilla-skin agent left the soundstage in a huff, taking his pelt with him.

Three days passed. Not a camera was grinding and the costs were mounting while the studio executive frantically combed the town for another gorilla skin. Alas, there were none to be had.

At last, the ape man, ill at ease outside a furry pelt, tracked down a man in San Diego who had an orangoutan skin. Even a child knows that an orangoutan is much smaller than a gorilla, but strangely enough the ape man didn't, and he impetuously bought it without trying it on. We gave him every chance to squeeze himself into the skin, but it was hopeless. When he finally realized he was too big for the pelt, he broke down and cried like a baby gorilla. However, this was no time for sentiment. We were faced with reality, and also with the head of the studio. There was a picture to be finished, and we were obliged to engage a smaller monkey man who specialized in impersonating orangoutans in and around San Diego. Moreover, because of the demands of the union, we had to pay the original ape man standby salary, portal to portal, and psychiatric treatment.

From Groucho and Me

304 Florence Rice, featured in the picture, was the daughter of Grantland Rice, the great sportswriter, who was a good friend of ours.

306 Miriam visits the set.

308 With Eve Arden. She'd been chased all over the Broadway stage in *The Ziegfeld Follies of 1935.* Bob Hope was the chaser, singing as he pursued her, "I can't get started with you."

304

306

308

311 When Eve as Peerless Pauline and I as J. Cheever Loophole did our upside-down walk, we were outfitted with huge suction cups on our feet. I was almost fifty years old at the time, and I should have known better, but I was heels over head.

313

312

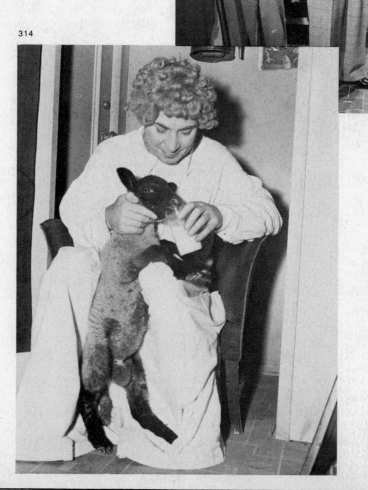

314

312 Chico, me and the gorilla skin.
313 With Chico and Nat Pendleton.
314 Harpo and the lamb that appeared in
   several scenes with him.

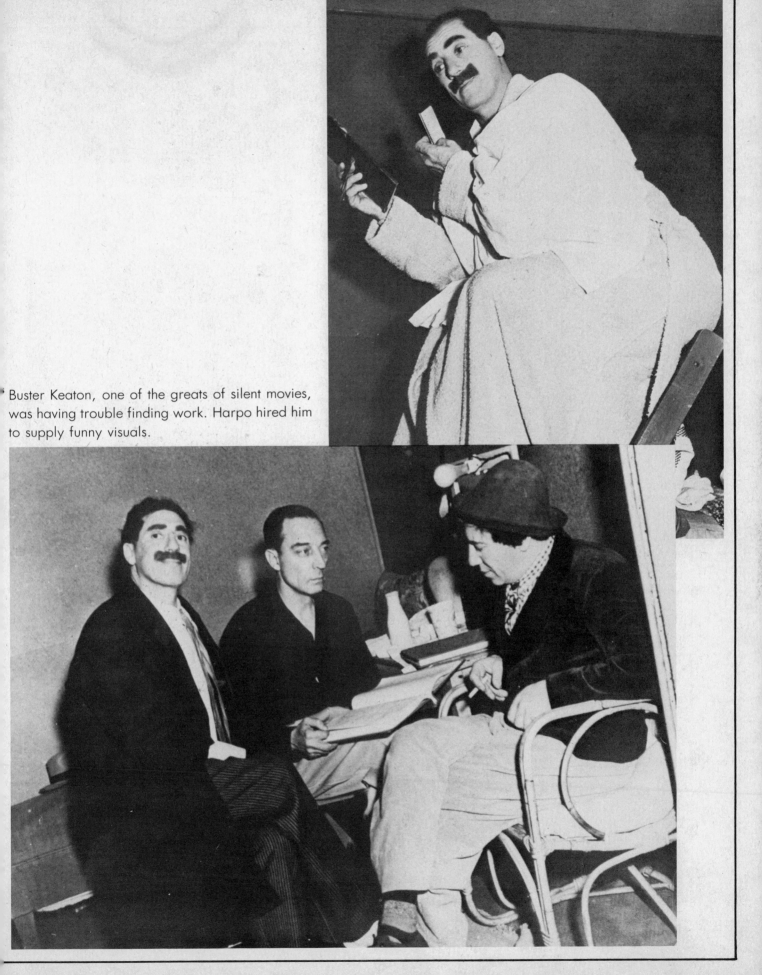

315

Buster Keaton, one of the greats of silent movies, was having trouble finding work. Harpo hired him to supply funny visuals.

Where else, I ask you, will you find an actor of my caliber?

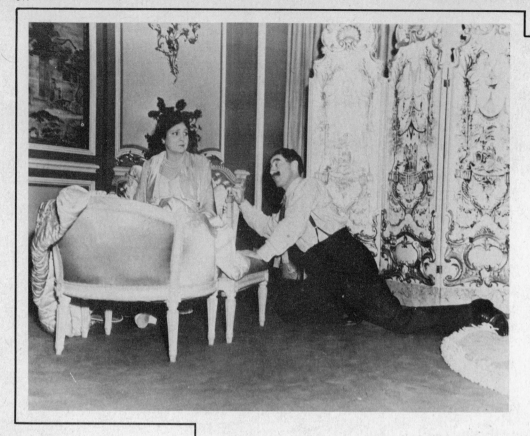

323 Uncle Al visited us on the set. He was making a name as a serious actor, playing a priest in *Father Malachy's Miracle*. The action backstage was anything but celibate. George Kaufman caught Uncle Al with a female visitor. "I just saw a priest buttoning his fly," he reported.

325 Rube Goldberg, a good friend, was another visitor to the set. One New Year's, I went to a party at his house. James Thurber got drunk and tried to hit me over the head with a beer bottle. He was such a cutup.

326

327

174

326 Lunch in the commissary with Messrs. Simon and Schuster, the well-known publishers. Also at the table are Irv Brecher (far right) and Rube Goldberg (second from right).

It was during this period that my social life revolved around the writers about town. What talent. A group of us formed the West Side Writing and Asthma Club. Perelman invented the title. Others in the group were Robert Benchley, Donald Ogden Stewart and Charles Butterworth. We'd meet at Lyman's, across the street from the Hollywood Brown Derby. As the Algonquin wits gravitated West, they were taken up by the group. Charles MacArthur had come to Hollywood at about the same time as his sometime collaborator, Ben Hecht. I was in love with Charlie, as was everyone else who knew him. He was without doubt the most

charming guy I ever met. Hecht was another matter. In later years he would visit me at my house on the desert. I once asked him what he thought of Palm Springs. "There's nothing here but old sunburned Jews," he said, as he continued rubbing on a double layer of calamine lotion.

327 In the late 1930s, Chico and I took another stab at radio. This time we were joined on the Kellogg Radio Show by such regulars as Cary Grant, Lawrence Tibbett, Ronald Colman and Carole Lombard.

328 Noël Coward was our guest star one week. This picture was taken at rehearsal. Years later, I danced in the new year with Noël on a table at the Savoy Hotel in London. I split my pants. This, of course, inspired Noël to write a play, *Brief Encounter*.

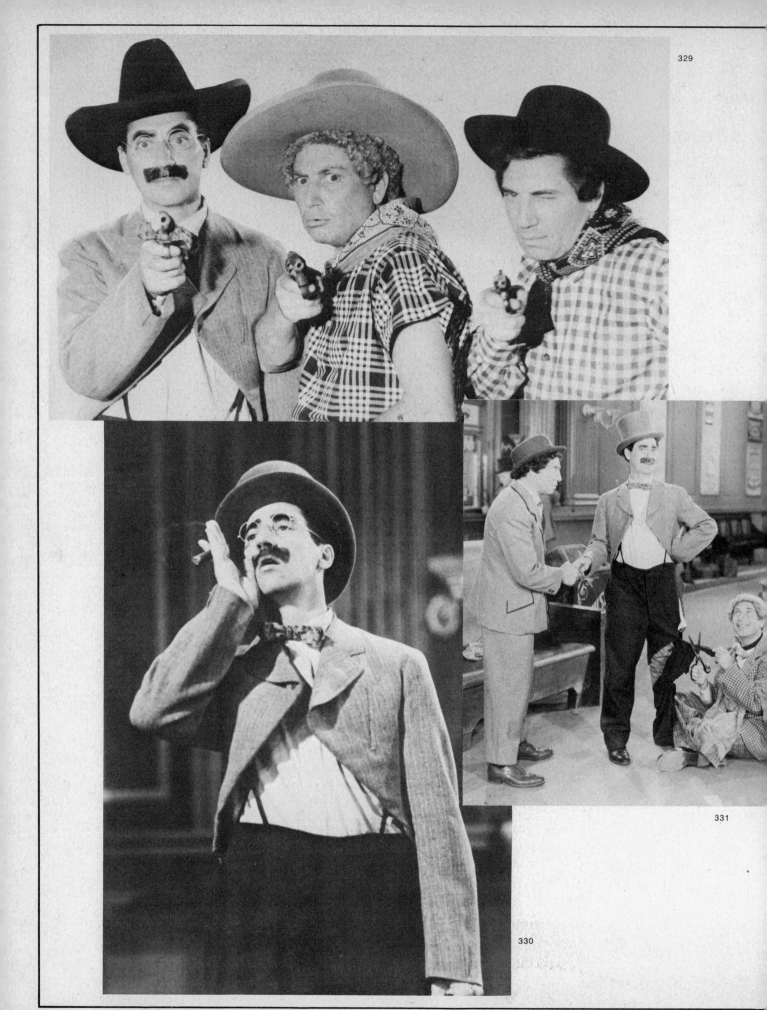

329

330

331

GO WEST

GROUCHO: Someday this bitter ache will pass, my
sweet . . . Time wounds all heels.

To son Arthur

Summer, 1940

Dear Arthur,

. . . Go West has again been postponed. I don't know why the studio doesn't come right out and say they're afraid to make it. All I get from them is a weekly announcement to come to the wardrobe department and be fitted for a pair of early-American pants. The writers have been taking some big hacks at the story, and from what I hear, once we begin we should be able to shoot the whole thing in three days, and get the Academy Award. Irv Brecher says this picture will be known as the longest short ever made. Well, it doesn't bother me. My attitude is, take the money and to hell with it. I had my hair darkened to match my greasepaint mustache, but it has been so long since the scheduled starting date that the dye has faded and now I will have to have it done all over again. So you see my theatrical career has dwindled to being fitted once a week for a pair of early-American pants and having my hair dyed every three weeks. This is a fine comedown for a man who used to be the Toast of Broadway . . .

Love,
Padre

From *The Groucho Letters*

Buzzell again directed us in 1940, when we finally made *Go West*. The producer, Jack Cummings, was Mayer's nephew. I've always believed in nepotism; I can't think of anyone who could play a Marx Brother like a Marx Brother. There are exceptions, however, that prove the rule. Cummings was a nice man, I suppose, but he was no Thalberg.

During that period, there was a term for under-age girls. They were called "jailbait," but in California they were also called "San Quentin Quail." Brecher came up with my character's name: S. Quentin Quale.

332 This is known as shooting off your mouth.

336

335 With June McCloy.

335

337

338 With director Eddie Buzzell, seated at center.

340

341

342 Harpo was the linkup between two trains. This may
be the only time he let me step all over him.
343 A wardrobe shot.

345

347

348

THE BIG STORE

MARGARET DUMONT: I'm afraid after we're married awhile, a beautiful girl will come along and you'll forget all about me.

GROUCHO: Don't be silly. I'll write you twice a week.

In May of 1941, the month before *The Big Store* was released, Rudolf Hess arrived at the Duke of Hamilton's estate by parachute. He had an offer from Hitler. The Germans would drop their war against England if Churchill would allow Hitler to go to war with Russia unopposed. That night, 1,200 Nazi bombers strafed London in the heaviest attack of the two-year war, a not-so-subtle message to the British. Churchill was spending the weekend at Ditchley Park. He wrote later in his memoirs,

After dinner, news arrived of the heavy air raid on London. There was nothing that I could do about it so I watched the Marx Brothers in a comic film which my hosts had arranged. I went out twice to inquire about the air raid and heard it was bad. The merry film clacked on, and I was glad of the diversion.

The merry film was *Monkey Business,* not *The Big Store.* We brothers decided this would be our last picture. All of us were in our fifties, and didn't have to work at such a frantic pace any longer. We were comfortably set. Even Chico, who always needed money, must have hit the daily double, because he agreed to slow down too.

Nat Perrin wrote the story for our farewell film, which was directed by Chuck Reisner. It was all about life in a department store. Previous titles were *Bargain Basement* and *Step This Way.* I objected to the first title, because it implied—correctly, as it turned out—that this wasn't one of our better efforts. As for *Step This Way,* that title was an invitation to disaster. Critics might point their arrows to the edge of a cliff. I was playing Wolf J. Flywheel. Flywheel, you'll recall, was the name of the character I played on radio in the early 1930s. One of

the funniest things in the picture—unintentionally—was Tony Martin singing "Tenement Symphony." It was the most godawful piece of music I'd ever heard.

After thirty years as a team, the Marx Brothers disbanded with a whimper. *The New York Times* review of June 27, 1941, condemned us with faint praise: "As the last remnant on the counter, it's a bargain."

346 We were men of many hats—none of which fit.

183

349

350

353

351

351 The girl is Norma Thelan.
352 Tony Martin, Harpo, me, Douglas Dumbrille and Chico.

352

354 Miriam at thirteen.

GROUCHO MARX

who says

"My Best Friend is a Dog . . . ."

Connoisseurs of the humour known as "crazy" will have heard with regret the news that the Marx Brothers have "split", and are to make no more films together. As consolation here is a glimpse of the larger lunacy by that nimble wise-cracker—

A MAN in my position (horizontal at the moment) is likely to hear strange stories about himself. A few years ago they were saying that I made a pig of myself drinking champagne out of Miss Garbo's slipper. Actually it was nothing but very weak punch.

And now they say I am not a dog lover. Not a dog lover indeed!

Why, if I have a friend in the world it's my Great Dane named Bowser. We have been absolutely inseparable for years. The only reason he didn't come with me when I went to New York recently was that he didn't have money enough for a railroad ticket.

Meanwhile, New York is a very lonely place without my dog. Actually so lonely that when I see a girl with a pretty dog in the hotel lobby, tears come into my eyes and I invite the pup into the lounge for a drink.

Maybe I'm a sentimental old fool. My wife says I spoiled Bowser by letting him sleep in my bed at home, while I slept in the doghouse outside. But I'd do the same thing again. To turn a Great Dane out of my bed would take a harder heart than mine, and stronger muscles.

In the eight years we've been together, Bowser and I have never quarrelled. I don't spend any more on his wardrobe than I do on my wife's, but he has never once asked for a new collar just because Archie Mayo's dog across the street dresses better.

Bowser has never sat in a night club with me and whined that George Raft is a wonderful dancer. Just because George is light on his toes, does that make me a heel? Let's not have a hasty answer.

I give you my word that Bowser has never said, "Dear, why don't you take a few dancing lessons? Really, nobody does the Bunny Hug any more."

Well, *I* do the Bunny Hug. Is it my fault that I'm crazy about rabbits?

Don't misunderstand. I am not suggesting that dogs should replace wives in the home. That is something every man will have to decide for himself. Personally I don't see why a man can't have a dog *and* a wife. But if you can afford only one—

Well, to help you decide, I might point out that a dog already *has* a fur coat. It lasts a lifetime. And if you and your dog ever split up, he doesn't go to court and ask for ten bones a week more than you earn.

Only once has a dog disappointed me. That was the time I took Alonzo, a big St. Bernard, home from the studio. He had been working in a picture, earning 12 dollars a day, and he seemed lonely. I would have been even happier to get a dog with the spirit of the late Rin Tin Tin, who used to bring home 1,500 bucks a week.

However, Alonzo was a very intelligent beast and his habit of running off with our brandy was, I suppose, typical of St. Bernards, although many of my two-footed guests have done the same thing.

I was a little annoyed when Alonzo refused to eat our food, preferring to take his meals at a near-by delicatessen. (Not that the food at our house is good;

I don't want people to get that idea.) But I kept my trap shut. After all, Alonzo was earning 12 dollars a day, which was 12 dollars more than I was getting at the time.

After he had been with us a week, I had the shock of my life. On a Saturday night, just as I got through marking the liquor-level on my brandy bottles, a little man stuck his head out of Alonzo's skin and asked for his salary—12 dollars a day!

Of course I should have suspected that something was wrong the day my wife came into the living room with the cat. Instead of chasing the cat, as a dog should, Alonzo chased my wife.

Possibly it was this incident which gave rise to the ugly rumour that I was not a dog lover. People stopped inviting me to their homes—just as they had once before (1907 to 1940); ladies walked by without troubling to curtsy, and even my barber cut me. That hurt. Nevertheless, to me it was enough that my dog kept faith in me.

My overwhelming affection for dogs does not mean, of course, that I have no love for other pets. All my life I have had animals of one kind or another around the house, even if it was only a small distant relative, or a termite.

Once, when I was a child, I was given a pair of guinea pigs which, with only a little difficulty, I learned to love like brothers. (Learning to love my brothers wasn't easy either.)

Well, the guinea pigs settled down in

our cellar and one afternoon I found the cellar floor literally covered with pets.

In those days my heart was smaller than it is now and I was able to love, at most, no more than 30 or 40 guinea pigs. I was in a quandary. Did you ever spend an afternoon in a quandary with 96 guinea pigs?

"Sell them," my brother Harpo suggested.

"If that," I replied, "is all you have to say, you ought never to bother to speak again."

And to this day Harpo has remained silent, and I can't tell you how pleased I've been.

Another brother, Chico, came into the cellar and he, too, said, "Sell them." (When I suggested that he, too, remain silent from then on, he compromised by offering to speak in broken English, which he, too, does to this day.)

Anyway, being overruled, I went out with Chico to a near-by pet shop and offered to sell 96 fine guinea pigs for 20 dollars.

"I'll do better than that," the dealer said. "I'll give you 100 guinea pigs for nothing,"

For a good, all-year-round pet, I don't believe there is anything to compare with a simple, unpedigreed chorus girl. Like the Maltese cat, the chorus girl becomes attached to any man who feeds her. But there the resemblance ends.

For, whereas you can take the Maltese cat to the basement for a saucer of milk, the chorus girl insists on eating on the roof, where there is dancing and a $9 cover charge.

Not a poor man's pet, the chorus girl. But I am saving my money.

From This Week, U.S.A.

During the 1941–1942 radio season I made several appearances on Rudy Vallee's Sealtest show. John Barrymore was a semi-regular on the series, playing the ham actor buffoon. This was shortly before his death. His ankles were swollen from drink.

I asked him once where he was born. "In Rangoon," he replied. "I was suckled by a goat." With that kind of logic, he could have been a Marx Brother. One evening, knowing I'd be there, Barrymore called Harpo and asked if he, too, could be invited to dinner. That was fine. "One thing though," Barrymore said. "I have to bring a girl friend."

The host said, "Then there'll be two of you."

Barrymore continued, "And my girl friend's boy friend." There would be three? "And her boy friend's mother." Then there would be four. "And the mother's boy friend." That made it five. "And the boy friend has a cousin." Six people came to dinner as part of the entourage. The cousin carried in a case of bourbon. Barrymore got stiff and fell

over. The five others folded him up and carried him away.

My second book, *Many Happy Returns*, was an indictment of the Internal Revenue Service. It was published, however, just as the Japanese attacked Pearl Harbor. Legitimate protests about taxation were shouted out by waves of patriotism. Someday this book will be rediscovered, and armies will march on Washington.

The book carried this thumbnail biography of me:

Always precocious, Groucho Marx, author, actor and tax wizard, was born in Manhattan at the age of five. He was immediately signed up as a member of the Four Marx Brothers.

Unlike that of H. G. Wells and other lesser economists, Mr. Marx's mustache is painted on. When writing, he uses simple black Duco (two coats in winter and a polo shirt in summer).

Destiny and a small advance royalty were responsible for Mr. Marx's new book. It was written during a sandstorm at Palm Springs and started out as a serious novel. Sand kept flying into Mr. Marx's typewriter. To his surprise, he discovered that the finished manuscript was a book on the income tax.

Let me illustrate what havoc the upper bracket has brought into homes with million-dollar incomes.

Out of that million which, offhand, seems like a lot of moolah, the government's cut is $850,000. That leaves you with $150,000 to play with. Don't think this is all clear. You can't get away with under $1.75 for your laundry, unless you wash your own underwear.

The underwear problem has never affected me. Being a conservative dresser, I have never varied my custom of sewing myself into a woolen suit of underwear in October and emerging from my cocoon at the first blush of spring. This is a practice followed by few millionaires, and hardly any of them have learned how to press their pants under the mattress.

So, don't be too envious of the rich man, sitting in the back of his Rolls Royce, swathed in a raccoon coat, with a beautiful blonde on his arm. How does he know that she loves him for himself alone, and is not just after his fur coat?

It isn't only the businessman who has been hit by the higher brackets. Even a man like Joe Louis, who used to have a bum-of-the-month whom he clubbed into a frazzle, has had to cut down on bums, because, as the Chinese poet, Ah Ling, put it (in the wastebasket):

The more the moolah
You make in your racket,
The quicker you go
In a higher bracket.

The case of Mr. Clark Gable is, if he won't mind my saying so, a very touching example. Mr. Gable makes love to Lana Turner twice a year on the screen. He has time enough, heaven knows, to make love to Miss Turner four times a year. But he can't afford to. He realizes that a third and fourth session with the lovely Lana would take him right into higher and prohibitive brackets. Instead of making those extra pictures, Mr. Gable spends his spare time steering a mule around his 200-acre farm.

When you see Mr. Gable throw his strong, hairy arms around Miss Turner, what do you suppose he is thinking of?

(Paragraph deleted by Simon and Schuster.)

Obviously the Messrs. S. & S. didn't read that paragraph very carefully. How do they expect to get an authoritative book on income taxes if I can't illustrate a point without interference? Mr. Gable is one of my dearest friends. He brings all of his tax problems to me. If I haven't been able to convince him that Miss Turner is a tax problem, that is a mere academic point that can be thrashed out later.

The fact remains that Mr. Gable is a typical American. He realizes what the extra screen kisses cost him. He knows that every time he kisses Miss Turner, the government gets sixty percent.

Do you think Dante could have made love to Beatrice under the circumstances? Do you suppose Casanova could have been hotfooting it around Europe so successfully if he had his mind on taxes? Take any of the great lovers of history—Lord Byron, Abelard, or Cesar Romero; they have made a success of love only because they have lived love. They were not thinking of Schedule B and Tax Item 7 when responding to la grande passion ("love" to you and the rest of the family. P.S. I expect to be home for the holidays).

From Many Happy Returns

CO

NORTH ENTRANCE

Mr. Groucho Marx

will please present this card at

The White House

April 30, 1942

at five o'clock

NOT TRANSFERABLE

Mrs. Roosevelt

At Home

on Thursday afternoon

April the thirtieth

at five o'clock

360 The first time I was invited to the White House, a Marine band was playing. I'd heard better musicians. These were Marines that should have stayed in the halls of Montezuma. When I met Mrs. Roosevelt, I commented on the band, adding, "Now I know why you travel so much."

361 In 1942, Ruth and I were divorced. She'd weighed 118 pounds when we were married; now she weighed 150—from alcohol. Our life together had become untenable. After much agonizing, I sued for divorce. We'd been married twenty-one years. Arthur was on tour, playing tennis. I received custody of Miriam, who was then in her mid-teens.

361

Going It Alone

The Marx Brothers as a team were officially *phfft*.
We went our separate ways: I got custody of
the mustache, Harpo kept the blond wig and Chico
bought a new Buick. We continued working,
however—sometimes together, other times alone.
America had entered the war, and we set out on
tours to raise money for the war effort.

Percy Hammond was the toughest theater critic
around. When the war broke out, his publisher
considered sending Hammond to cover the war.
"No, you can't do that," Ring Lardner protested.
"Suppose he doesn't like it?"

The names I toured with were the great stars of
the age. Harry Ruby was also along. He wrote a
parody of a famous lullaby for me:

> *Rockabye, baby,*
> *Gurgle and laugh,*
> *Mother is making*
> *Time and a half.*
> *I'll cook the meals*
> *And keep the house clean*
> *While Mom helps to build*
> *A B-Seventeen.*

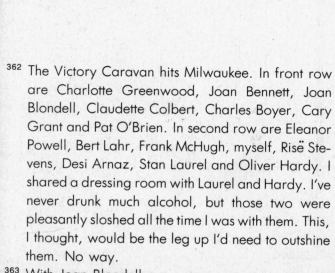

363

362

362 The Victory Caravan hits Milwaukee. In front row are Charlotte Greenwood, Joan Bennett, Joan Blondell, Claudette Colbert, Charles Boyer, Cary Grant and Pat O'Brien. In second row are Eleanor Powell, Bert Lahr, Frank McHugh, myself, Risë Stevens, Desi Arnaz, Stan Laurel and Oliver Hardy. I shared a dressing room with Laurel and Hardy. I've never drunk much alcohol, but those two were pleasantly sloshed all the time I was with them. This, I thought, would be the leg up I'd need to outshine them. No way.

363 With Joan Blondell.

GROUCHO MARX
TURNS HIMSELF IN FOR SCRAP

"I, too, was once a 90-pound weakling — but I lost weight"

"The present human body is already obsolete," says this dubious authority. Here he tells what the man of the future will look like, complete with built-in suspenders, chromium trim and rotating hair crops

by Groucho Marx

I'M ALWAYS reading enthusiastic articles describing the new automobiles that will appear after the war. It is predicted they will have engines in the rear, seats made out of soy beans, plastic bodies and steering wheels made out of French pastry, in case you get hungry on a long trip.

Why doesn't someone manufacture a new man? If there ever was a contraption that needed improving, it's the human body. If this current model is old Mother Nature's masterpiece, obviously the old girl is a little on the jerky side and needs a few years at a good engineering school.

Let us begin at the bottom and work our way up. Here we find the feet. Feet are utterly without beauty. Would any man reading this piece go out with a girl who resembled his feet? Of course not. **They are usually gnarled and misshapen from being whacked against furniture and high curbs and they require shoes, socks, arch supports and adhesive tape.**

Now, suppose your feet grew in the shape of wheels? You'd really have something then. You could roll around and see your friends, you could roll to the vegetable market, and in the evening when you came home from work, your wife could tie a suction bag around your neck and use you for a vacuum cleaner.

Now, friends, move up 18 inches and what do we encounter? That's right — the knee. No one has ever been able to figure out what purpose the knee serves. It toils not, neither does it shin. (This is known as a literary pun, and is always greeted with about five minutes of dead silence.) The knee is hardly worth discussing. Functionally it's a disgrace. It is constantly getting out of joint and requires almost as much attention as a second-hand lawn mower.

Out-of-Date

IT IS true that in the olden days the knee played an important part in love making. Lovers used to slide off the parlor sofa and plop down on one knee when declaring their affection. The invention of the gasoline motor, however, gradually changed all this. The rumble seat of an automobile proved itself a much more effective setting and, in a few short years, the parlor sofa deteriorated into a useless and moth-eaten antique.

The stomach, or paunch, is a prominent part of the human body, particularly if you drink a lot of beer. But I am sure a smart designer could have rigged it up more effectively. The stomach serves two purposes: it holds your dinner and, what is much more important, it is supposed to hold up your trousers. Unfortunately, we have to breathe, and whenever we inhale, the trousers drop from two to four inches. This could easily have been avoided had the hip bone been extended six inches on each side. The trousers would then hang naturally, without the aid of belt or suspender, and the rear end of a man's pants wouldn't sag as though it were filled with rocks.

The less said about the arms, the better.

They grow out of nothing, they swing aimlessly back and forth, and they give the wearer a grotesque and unfinished appearance. Even the ugly baboon, supposedly several notches lower than man in the social scale, is better equipped. A full-grown baboon's arms are long enough to reach the ground without stooping over and enable him, when strolling down the street, to pluck bananas, cigar butts and small coins out of the gutter with little or no loss of dignity.

The neck is a short drain pipe that rises up out of the shoulders and disappears into the bottom of the head. It is usually decorated with an Adam's apple and a collar. The Adam's apple is a medium-sized meat ball that keeps running up and down the front of the neck looking for its mate. It is a monstrosity that nature has left on our doorstep and there is nothing we can do about it. Many people attempt to hide it by wrapping a necktie around it, but in most cases, the necktie is even uglier than the apple.

The neck would be much more useful if it were equipped with ball bearings. This would enable the head to swing completely around on its axis and eventually return to its original position. Equipped with a revolving head, a man could walk down the street and if he noticed a choice number strolling past in the opposite direction, he could quickly swing his head toward her and speculate if that's the way he wanted to spend the afternoon. By spinning the head occasionally in the other direction, he would also reduce the danger of bumping into strange pedestrians and, perhaps, his wife.

Mouthful

THIS brings us to the teeth, the sentinels of the mouth. The average man spends 50 per cent of his salary on his family, 25 per cent on chorus girls and 25 per cent on his teeth. Let us look into the mouth of a man who has just celebrated his 50th birthday. What do you see? In addition to a small piece of birthday cake, you will see a miscellaneous collection of inlays, concrete fillings, porcelain jackets and a tongue. In fact, you will find practically everything but teeth.

But should the teeth be blamed for this? Of course not! The teeth are innocent bystanders — they didn't ask to be part of the mouth. Had we been built scientifically, there wouldn't be any mouths at all. You naturally ask, "How would we eat?" Frankly, I don't know, but I'll give it some thought over the week end.

We now come to man's crowning glory — the hair. The top of the head is apparently the only spot where hair cannot be grown successfully. In most cases all the scalp acquires is a smooth, slippery surface as bleak and desolate as Death Valley.

Perhaps agriculture can solve this problem. Farmers long ago discovered that the soil deteriorates unless they rotate their crops. For example, if one year they raise corn, the following year, they will raise wheat or cabbage or, in desperate cases, even eggplant. The scalp might respond to similar treatment. In the winter we could grow hair on our heads and then in the spring, as the hair began thinning, the scalp could be plowed up and string beans planted. I particularly recommend string beans as they are green and curly, grow to a good height and require very little attention. Around October, they could be clipped and made into a nice salad. The next year the same thing could be tried with cabbage — six months hair and six months cabbage. A man would then have a head of hair in the winter and a head of cabbage in the summer. This same joke can also be used for a head of lettuce, but there's no point in whipping a dead horse.

I could go on endlessly pointing out the hideous mistakes that Nature has made, but my time is short, and if my readers will examine each other carefully and honestly, I am sure they'll be willing to admit that everything I've said about the human body has been, if anything, an understatement.

The End

365

365 At home, Miriam had just graduated from high school. She, like Arthur, decided to become a writer, and planned to go to college at Bennington. By this time, Arthur was in the Coast Guard.

366 With Veronica Lake, Fay McKenzie waiting to cut in. We tripped the light—fantastic!

367-368 With Lucille Ball. She was a glamour girl then and not yet the great comedienne.

369

370

369 A ragtag chorus line consisting of Jerry Colonna, myself, Bing Crosby and Bob Hope.

370 Harpo with Lucy. By the time our bandwagon had reached Minneapolis on our cross-country tour in May 1942, we'd raised $40 million for the war effort. There was no theater big enough in the area to hold the show, so we entertained at Union Station. "I knew a girl in Minneapolis once," I told the huge crowd. "She used to come over to see me in St. Paul. She was known as the tail of two cities." Somebody pulled the microphone cord on me. I was canceled.

371 At the Great Lakes Naval Training Center.

373 I played Santa Claus many times, and if you don't believe it, check out the divorce settlements awarded my wives.

371

372

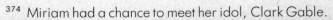

373 374 Miriam had a chance to meet her idol, Clark Gable.

375 With Virginia O'Brien. In March of 1943, I again went on radio with a variety show called *Blue Ribbon Town*, sponsored by Pabst Beer. Virginia was one of the regulars on the series, along with Kenny Baker, Donald Dickson and Fay McKenzie. The regulars also appeared with me in the camp shows. When we first started entertaining the troops, I usually went on after Fay McKenzie. But she had such big—I mean, her act was such a standout that my routine was drowned out by whistles and wolf calls. A solution was worked out. I would go on before Fay, winding up my act by introducing her. I was no withered anachronism; I kept abreast of the times. Recently, I dug up one of my old extemporaneous routines. It went this way:

Good evening, soldiers, sailors, Marines, doctors, nurses, hospital attendants. You know, ever since I started appearing before audiences without my mustache, a lot of people don't recognize me as Groucho Marx. Some of them think I'm Errol Flynn . . .

I don't know why that should strike you as particularly amusing. Just because Flynn became a father in two or three places recently . . . It's no trick, you know . . . My grandfather had twenty-three children. Of course, that was before Ovaltine was invented. But enough of this irrelevant chatter. When I first decided to come here I was in doubt as to what subject I could talk about that would be of interest to you fellows. Maybe I could talk to you about Hollywood. Probably, since I haven't made a picture recently, you may think that, as Winchell would put it, Hollywood and I have *phfft*. Hmm, *phfft*—sounds like somebody opening a warm bottle of Pabst Beer. At any rate, I nearly made a picture recently. They tested me for the part of the man who makes love to Betty Grable in the picture version of *They Knew What They Wanted*. But they turned me down—they knew what *I* wanted. But you have to take your hat off to Hollywood for the educational pictures they've made. Why, Twentieth Century–Fox alone has made pictures about Alexander Graham Bell, Robert Fulton and his steamboat, Jesse James—in fact, they've filmed the lives of almost every historical character but Lady Godiva. But then, Lady Godiva doesn't need any help from Twentieth Century–Fox. She already had her chance, Sixteenth Century Bare . . .

I *did* do a little work in Hollywood before I left. I worked at my draft board as a model. Don't laugh. I really was a model. Anyone who came in and looked like me was automatically rejected. While I was working there, I met the most wonderful girl—I can hardly wait to get back to her. Of course, she's homely, stupid, fat and bowlegged, but I sure am lucky to know her. Boy, can she wash and iron a shirt! . . . She's really kind of attractive, though. In fact, she's got everything Dorothy Lamour's got. I'll go farther than that. She's got *more* than Dorothy Lamour . . . only it's in the darnedest places! . . . which brings us around to the subject I'd hoped we'd finally get around to—women. First of all, what are women? According to Kipling, women are a rag, a bone and a hank of hair, which is a pretty accurate description of some of the women I go out with. Now let's take the custom of marrying women. Some people claim that marriage interferes with romance. There's no doubt about it. Anytime you have a romance, your wife is bound to interfere . . . I'll never forget when I first got married. We went to Niagara Falls, just the two of us, me and my wife's mother. My wife wanted to come along, but I felt it took an older person to appreciate scenery. . . . Besides, what did I want *her* along for? When I was a few years older I found out . . . The reason it took me so long to find out was that my wife's mother was very strict . . .

My experience with women has been very limited, though. As a matter of fact, I come from a very strict family, and I didn't go out with girls until I was twenty-one because my mother objected. After I was twenty-one, the girls objected! . . . Even then, when I had a date, we always had to have a chaperone. You know what a chaperone is—that's a French word meaning, "Brother, are you in for a dull evening!" . . . I don't want you to get the impression that I still can't get a date, because back in Hollywood there are plenty of girls who are ready, willing, and able to go out with me. That is—I'm always ready, but the girls that are willing aren't able, and those that are able aren't willing! . . . The way I've been talking about women so much you're probably thinking that that's all I'm interested in—women. But that's not true. There are any number of things I'm interested in besides women. For instance, there's uh . . . that is, uh . . . darn it, I could have sworn there was something! . . . Ah, wonderful women! Just give me a comfortable couch, a dog, a good book, and a woman. Then if you can get the dog to go somewhere and read the book, I might have a little fun! . . . And right now I want you to meet a girl who is always fun—the ingenue of *Blue Ribbon Town*—Fay McKenzie!

376 Pabst Beer celebrated its 100th anniversary while we were still doing the show. We all went to Milwaukee to celebrate. I'm seen here with Fred Pabst.

377 At the same celebration with Edward Pabst, Fay McKenzie, Gene Lockhart and Kay Gorcey, whom I was seeing steadily. Mr. Pabst was a fine old gentleman, almost eighty at the time. He wasn't much of a drinker. Later it was discovered that the beer I'd been forcing down Mr. Pabst was Miller High Life. Before you could say "convertible debenture," I was canceled from the show and a rising young comedian named Danny Kaye was hired to replace me. I wonder whatever happened to him.

378

377

380

379

379 To many of us in show business, getting Roosevelt reelected in 1944 was as much a part of the war effort as any of the camp shows we'd done. Here I'm seen with Danny Kaye, proving there were no hard feelings about my fizzled Pabst Beer, and John Garfield.

380 With Dorothy Lamour. Pretty girl.

381 There wasn't anything we wouldn't do for FDR and his running mate, Harry Truman. That included dressing up like dames, as Edward G. Robinson and I did, seen here with Jane Wyman.

382

383 On the campaign trail with Robert Benchley (adjusting his tie), Walter Huston (chin in his hand), Eddie Robinson and myself (at far right). The others are at this point unidentifiable, though I'm sure they were all quite prominent. Bob Benchley was one of the few writers I knew who always laughed at other writers' lines. I always laughed at one of his. When he returned for his twenty-fifth homecoming at Harvard, he stated to underclassmen, "I feel as I always have, except for an occasional heart attack."

384 One war was about to end and another one about to begin when, on July 21, 1945, I married Kay Gorcey. She was an aspiring singer and dancer, a pretty kid who'd been married to Leo Gorcey, one of the Dead End Kids. I'd met them during one of the band tours. It was very easy to get stuck on her.

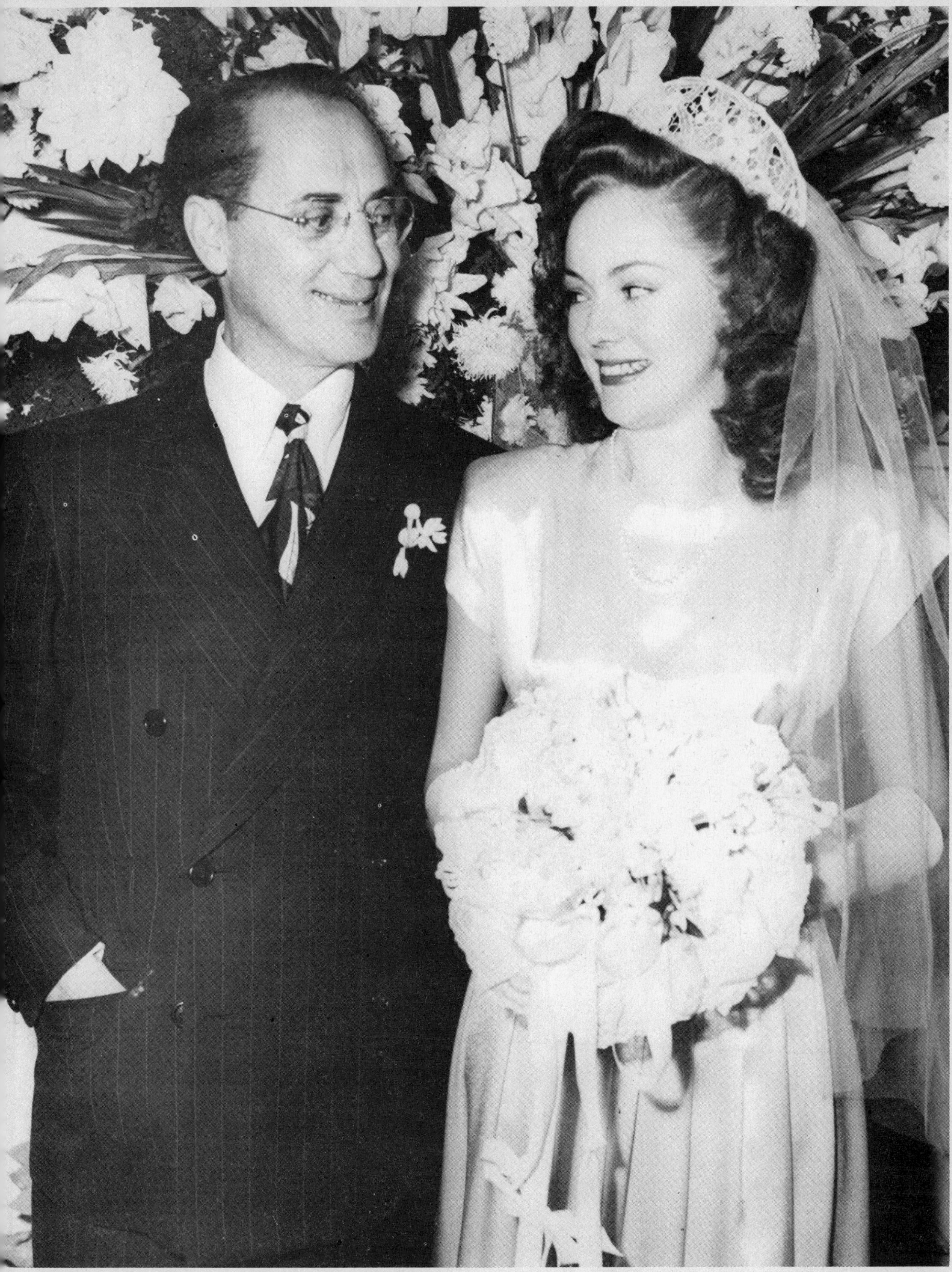

A NIGHT IN CASABLANCA

FEMALE: I'll be in the supper club tonight. Will
            you join me?
GROUCHO: Why? Are you coming apart?

Chico, Harpo and I probably wouldn't have teamed up again if Chico hadn't needed the money. I was about to begin raising a second family, and, at my age, that was a full-time occupation. But we allowed ourselves to be talked into returning to the screen. Our return to movies after a five-year absence was to be an epic called *Adventure in Casablanca*. When word of our plans spread, we were bombarded with letters—some of them friendly, but not all.

Running battle with Warner Brothers

When the Marx Brothers were about to make a movie called A Night in Casablanca, there were threats of legal action from the Warner Brothers, who, five years before, had made a picture called, simply, Casablanca (with Humphrey Bogart and Ingrid Bergman as stars). Whereupon Groucho, speaking for his brothers and himself, immediately dispatched the following letters:

Dear Warner Brothers:

Apparently there is more than one way of conquering a city and holding it as your own. For example, up to the time that we contemplated making this picture, I had no idea that the city of Casablanca belonged exclusively to Warner Brothers. However, it was only a few days after our announcement appeared that we received your long, ominous legal document warning us not to use the name Casablanca.

It seems that in 1471, Ferdinand Balboa Warner, your great-great grandfather, while looking for a shortcut to the city of Burbank, had stumbled on the shores of Africa and, raising his alpenstock (which he later turned in for a hundred shares of the common), named it Casablanca.

I just don't understand your attitude. Even if you plan on re-releasing your picture, I am sure that the average movie fan could learn in time to distinguish between Ingrid Bergman and Harpo. I don't know whether I could, but I certainly would like to try.

You claim you own Casablanca and that no one else can use that name without your permission. What about "Warner Brothers"? Do you own that, too? You probably have the right to use the name Warner, but what about Brothers? Professionally, we were brothers long before you were. We were touring the sticks as The Marx Brothers when Vitaphone was still a gleam in the inventor's eye, and even before us there had been other brothers—the Smith Brothers; the Brothers Karamazov; Dan Brothers, an outfielder with Detroit; and "Brother, Can You Spare a Dime?" (This was originally "Brothers, Can You Spare a Dime?" but this was spreading a dime pretty thin, so they threw out one brother, gave all the money to the other one, and whittled it down to "Brother, Can You Spare a Dime?")

Now, Jack, how about you? Do you maintain that yours is an original name? Well, it's not. It was used long before you were born. Offhand, I can think of two Jacks—there was Jack of "Jack and the Beanstalk," and Jack the Ripper, who cut quite a figure in his day.

As for you, Harry, you probably sign your checks, sure in the belief that you are the first Harry of all time and that all other Harrys are imposters. I can think of two Harrys that preceded you. There was Lighthorse Harry of Revolutionary fame and a Harry Appelbaum who lived on the corner of 93rd Street and Lexington Avenue. Unfortunately, Appelbaum wasn't too well known. The last I heard of him, he was selling neckties at Weber & Heilbroner.

Now about the Burbank studio. I believe this is what you brothers call your place. Old man Burbank is gone. Perhaps you remember him. He was a great man in the garden. His wife often said Luther had ten green thumbs. What a witty woman she must have been! Burbank was the wizard who crossed all those fruits and vegetables until he had the poor plants in such a confused and jittery condition that they could never decide whether to enter the dining room on the meat platter or the dessert dish.

This is pure conjecture, of course, but who knows—perhaps Burbank's survivors aren't too happy with the fact that a plant that grinds out pictures on a quota settled in their town, appropriated Burbank's name and uses it as a front for their films. It is even possible that the Burbank family is prouder of the potato produced by the old man than they are of the fact that from your studio emerged *Casablanca* or even *Gold Diggers of 1931*.

This all seems to add up to a pretty bitter tirade, but I assure you it's not meant to. I love Warners. Some of my best friends are Warner Brothers. It is even possible that I am doing you an injustice and that you, yourselves, know nothing at all about this dog-in-the-Wanger attitude. It wouldn't surprise me at all to discover that the heads of your legal department are unaware of this absurd dispute, for I am acquainted with many of them, and they are fine fellows with curly black hair, double-breasted suits and a love of their fellow man that out-Saroyans Saroyan.

I have a hunch that this attempt to prevent us from using the title is the brainchild of some ferret-faced shyster, serving a brief apprenticeship in your legal department. I know the type well—hot out of law school, hungry for success and too ambitious to follow the natural laws of promotion. This bar sinister probably needled your attorneys, most of whom are fine fellows with curly black hair, double-breasted suits, etc., into attempting to enjoin us. Well, he won't get away with it! We'll fight him to the highest court! No pasty-faced legal adventurer is going to cause bad blood between the Warners and the Marxes. We are all brothers under the skin, and we'll remain friends till the last reel of *A Night in Casablanca* goes tumbling over the spool.

> Sincerely,
> Groucho Marx

For some curious reason, this letter seemed to puzzle the Warner Brothers legal department. They wrote—in all seriousness—and asked if the Marxes could give them some idea of what their story was about. They felt that something might be worked out. So Groucho replied:

Dear Warners:

There isn't much I can tell you about the story. In it I play a Doctor of Divinity who ministers to the natives and, as a sideline, hawks can openers and pea jackets to the savages along the Gold Coast of Africa.

When I first meet Chico, he is working in a saloon, selling sponges to barflies who are unable to carry their liquor. Harpo is an Arabian caddie who lives in a small Grecian urn on the outskirts of the city.

As the picture opens, Porridge, a mealy-mouthed native girl, is sharpening some arrows for the hunt. Paul Hangover, our hero, is constantly lighting two cigarettes simultaneously. He apparently is unaware of the cigarette shortage.

There are many scenes of splendor and fierce antagonism, and Color, an Abyssinian messenger boy, runs Riot. Riot, in case you have never been there, is a small nightclub on the edge of town.

There's a lot more I could tell you, but I don't want to spoil it for you. All this has been okayed by the Hays Office, *Good Housekeeping* and the survivors of the Haymarket Riots; and if the times are ripe, this picture can be the opening gun in a new worldwide disaster.

> Cordially,
> Groucho Marx

Instead of mollifying them, this note seemed to puzzle the attorneys even more; they wrote back and said they still didn't understand the story line and they would appreciate it if Mr. Marx would explain the plot in more detail. So Groucho obliged with the following:

Dear Brothers:

Since I last wrote you, I regret to say there have been some changes in the plot of our new picture, *A Night in Casablanca*. In the new version I play Bordello, the sweetheart of Humphrey Bogart. Harpo and Chico are itinerant rug peddlers who are weary of laying rugs and enter a monastery just for a lark. This is a good joke on them, as there hasn't been a lark in the place for fifteen years.

Across from this monastery, hard by a jetty, is a waterfront hotel, chock-full of appla-cheeked damsels, most of whom have been barred by the Hays Office for soliciting. In the fifth reel, Gladstone makes a speech that sets the House of Commons in an uproar and the King promptly asks for his resignation. Harpo marries a hotel detective; Chico operates an ostrich farm. Humphrey Bogart's girl, Bordello, spends her last years in a Bacall house.

This, as you can see, is a very skimpy outline. The only thing that can save us from extinction is a continuation of the film shortage.

> Fondly,
> Groucho Marx

After that, the Marxes heard no more from the Warner Brothers legal department.

> From *The Groucho Letters*

It might have been better if we'd filmed the letters to Warner Brothers and left the picture we made in the can. While we were making the movie, I had occasion to write another letter to the Brothers Warner. I'd heard that they were planning to film Cole Porter's life story, and that it had tentatively been titled *Night and Day*. That they couldn't do, I wrote them. The Marx Brothers had prior claim to the title through two of our previous pictures: *A Night at the Opera* and *A Day at the Races*.

385 -86 United Artists had plans to make Lisette Verea the next greatest European import since the Volkswagen. Or maybe it was before. *A Night in Casablanca*—as the picture was retitled—may have been the only movie she ever made.

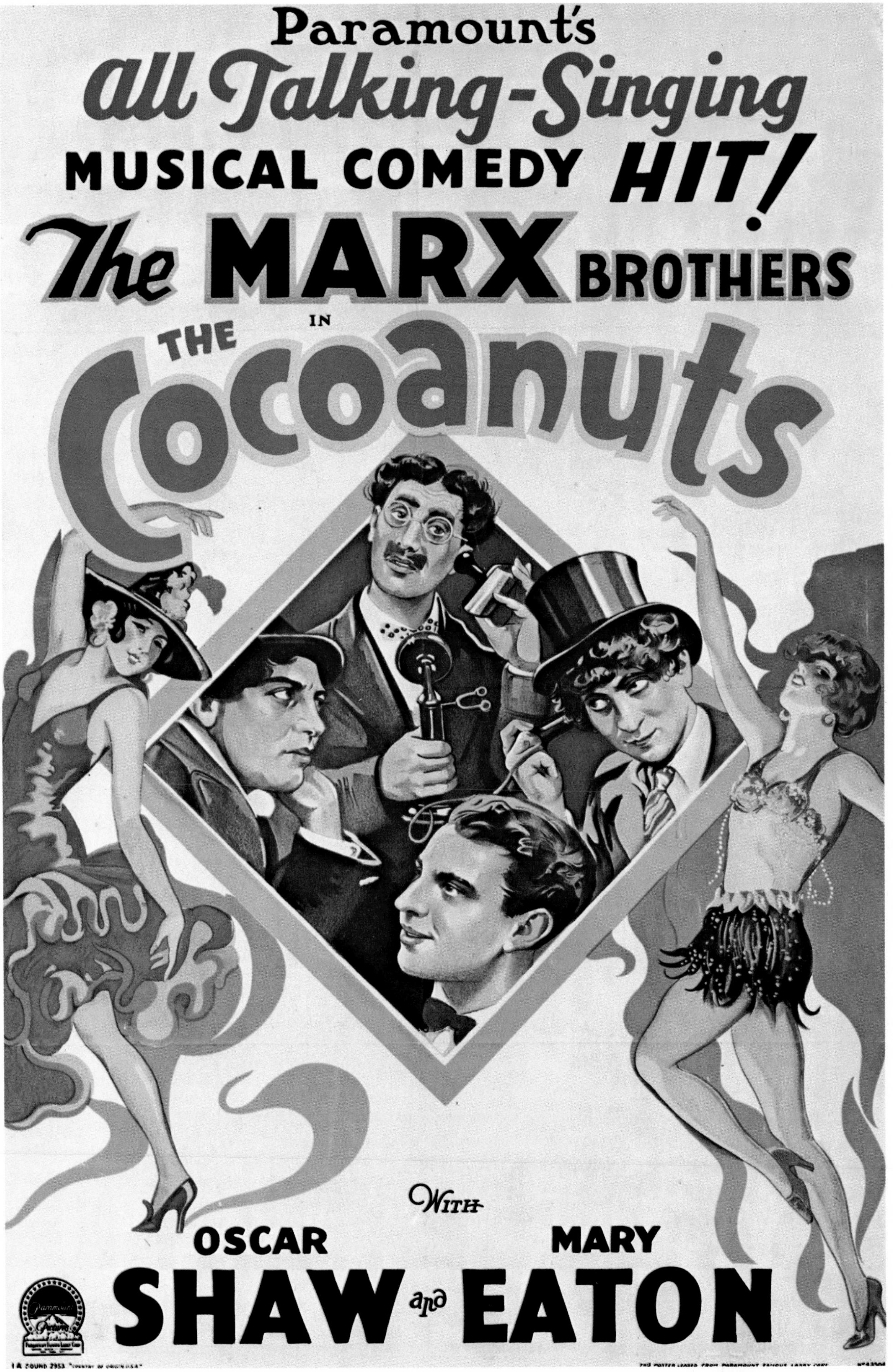
Paramount's
All Talking-Singing
MUSICAL COMEDY HIT!
The MARX BROTHERS
IN
THE
Cocoanuts
WITH
OSCAR
MARY
SHAW and EATON

THE
MARX
BROTHERS
"ANIMAL
CRACKERS"
LILLIAN ROTH
A Paramount Picture

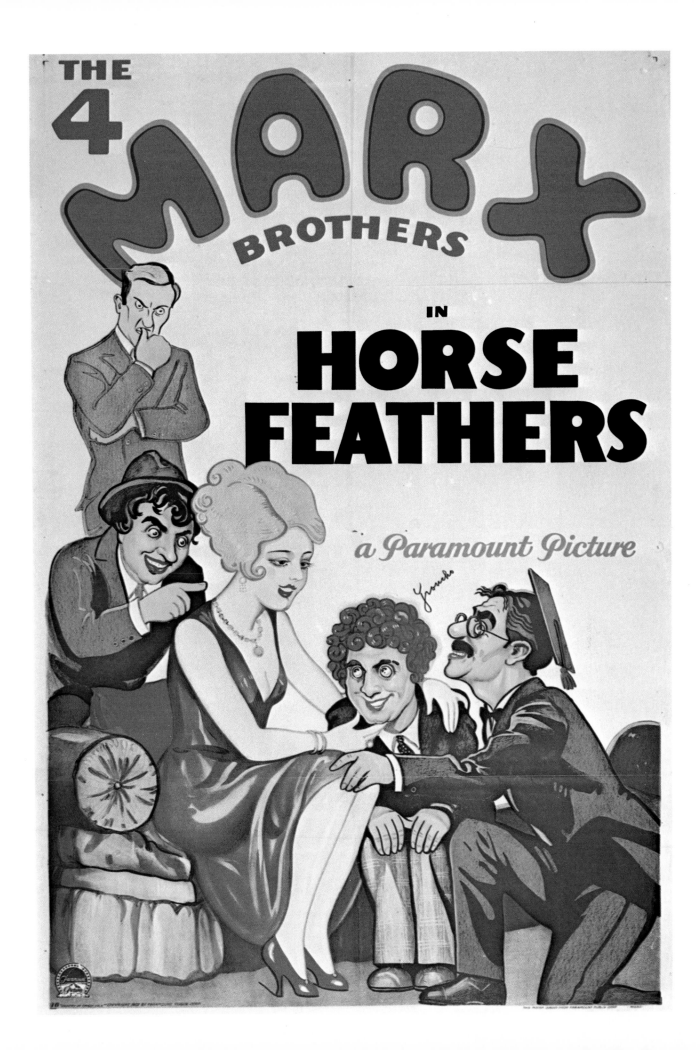

John Decker, who was a close friend of John Barrymore's and also a good drunk, was commissioned to paint the Marx Brothers.

A promotional cartoon for A Night at the Opera.

GROUCHO
CHICO·HARPO
MARX BROS.
GO WEST

"This is a genuine beaver... the last of its kind. The beavers have stopped making them!"

A Metro-Goldwyn-Mayer Picture

New Musical Girlesque!!!

LOVE
HAPPY

starring **The MARX BROS.**

Co-Starring
ILONA MASSEY · VERA-ELLEN · MARION HUTTON

with Raymond Burr · Melville Cooper · Leon Belasco · Paul Valentine · Eric Blore · Bruce Gordon

MARY PICKFORD'S Presentation of A LESTER COWAN Production

Directed by DAVID MILLER · Musical Score & Lyrics by Ann Ronnell · Released thru United Artists

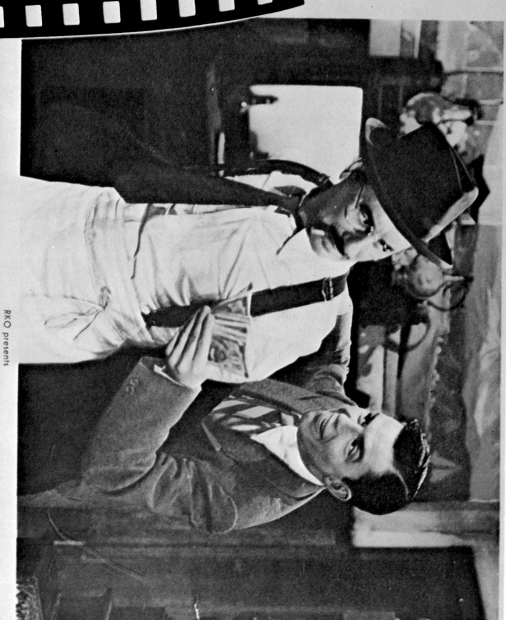

Double Fun!
Double Joy!
Double Everything!

JANE RUSSELL · GROUCHO MARX
FRANK SINATRA IN

RKO presents

DOUBLE DYNAMITE!

*In 1960, I played Ko-Ko, the Lord High Executioner, in the
Bell Telephone Hour production of The Mikado. This fulfilled a lifelong
ambition. Gilbert and Sullivan have been my favorites for years.*

The hall tree in the foyer of my house holds my collection of headgear. Some people say I got it from Hedda Hopper. If you look closely, you'll find Harpo's blond wig.

My third wife Eden dabbled in the arts. So did I, as this painting will show. Having perfected my art, I put away my paint brushes and went on to conquer other fields.

When my house was redecorated a few years ago, my decorator Peter Shore brought over a painting of a little boy. The picture is as old as I am, having been painted in 1890. We also have something else in common: the boy and I both like red berets.

With Peter Shore in my living room.

My dining room.

387 Chico with Karen Reeves and Ethelreda Leopold.
388 With Ruth Roman, who was just starting out in films
and played a small part in the picture.

392

390 During the filming, Kay gave birth to a daughter. We named her Melinda, and this is her first picture, taken August 29, 1946.

391 Melinda, age eighteen months.

392 With Miriam.

393 With Harpo's children on the set: Chico, Alex, myself, Jimmy, Billy, Harpo and Minnie. Harpo married late, a pretty actress named Susan Fleming. They adopted four children, all of whom they raised successfully.

394 With Kay on the set. She's the one on the camel.

395

395 Who said the script was rotten to the core?

396 A dressing-room shot before being made up. (Refer to page 192)

397 With Kay and Cary Grant at a Hollywood party for the Braille Institute. Cary has always been a great gentleman.

398 This shot was taken when I was announcer for the "Out of This World Series" benefit ball game at Gilmore Park.

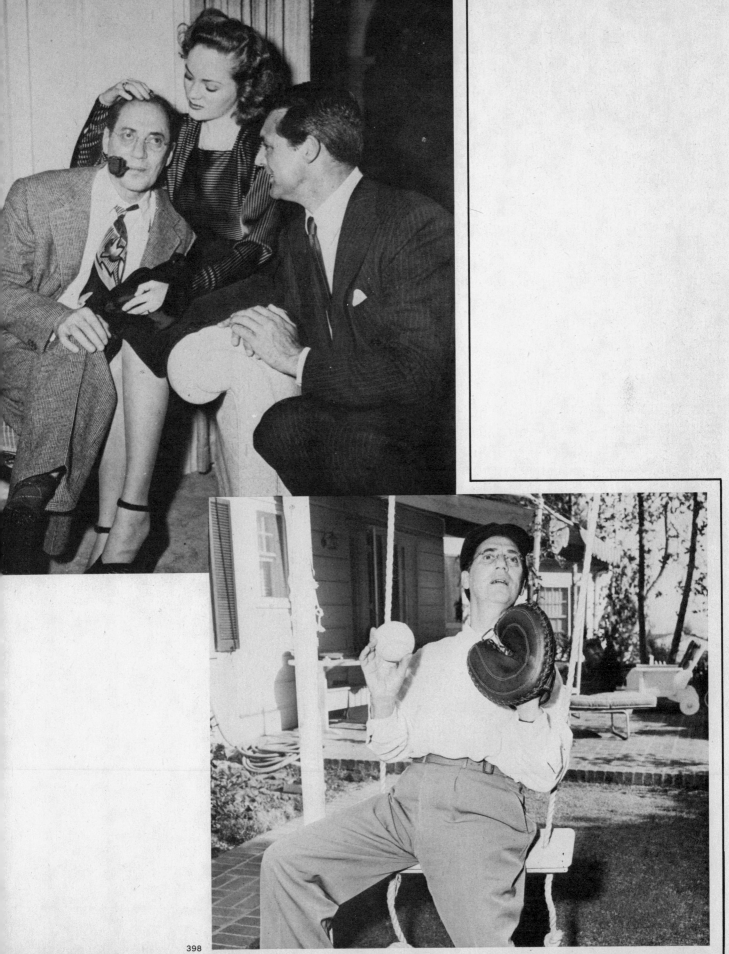

399

L'Amour the Merrier

The romantic teams, the love interests, the dazzling duos. Almost every Marx Brothers film needed a love story to bounce the craziness off of. The characters were sometimes banal, but always pretty.

399 Oscar Shaw and Mary Eaton in *The Cocoanuts*.
400 Ruth Hall and Zeppo in *Monkey Business*.
401 Kitty Carlisle and Allan Jones in *A Night at the Opera*.
402 Allan Jones and Maureen O'Sullivan in *A Day at the Races*.

401

403 John Carroll and Diana Lewis in Go West.
404 Tony Martin and Virginia Grey in *The Big Store.*
405 Lois Collier and Charles Drake in *A Night in Casablanca.*
406 This is one romantic team that, I hope, needs no further introduction.

COPACABANA

For the first time in my film career, I appeared without my brothers. They must have known something I didn't. It was another United Artists picture, featuring a fiery Brazilian named Carmen Miranda. Also in the cast were singers Andy Russell and Gloria Jean.

407 Carmen Miranda was a warm and generous woman. She seemed to have hundreds of relatives back in Brazil, all of whom she supported. In the picture, I seemed to be playing second banana to the tropical fruit on her hat.

408 Clothes make the hombre.

409 In the picture, Carmen played a dual role, a French chanteuse and a Brazilian bombshell. I called it a duel role because the chanteuse and the bombshell fought for my affections.

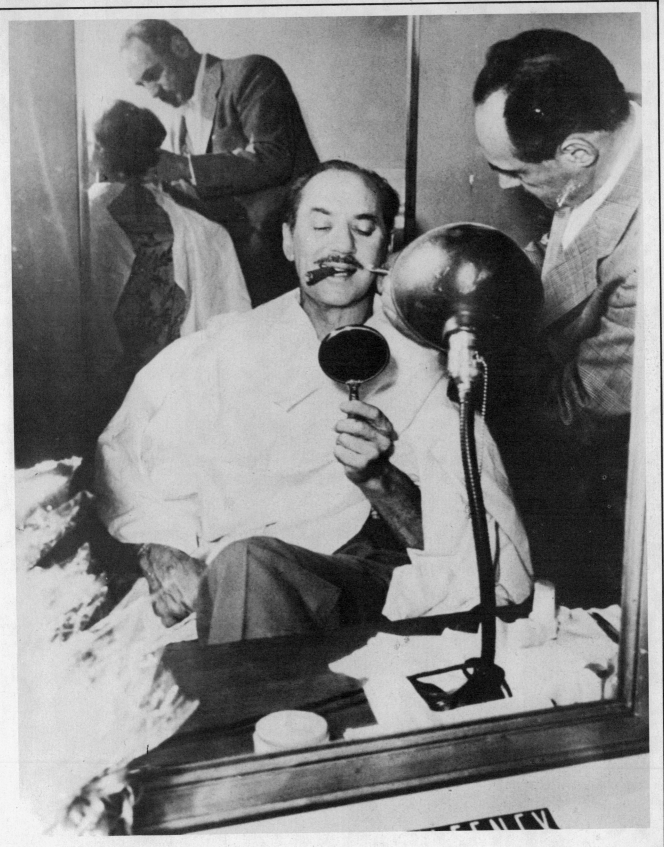

410 This is how I look the first thing in the morning,
without pancake makeup and mascara.

411 Putting on the finishing touches.

412 With Andy Russell and Carmen.

413 Adjustments had to be made—the horse wore a EEE shoe.

414 Kay, seen here with Carmen and me, had a small role in the picture.

To Earl Wilson

October 18, 1949

Dear Earl:

I found your reference to the picture *Copacabana* in shockingly bad taste. One doesn't speak disparagingly of the dead. The fact of the matter is, I did very well on *Copacabana*. It gave me an opportunity to rise every morning at 6 o'clock, glue on a fake mustache, eat an extraordinarily bad lunch in the studio restaurant and get home in time to miss dinner. Plus all this, it gave me a chance to look at my producer fourteen hours a day. No other picture can make that statement.

Regards,
Groucho

From *The Groucho Letters*

417 George Jessel and Al Jolson. This is one of the last pictures taken of Jolson before his death. Both were guest stars on Bing Crosby's radio show, which broadcast from San Francisco. Jolson made movie history in the first talkie, *The Jazz Singer*. Jessel had written the show and starred in it on Broadway, but didn't do the movie because of some differences with the Warner Brothers. Instead, he went out and raised $150 million for the State of Israel. As a result, Israel has more money than the Warner Brothers.

418 With some well-known radio stars of the late 1940s: George Montgomery, Mary Livingston, Dinah Shore and Jack Benny.

418

THE PLAY IN INTERVIEW

Groucho Marx Confirms the Rumor That His Knock-About Team of Foolish Brothers Has Broken Up for Good—To Act in Own Show Smooth Shaven

By BROOKS ATKINSON

An ugly rumor has been going around the country. People say that the Marx Brothers have broken up their slap-stick team. Rialto Gossip, which hears all evil and tells a good part of it, printed a melancholy confirmation of the rumor signed by Groucho Marx a fortnight ago. But this column believes the worst slowly, reluctantly and skeptically, for show business is an asylum of fraudulent rumors. Since Groucho had secluded himself in an anonymous hotel at the corner of Sixth Avenue and Fifty-fourth Street, directly across from the Ziegfeld Theatre (Suite 17E), this column trotted up yesterday afternoon to make inquiries at the source.

* * *

Groucho was stalking about the living room in what would have been his shirt sleeves if he had not been wearing a ducky little sweater cutely buttoned at the neck. Gray pants, cut rather high, supported chiefly by suspenders. Over the back of a chair hung a casual sports jacket of cultivated pattern. Bushy hair, thin at the forepeak, but flaring with considerable bravado astern, and rimless spectacles of dynamic design. Except for the resonant voice which has shot a lot of impudence into theatres and films and except also for the panther style of walking, you would hardly have recognized the illustrious Flywheel who has been playing low comedy in the grand manner for more years than any of us likes to think about.

"Come on, Groucho, how about it?" the interview began. "Are these rumors on the level or not?"

"Absolutely authentic," he growled as he sullenly turned off the radio. "Right from the feedbag. Part of the historical truth."

"You mean, never again?"

"I mean I'm never going to put on the prop coat again as long as I live," he said decisively.

"You mean, in the pictures, don't you?"

"I mean pictures, theatre, airplane, submarine, jeep-car and pogo-stick," he said. "I'm never going to get behind that phony mustache again. I'm through with the whole racket."

Well, probably the boys would be on the radio from time to time as a unit.

"No radio units, I'm telling you," he said, "and, I know what you're going to say, not in television either. I wouldn't go through that stuff again if they could inject it into your arm with a hypodermic needle."

* * *

So long, Groucho, the sardonic buffoon. At the age of 49 Mr. Marx of stage and screen may go on the radio in a personal program. He has a soft spot in his heart for studio audiences because they laugh at him without the mustache. But he has just come East with a play that he and Norman Krasna have written, and if his friends do not think too badly of it he may appear in it in New York this season.

"It's about a guy who is, you know, trying to fix things up when things, you know, get sort of this way and that," Mr. Marx explained. "He comes in in the first act and he runs into this situation which, of course, puts him on the par and he sees all these

THE MUSTACHE IS OUT
Groucho Marx emerges at long last as Julius Marx
New York Times

lugs and dames around there and used to say."

then he kind of dives in and goes on from there the best way he can."

"Fine," this department responded after some swift reflection. "Comedy?"

"Uh-huh, comedy. Still, some drama, you know, here and there the way things are," said Mr. Marx to fill out the outlines of the picture.

"You figure on playing it straight?"

"Just get that grease-paint mustache out of your mind, will you?" he interjected with a flash of temper. "The mustache is out for good."

* * *

Mind you, this department wholly sympathizes with Groucho's situation. He and Harpo and Chico have worked at the same trade all their lives with nothing but a fortune to show for it. They have covered about as much comic ground as three fantastic characters with separate personalities are able to do without bogging down in formula. Form removes the spontaneity from clowning, and this department understands perfectly.

"Now, in this play you say you have written, although no one seems to have seen it yet," the interview continued, "would it be entirely out of character—we'll say in just the last scene—for you to come in smoking a cigar and wearing, for instance, a black cutaway?"

"Well, now that you mention it," Mr. Marx said thoughtfully, "it wouldn't be absolutely impossible. Nothing is impossible, as my grandfather, who lived to be over a hun-

"Now, let's get one more thing straight. Did I hear you say you are going to play smooth-shaven?"

"Look here, chum, the mustache is out," Mr. Marx said irritably. "You take the mustache. It would be an improvement."

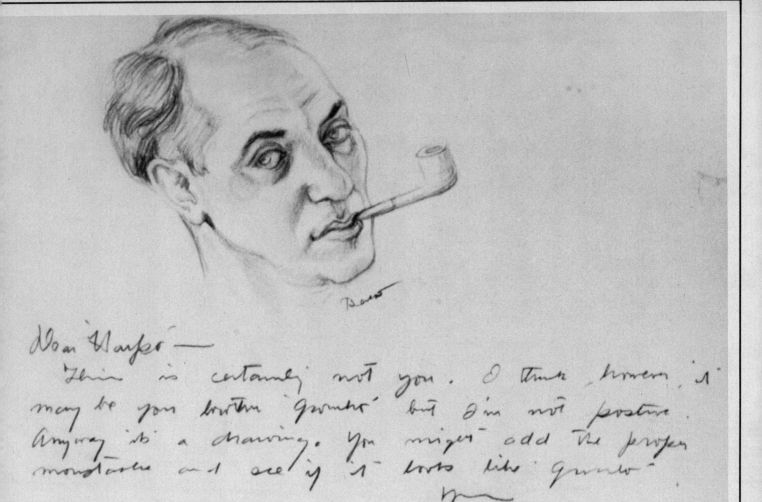

Dear Harpo —

This is certainly not you. I think, however, it may be your brother 'Groucho' but I'm not positive. Anyway it's a drawing. You might add the proper moustache and see if it looks like 'Groucho'.

Yours
Thomas H. Benton

420 In 1947 Kay and I had a costume party. Many people came dressed as Groucho. I did my Harpo imitation. (That's me as Harpo near the top of the stairs.) The Red scare had the whole movie colony nervous, and this picture had another incarnation when, in 1973, *The Way We Were* was released. Our costume party was re-created in the film. (See picture 610.) This photo was taken by Charlotte Granet, and was published in *Life*. The others, sort of clockwise, are Harry Tugend, Nat Perrin, Bert Granet, Harpo as Groucho at center, Hy Kraft at far right, Norman Panama, Mrs. Frank Loesser and, at bottom left, Alan Boretz.

421 Bert Granet took this picture at the same party: me, Charlotte Granet, Kay, Nat Perrin.

422 A sketch arrived for me in the mail one day. Thomas Hart Benton claimed he'd drawn Harpo and it looked like me without a mustache.

YOU BET YOUR LIFE

The time was April 1947. Bob Hope was master of ceremonies for an all-star radio special. The spots were running longer than usual, and I had to cool my heels—and other nether regions—waiting to go on to do my two-spot with Hope midway through the program.

We were to do a sketch in which Hope was running a radio station in the middle of the Sahara, and I would be playing a traveling salesman. Since I'd played traveling salesman to many a farmer's daughter, it was type casting.

I came on to a deafening roar of applause.

"Why, Groucho Marx!" Hope read. "What are you doing out here in the Sahara Desert?"

"Desert, hell!" I extemporized. "I've been standing in a drafty corridor for forty-five minutes."

This broke up the audience, as well as Hope, who in his hilarity dropped the script. I casually stepped on it.

"Hope, a pretty fair ad libber himself," my son Arthur wrote in *Life with Groucho*, "quickly entered into the spirit of the thing, and before Mannie Manheim or Charlie Isaacs (the show's writers and producers) could figure out how to stop them, the two comics had made an absolute shambles of their carefully prepared show. The spot ran twenty-five minutes over length, and much of it would never have passed the censors. Among a great many other off-color remarks, Groucho and Hope, all through the spot, had made frequent references to a notorious Los Angeles madam of a few years back."

JOHN GUEDEL (producer): Afterwards I went up to Groucho in the dressing room. I said, "Hiring you to do a show in which you read the script is like buying a Cadillac to haul coal. You're not getting all out of you that is desired. In other words, you're so much better ad libbing than talking to another stooge." I also said, "It gives you more reality. You might talk to real people for a change—a real old maid and a real truck driver and a real librarian rather than other people holding scripts— because your character comes over thin and brittle, just jokes and that's all, whereas I think you have a certain warmth."

So Groucho said, "What do you have in mind?" I said, "I want you to do a quiz show." He answered, "I've flopped four times on radio before. I'm interested in anything. I might as well compete with refrigerators. I'll give it a try."

From *The Secret Word Is Groucho*

The implication that I went on radio with my tail between my legs is substantially true. Maybe I thought I was slumming, but I needed the work. *Newsweek*, in noting my capitulation to do a quiz series, observed that it was like selling Citation to a glue factory.

The show started at the American Broadcasting Company, known as the third network. It had formerly been part of the National Broadcasting Company, but that network had become such a monopoly that it was divided into two new networks.

With Kay backstage.

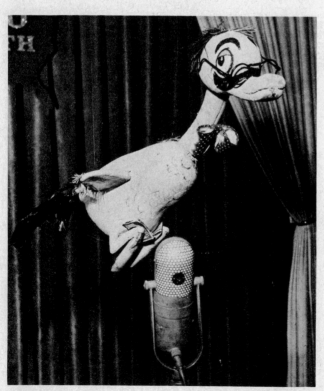

423

424

234

426

427

236

426 I hadn't given up entertaining the troops just because the war was over. Here, Kay and I are greeted by Evelyn Young, manager of the Hollywood USO Camp Shows Office, when we returned from a tour of veterans hospitals on the Pacific coast. We'd entertained thirty thousand wounded veterans at five hospitals.

427 Two of our earliest jackpot winners on *You Bet Your Life:* Bertha Paul, a housewife from Inglewood, California, and Mike Levy, a Hollywood grocer. They received a $3,710 jackpot.

428 In 1948, when *Time for Elizabeth* first opened on Broadway, we went back to New York for the opening. Here I'm with Norman Krasna and his wife Ruth. Norman and I had written the light comedy specifically for me, but other commitments forced me to bow out, and Otto Kruger took over the part. It closed after eight performances.

428

After only three years of marriage, Kay and I decided to divorce. She had emotional problems she would have to work out on her own. I got custody of Melinda.

Because of this unhappy marriage, I had added reason to throw myself into the quiz show and try to make it a success. The low ratings gradually climbed. Our sponsor—Elgin-American Compacts—sold out its complete line of merchandise each of the two seasons it was associated with us. The intellectuals had adopted the program. At last, after four or five previous efforts, I was secure as a radio star. There was talk about the impending threat of a one-eyed monster, but I laughed it off. In April of 1949, I wrote a substitute column for Arthur Engel of *The Hollywood Reporter.* From my secure vantage point, I took a condescending look at the upstart:

Run for your career, boys. A new monster has arrived, scaring the daylights out of actors, producers, theater owners, sports promoters and sponsors. According to some of the prophets, within six months most of the theaters, nightclubs and sports arenas will be dismantled and converted into parking lots. We may not need the parking lots, because no American with a television set is ever going to go outdoors again.

To hear them tell it, we will soon be a nation of squint-eyed hermits huddling around wooden boxes with glass fronts. Only a lower-case cretin will ever go to a movie again. Who in his right mind is going to look at *Letter to Three Wives, Johnny Belinda* or *Hamlet* when he has the choice of sitting home and watching a 20-year-old Western with the same story, plot and cast that he saw not only the night before, the month before, but the year before? Can you conceive of anyone journeying to a ball park, sitting in that awful fresh air eating hot dogs and drinking beer, when, by just flicking a switch, he can remain at home and see the catcher's left shoulder, the first baseman's right ear, the third finger on the left hand of the right fielder and, if he keeps his eyes peeled, sometime during the evening he may even see the baseball?

What young lover is going to take his girl out for an evening of dancing, and whatever the current equivalent is for necking, when he can watch a chorus of six girls without faces dancing hazily on Kinescope?

As for the poor old theater, it's dead again. This happens every ten years. It was killed long ago by the movies, then by radio, and now, the coup de grace, by television. It is sad but it's true. Who wants to see *Death of a Salesman, South Pacific, Born Yesterday* or any of the great plays when that same time can be consumed in watching a seal juggling a rubber ball, puppets with dialogue out of the first reader by Joe Miller, and second-rate plays with stock company actors in papier mâché sets?

I am not denying the potentialities of television, or the two or three shows that come out of the East. I am sure television will grow bigger and more professional each year, but people will still want action. They will still want to smell the turf at Santa Anita, the rush to the betting window, the fun of personally cursing the umpire, and the drama and crowd of the fight arena.

This is America, my fine calamity howlers. This is still the land of the pioneer and the adventurer; of Daniel Boone and Lewis and Clark; of the jet plane test pilot; of Johnny Appleseed and Errol Flynn. Bascially we are a gregarious and crowd-loving nation, and no mechanical invention will ever plant us permanently in front of a fireplace. Home is unquestionably where the heart is, but it is also the place where you bathe, change your clothes and get the hell out of as quickly as possible.

429 In the fall of 1949, we moved to CBS Radio. *You Bet Your Life* shot up to Number Six in the ratings. When both major networks—NBC and CBS—approached us about going on television, a bidding war started. Since we were already at CBS, it seemed likely we'd stay there. One of their star directors, Ralph Levy (left), helped us with the pilot show. With him are announcer George Fenneman, co-director Robert Dwan, and myself. When the dust settled, NBC was the high bidder. Levy stayed on at CBS, becoming the director of Jack Benny's television show for many years.

430 With Olivia de Havilland. I was crazy about her, but she was crazy about John Huston. Olivia and I were members of the Independent Citizens' Committee of the Arts, Sciences and Professions. We'd traveled to Seattle to support some liberal candidates. A local newspaper headlined our visit: "Liberals Invade Seattle." Olivia laughed it off, but I didn't understand why "liberal" should be considered a dirty word. These were the witch-hunting days of McCarthy and Nixon, however, and suddenly those with liberal viewpoints were being called pinkos. I've been a liberal Democrat all my life. The only time I've ever voted for a Republican for President was in 1940, for I had great respect for Wendell Willkie and was concerned about Roosevelt's breaking precedent in running for a third term. Four years later, however, I'd reverted to FDR because we were in the middle of the war and a changeover at that time didn't seem advisable. Even at the height of the hysteria and the blacklisting, I never apologized for my political convictions. Many times my crusades have been as effective as Don Quixote's mad lunges at windmills. Such was probably the case with McGovern in 1972. Yet, I frankly find Democrats a better, more sympathetic crowd. It's been said often before, and until I have greater evidence to the contrary, I'll continue to believe that Democrats have greater regard for the common man than Republicans do. One of my closest friends—Morrie Ryskind—disagrees. He's as far to the right as I am to the left. We remain close despite what each of us considers an aberration in the other. It's reached a point where we tease each other about our political beliefs rather than discuss them seriously.

429

430

Be it known that the **George Foster Peabody Radio Award** *is hereby presented to* The Groucho Marx Show and American Broadcasting Company,

for outstanding entertainment

during 1948,

upon recommendation of the Henry W. Grady School of Journalism, University of Georgia, and the Peabody Advisory Board, by authority of the Regents of the University System of Georgia, in conjunction with the National Association of Broadcasters.

April 21, 1949

Edward Weeks,
Chairman of Peabody Board

John E. Drewry,
Dean of School of Journalism

By and large, my convictions haven't gotten me into trouble. There was one exception, however. During Nixon's first term, I was quoted as saying the only thing that would save the United States would be Nixon's assassination. I was immediately put on the infamous Enemies List and, as I was informed later, put under FBI surveillance. Later events proved that Nixon was indeed a storm trooper trampling over our personal freedoms, but I still shouldn't have said what I did. The language was intemperate and no better than some of Nixon's appalling statements over the course of his political career. An earlier quote of mine about Nixon was more in the Groucho character. After Kennedy defeated him in the 1960 election, the Nixon family moved to Trousdale, the section of Beverly Hills in which I live. I was asked about my new neighbor. "I'd rather have him here than in the White House," I remarked. After all, if I could accept Elvis Presley as a neighbor, why not Tricky Dick?

431 The ultimate broadcasting award, the Peabody for 1948, which we received the following year.

LOVE HAPPY

While *You Bet Your Life* was ending its run at CBS, I signed to make a film for United Artists, *Love Happy*, which was released later that year. It was a terrible picture, and I tried to blot it out of my mind.

One memory, however, lingers. The producer called me one day. "We have three girls here," he said. "Why don't you come and pick one out?" No, this wasn't part of some new giveaway program. I would be picking the girl who would be doing a sexy vignette in the picture.

Three girls were lined up in the producer's office when I arrived the following day. Each was required to walk up and down the room. Then the three girls left.

"Which one do you like?" the producer asked.

"You must be crazy," I replied. "There's only one, as far as I'm concerned. The blonde."

The girl was signed for the part. For her one scene, she wore a dress cut so low that I couldn't remember the dialogue. Very soon, other men throughout the world were suffering similar fevers, for the girl was Marilyn Monroe.

From *The Secret Word Is Groucho*

434 *Love Happy* marked the last time the Marx Brothers acted together in film. The most memorable thing about the picture to me was the birthday party for co-star Ilona Massey on the set. It was then that the informal pictures with Marilyn were taken, as was this one with Ilona and Harpo.

435 Marilyn's one line became a cinema classic. Well, maybe it wasn't so hot, but *I* liked it: "Mister Grunion, I want you to help me . . . some men are following me." Then she sashayed away. I would have followed her too, but I was called back for a double take.

The Picture That Discovered **MARILYN MONROE**

Two Laugh-Happy Hits IN ONE Hilarious Show!

The Picture That Discovered MARILYN MONROE

LOVE HAPPY

THE MARX BROS.

ILONA MASSEY
VERA-ELLEN
MARION HUTTON

ABBOTT and COSTELLO AFRICA SCREAMS

3-SHEETS AND 6-SHEET SNIPE AVAILABLE INDIVIDUALLY

THE "HAPPIEST" HIT SHOW OF THE YEAR!

Wait'll you see those JOY BOYS in a JUNGLE JAM!

Their FUNNIEST musical!

The Marx Bros. are LOVE HAPPY

ILONA VERA- MARION
MASSEY-ELLEN-HUTTON

ABBOTT COSTELLO "Africa Screams"

CLYDE BEATTY   MAX and BUDDY BAER

FRANK BUCK

The picture that discovered MARILYN MONROE

UNITED ARTISTS PRESSBOOK

436 With character actor Eric Blore and the CBS eye.

438 Ilona and her velvet glove.

439 When the picture was re-released as part of a double bill with Abbott and Costello in *Africa Screams,* the ad campaign was somewhat changed.

440 I don't recall the circumstances of this letter from one of history's great men, but I suspect it has something to do with the comedy writer I fired.

THE WHITE HOUSE
WASHINGTON

October 27, 1950

Dear Mr. Marx:

Thanks very much for your note of the twentieth. I was very certain that the joke referred to was not of your making.   You can make much better ones than that, as I have heard you on many an occasion.

I appreciated your note most highly.

Sincerely yours,

Harry Truman

Mr. Groucho Marx
1150 South Beverly Drive
Los Angeles 35, California

MISTER MUSIC

441
-42 I returned to Paramount Studios after an absence of fifteen years to do a guest spot with Bing Crosby in *Mister Music*. It was a 1950 Christmas turkey, based on Arthur Sheekman's *Accent on Youth*. One reviewer singled out my contribution: "The Groucho Marx bit is not up to the comic's usual standard, largely because of weak material." By this time, Adolph Zukor, one of the founders of the studio, was well past seventy-five (he died in 1976 at the age of 103), but he insisted on remaining professionally active. Zukor was a great old gentleman. One day George Jessel and I were talking about him, and Georgie snorted, "He considers the day a success if he can find his eyeglasses by three in the afternoon."

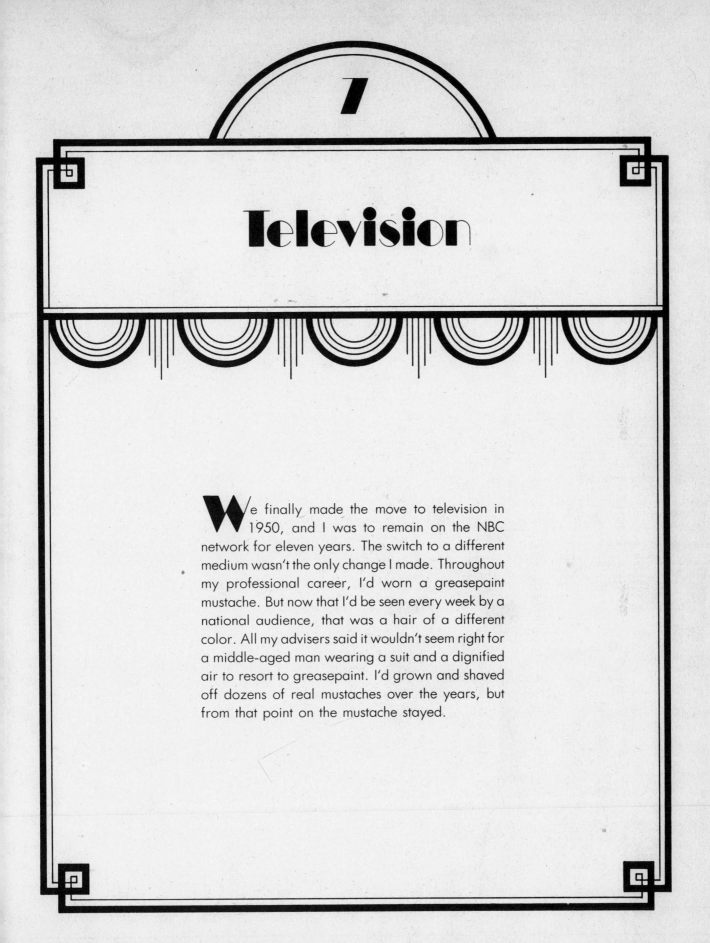

Television

We finally made the move to television in 1950, and I was to remain on the NBC network for eleven years. The switch to a different medium wasn't the only change I made. Throughout my professional career, I'd worn a greasepaint mustache. But now that I'd be seen every week by a national audience, that was a hair of a different color. All my advisers said it wouldn't seem right for a middle-aged man wearing a suit and a dignified air to resort to greasepaint. I'd grown and shaved off dozens of real mustaches over the years, but from that point on the mustache stayed.

King Leer

"I'm happy to be plunging into TV; but I'd rather plunge into a nutshell," says Groucho

By Groucho Marx

Groucho Marx "quizzes" a pretty contestant, Jane Easton.

Groucho chats with John Guedel, originator-producer of his show.

I MUST say I find television very educational. The minute somebody turns it on, I go into the library and read a good book.

That's a pretty cynical attitude for "the leer"—that's me, Groucho—and now that I'm a part of television, or "TV" as we say out here on the Coast, I don't mean a word of it.

TV presents a completely new set of problems to me. In my 35 years in show business, I've learned the intricacies of the stage, then the movies, then radio. Now comes television. I can't even learn how to turn it on!

At first, I thought it would be simple to put our show on TV. Just me and a few contestants gabbing. That's all.

Little did I know there would be four cameras staring at me, a makeup man frowning from the wings if I raise my eyebrows, the light crew glaring from the rafters if I cast a shadow in the wrong place, my director making frantic motions if I step out of camera range, the studio audience whispering if I step out of mike range, the sponsor screaming if I forget the commercial.

I suppose I'll get used to all this. After all, television is progressing rapidly. I notice the home sets are improving all the time. For instance, the old sets used to have about 35 tubes, but now the sets are down to 18 tubes. Now if they just eliminate the picture tube, they'll reach perfection.

I also notice that television screens are getting bigger. Thank goodness for those screens. They're the only thing that keeps the stuff from crawling into th eliving room.

I think the ideal television sets should be equipped with two screens. Then you could use the second screen to hide the television sets.

In a nutshell, I'm happy to be plunging into television. Although frankly, I'd rather be plunging into a nutshell.

Sure, we've got a lot of problems to lick, since we're doing our show for radio and TV simultaneously. This means everything we do for television must be plain to the listener who can't see it, the old-fashioned fellow with the radio receiver. It will limit our plans for the time being, but I'm sure everything will work out for the best. I wish I could say the same for Harpo, who isn't working out at all.

As for me, I'm going to keep my cigar, my leer and any old ad lib wisecracks I find kicking around. My mustache is my own now. I bought it from the upstairs maid. But the frock coat and the old Groucho who chases blondes will be missing. Even the new Groucho will be missing, but that's only until I can get my spark plugs cleaned.

All I can say is this: Walk, don't run, to your nearest television set in October, tune to KNBH and join us for our first TV session of "You Bet Your Life." I think you'll like it.

(At the time Tele-Views went to press, the exact date of Groucho's first telecast had not been announced—Ed.)

443

5

446

445 Melinda was also active in television. She appeared on Art Linkletter's *House Party*.
446 This time Melinda was on the Jimmy Durante show.

During the seven years we were sponsored by De-
Soto, I grossed many millions . . . which I seem to
have misplaced.

To show my appreciation I drove the sponsor
completely out of business.

447 George Fenneman, in his own way, was as great a straight man as Margaret Dumont was a straight woman. (pg. 246)

448 My signoff during the seven seasons we were sponsored by DeSoto-Plymouth.

450 Six months after I went on television, the Academy of Television Arts and Sciences, in its third annual awards, named me Outstanding Television Personality of 1950. Rosemary LaPlanche, a former Miss America, presented the Emmy.

spayed female dog. Answers name of "Shepard." Notify tuchen police.

LOST — Medium sized dog. Short haired, short ears. Reddish brown with white throat. Answers to name of Rex. Reward. CHarter

3. **Personals**

HOME window washing and janitorial service. Monite Bros. CH 7-3110. Free estimates.

ALEXANDER M. Jones earnestly and respectfully requests that his friends, business associates, relatives and all others refrain from telephoning his home, or otherwise disrupting its serenity, between 8 and 8:30 o'clock of a Thursday evening. These 30 minutes are regularly observed as the Groucho Marx Half Hour.

MILAZZO'S BEAUTY SHOP
298 George Street
CHarter

DRESSMAKING
And ALTERATIONS
SO. 8-3344-W

FREE home showing. Amazing Filter Queen Health Service. CH. 7-0010. A. M. only.

7. **Business Directory**

All Home Repairs

451 *The Big Show* was radio's last stand against television, a weekly ninety-minute all-star extravaganza starring Tallulah Bankhead. I appeared on the second program of the series, on November 2, 1950. On the first week, Tallulah had sung "Give My Regards to Broadway." On the second show, Broadway refused them. One of her lines to me was choice. I kissed her full on the lips. She growled, "Take that cheap cigar out of your mouth." Tallulah was very difficult, demanding and imperious. An all-around pain in the rear.

During rehearsals, Fanny Brice disappeared for twenty minutes. "Where have you been?" I asked when she returned.

"I fixed that SOB," Fanny said. "I went into her dressing room and took a leak in her sink."

452 With Melinda at home. We were now living in a Mediterranean house in the Beverly Hills flats.

453 We might have been living on the flats, but since it was a two-story house, we needed some horsepower to get upstairs. I installed an Inclinator on the staircase. Melinda and my grandson Steve Marx are seen in this picture.

TIME

THE WEEKLY NEWSMAGAZINE

TWENTY CENTS

DECEMBER 31, 1951

GROUCHO MARX
Trademark: effrontery.

454 After forty years in the business, I was finally accepted as a solo act. On December 31, 1951, I was on the cover of *Time* for the second time. I was called the zaniest and most durable of the Marx Brothers. They might have had a point—Harpo at the time was doing milk commercials on TV; Chico was performing in nightclubs. *Time*'s article read in part:

Unsquelchable effrontery has always been Groucho's chief stock in trade. During his stage & screen career, he played a succession of brazen rascals: fraudulent attorney, flimflamming explorer, dissolute college president, amoral private eye, cozening operatic entrepreneur, horse doctor posing as a fashionable neurologist ("Either this man is dead or my watch has stopped"), bogus Emperor of France—whatever the alias or whatever the rascality, he was always the same rascal, the con man who made no bones about the disdain he felt for the suckers he was trimming.

Married and divorced twice (two children by his first marriage, one by the second), he lives with a pair of servants in a 15-room Beverly Hills house. He does all the shopping. Afternoons, he works on the two dozen fruit trees that stand on his back lawn; he is a martyr to what Robert Benchley described as dendrophilism, which might be described as tree-tickling. Groucho takes excellent care of himself: he plays golf, never has more than two drinks at a party, and always leaves at midnight, even parties where he is the host. His only excess is cigars. One of his favorite occupations is sitting for long hours in his den strumming Gilbert & Sullivan (at which he is an expert) on his guitar. He is also an expert on the novels of Henry James. Having had hardly any formal education, Groucho, by dint of greedy reading, has made himself a well-read man. His friends are endlessly amazed at his mastery of the contents of magazines which they regard as highbrow (*Atlantic, Harper's, Saturday Review of Literature*, etc.).

455 Shortly after I went on television, Rube Goldberg sent me a sketch he'd drawn of me at a previous party—I think it was the Whigs.

DOUBLE DYNAMITE

In 1951 George Bernard Shaw's secretary wrote her autobiography. She quoted the great man as saying that the greatest actor of his time was . . . Groucho Marx. And here I'd been dissipating my talent on a television quiz show. When Howard Hughes, who now owned RKO, approached me about returning to the screen, I jumped at the offer. [456] The name of the picture was *It's Only Money*. That was a philosophy that Howard couldn't agree with, so the title was changed. Actually, there were two other reasons for the title change:

To Leo Rosten

December 14, 1951

Dear Leo:

  It's Only Money is now called *Double Dynamite* as a tribute to Jane Russell's you know what, and will open around Christmas at the Paramount in New York.

  The fact that your children want photographs comes as no surprise to me. You apparently have been living with your head in the sand and haven't the faintest idea what is going on in the world. Practically all children are crazy about me, particularly girls. Unfortunately, as soon as they emerge from adolescence, they look around for facsimiles of Jeff Chandler and other bounders who, I am sure, do not possess the wisdom and charm that makes me so attractive.

  I hope this answers all your questions.

Regards,
Groucho

From *The Groucho Letters*

[457] The four co-stars of the picture: Frank Sinatra, Jane Russell, and Groucho Marx. This was my first film under contract to Howard. He promised me a plane trip around the world if I'd go on tour to promote some other products of RKO. Quicker than you can say "Spruce Goose," I agreed. I made the personal appearance tour, but I never collected the trip.

[458] Sinatra watches as propman George McGonigle lathers me. RKO slyly promoted the fact that there was a bubble bath sequence in the picture.

Thousands stormed the theaters around the country, assuming Jane Russell was taking the bath. Sinatra's up-and-down career was mostly down during this period (though he would win an Academy Award the following year for *From Here to Eternity*). He nevertheless maintained the temperament of a great star. You never know when you might need it again. He'd keep us waiting on the set while he dawdled over the racing form in his dressing room. I finally got fed up. "I believe in being on time for work," I told him. "The next time you show up late, you'd better be prepared to act for two, because I won't be there." We had no more trouble after that.

[459] My acting career almost went down the drain.

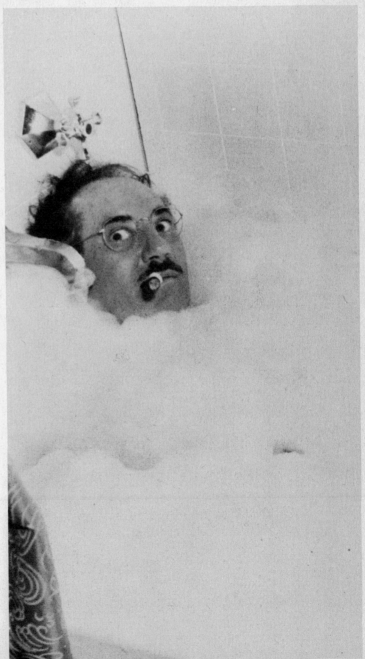

A GIRL IN EVERY PORT

Another RKO picture, this time co-starring William
Bendix, Marie Wilson and me. Bendix was a fine,
underrated actor, and Marie a good comedienne.
Maybe we were all too old to be involved in such
foolishness.

462 Marie was mad about the boy.

463 Bendix and me with one of the assistant directors.
This was the last straw.

464 Don't make waves.

465 Throughout the history of films, screen lovers have
been caught in awkward poses.

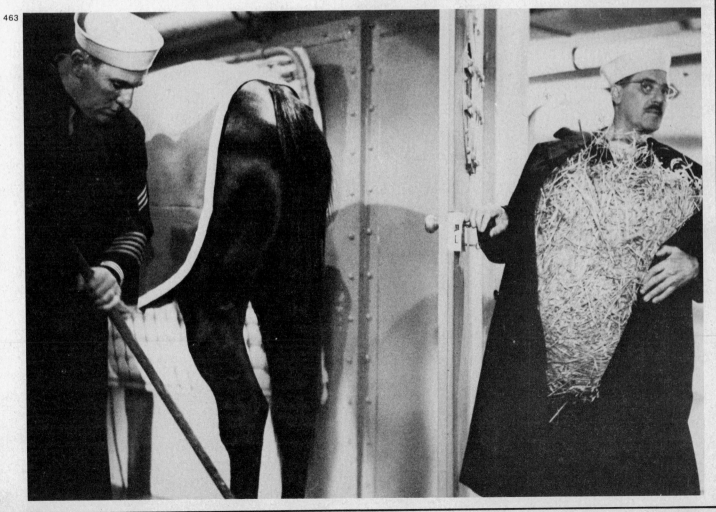

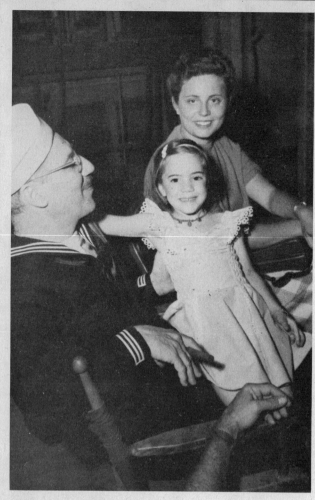

466 With Miriam and Melinda.

467 Melinda was a big hit with both of my co-stars.
-68

469 Bendix may have had a girl in every port, but thanks to my television sponsor, I had a DeSoto.

There's A Place Called Omaha, Nebraska

**By GROUCHO MARX
and HARRY RUBY**

HARRY RUBY MUSIC CO.
514 N. Elm Drive
Beverly Hills, Calif.

There's A Place Called Omaha, Nebraska

By GROUCHO MARX
and HARRY RUBY

Moderato

VERSE

A man sat by the fire - place The fire — it was out, It was

out be-cause the logs were soak-ing wet. _____ He then turned on the

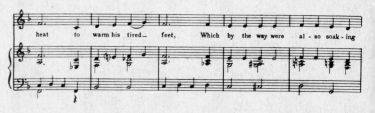

heat to warm his tired_ feet, Which by the way were al-so soak-ing

470-473 Still wanting to show my range—it was an O'Keefe and Merritt—I teamed up with Harry Ruby to write a popular song. It sold three copies—none of them in Omaha.

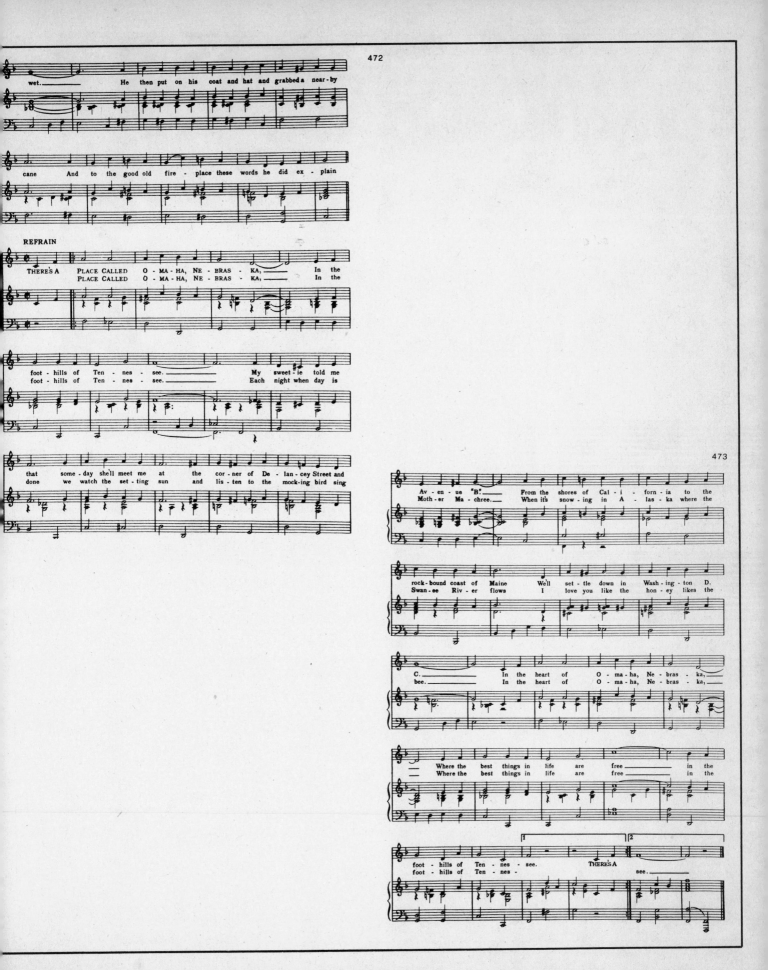

474 When Adlai Stevenson was campaigning in 1952, he was honored by the Hollywood moguls at a reception. Here he's flanked by William Goetz, Dore Schary, myself, and my daughter Miriam.

475 The American public was introduced to a second generation of performing Marxes on November 19, 1952, when Melinda appeared on *You Bet Your Life* for the first time. She would ultimately appear more than a dozen times on the show, tap dancing and singing as she did on her first appearance.

476 The Groucho pansies.

477 Meanwhile, back at NBC—

If you analyze it, the rules of the game were quite simple: Each pair of contestants was given twenty dollars. They could bet any of that amount on the first question, and as the amount increased on the three following questions so that the couple winning the highest amount would be eligible for the $2,000 grand prize question, not to mention the $100 they may have already won on the secret word, which if added to the four questions they could consecutively answer without missing two in a row, would give them $1,000 and make them eligible to spin the wheel, depending on if they picked the respective numbers previously selected by the contestants for the $5,000 and $10,000 questions, or they could bet on the basic amount by answering questions naturally paying off more, say $300 to the $100 pay-off on the question, even your Aunt Gladys could answer; however, if George Fenneman was recruited to help answer the questions, they were allowed to pick two questions from Column A and one from Column B, because after all George was born in China, and this added a novel slant to the game, not to mention the fortune cookies, none of which contained the right answers, because we were a rigidly honest show and no help from the audience was permitted. This was why our show was so distinctive.

From *The Secret Word Is Groucho*

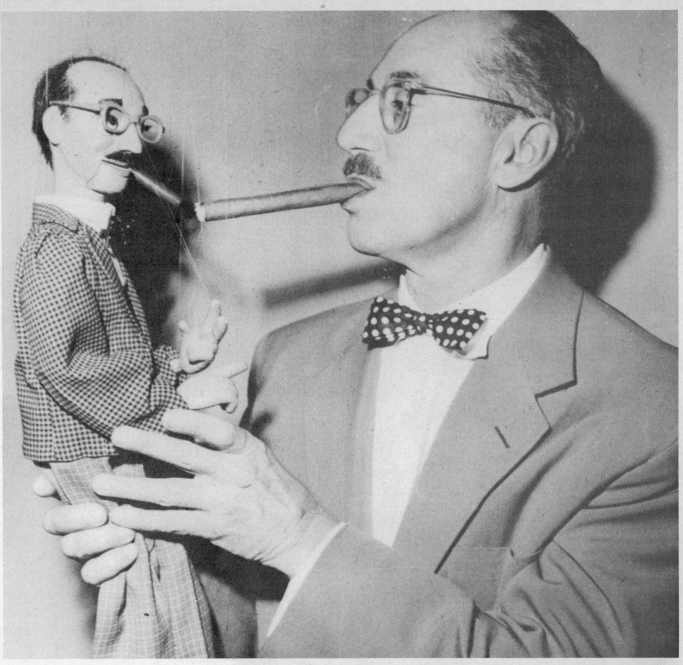

477

476

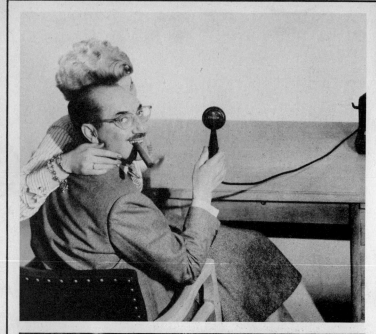

478 It's true—blondes do have more fun. After I was shown this picture, with the threat that my wife would also be invited to a future showing, blondes also had more funds.

479 With John Wayne and Red Skelton at one of those fabled Hollywood parties. How can I be standing between them, when everyone knows they're both to my far right?

480 With Leo Durocher at the 1953 spring training camp of the New York Giants in Phoenix. Leo gave me some advice, which I followed. He noticed that when fans asked for my autograph, I always signed my whole name. "Why don't you just sign your first name?" Leo asked. "Everyone knows who you are. There's only one Groucho, after all."

481 Ty Cobb was another visitor to the camp.

482 Back in Hollywood, the West Side Writing and Asthma Club had wheezed its last breath. Most of its writer members were now living in Switzerland— they wanted to be near their bank accounts. The action shifted to the Hillcrest Country Club. Lunch was a daily ritual, comics trying to top each other. Al Hirschfeld, visiting from the East, sketched a group of us for *The New Yorker*. Harpo hits a matzoh ball with his umbrella while standing on the table. Starting at bottom left, going clockwise, the others are me, George Burns , Jack Benny, Otto the waiter, Danny Kaye, George Jessel, Lou Holtz, the Ritz Brothers and Chico.

483 Some distinguished visitors backstage at the quiz show. Gummo, who was my agent, got together with Deborah Kerr, Eddie Robinson and me. I had a date later that evening with Deborah, and took her to a party. We'd met at the studio, so I didn't know she lived way out in the Pacific Palisades until the evening was almost over. There was no way I was going to drive forty miles to take the lady home, so I stood up and asked, "Is anyone going to the Palisades?" I secured a ride home for Deborah. And they say chivalry is dead.

484 Other studio visitors were Garson Kanin and his wife Ruth Gordon, Evelyn Keyes and her date Norman Krasna.

485 Prior to unveiling of the 1954 DeSoto, I went back to Detroit to give the assembled leaders a pep talk. "I have been through the plant and seen the new model," I said, "and I predict it will be just as successful as its predecessors. And you can bet that I will be in there pushing the '54 DeSoto as hard as I can. I only hope I won't have to push it as often as I did my '52."

During the 1953–1954 television season, I did a little moonlighting, appearing with Melinda, then seven, on *Person to Person*. Edward R. Murrow, the host of the program, was a great man with enormous dignity. I like to feel he appeared a little more human and warm after our exchange. First I got him to admit he had an eight-year-old son, and accused Murrow of trying to match him up with my Melinda. He took the teasing with good grace, but hurried along to the next question:

MURROW: Groucho, occasionally the skeptics say that your television and radio show is not ad lib. Is that right?

GROUCHO: That's not true. I've been ad libbing all my life, Ed. I don't know why I should stop just because I've been on a quiz show. Of course, we do have some preparation. If we have a governor or a mayor or a chief of police or a man who broke the sound barrier for Douglas who's an air pilot or something, then we do have some preparation for him. But for the people we pick out of the audience, we have nothing prepared. And I want to say here and now that I never see the contestants before I meet them at the mike. And I've been doing that for seven years. The first two weeks, I met the contestants, but I found it didn't work. It inhibited me. I found out it worked much better and more successfully if I didn't know what they sounded like.

MURROW: Groucho, do you have more fun doing television than you did movies?

GROUCHO: Oh, much more fun. To begin with, you don't have to get up early in the morning. I go down to the Brown Derby at seven o'clock at night and have dinner, and I go to the theater at eight, and I do the show at eight-thirty, and I'm home at ten. But I want to ask you about this ad libbing, Ed. Why don't you and I try it?

MURROW: Oh, no . . . this isn't fair . . . I mean . . . well, go ahead.

GROUCHO: Well, we could try it just a little bit. Let's say you were a contestant, and I'd say, "What is your name?"

MURROW: Murrow.

GROUCHO: Murrow—Ed Murrow?

MURROW: Yes.

GROUCHO: And are you married?

MURROW: Yes.

GROUCHO: How did you meet your wife, Ed?

MURROW: I met her on the train.

GROUCHO: Were you both on the same train?

MURROW: So far as I can remember—yes.

GROUCHO: Was this a sleeper?

MURROW: No.

GROUCHO: This was a day coach?

MURROW: Yes.

GROUCHO: And you were sitting opposite each other?

MURROW: Yes.

GROUCHO: Well, how did you happen to meet her?

MURROW: Uh . . .

GROUCHO: Did you ogle her?

MURROW: Uhh, yes.

GROUCHO: Oh, you did? You ought to be ashamed of yourself. You know, you're not supposed to pick up strange women on the train. And how did your wife react to this?

MURROW: Uh . . . favorably.

GROUCHO: Favorably, huh? Well, what did she say? What were your opening words to her?

MURROW: I can't remember. And if I did, I wouldn't tell you.

GROUCHO: I see. Well, you're not going to make a very good contestant. And there goes your chance to win $350, Ed . . . that your son could have given my daughter and we could have been enormously wealthy . . . on DeSoto money.

488 With Melinda. Because I was in my middle fifties when she was born, I've always tended to treat her like a granddaughter instead of a daughter. There has never been a time when she hasn't been able to wind me around her finger. If I spoiled her and indulged her every whim, I don't regret a moment of it.

488

492

493

489 Arthur and Irene were already the parents of two sons, Steve and Andy. This was during happier times, prior to their eventual divorce.

490 Melinda, keeping up her membership in AFTRA, appeared on a local television show. Its host was a fellow named Johnny Carson.

491 Melinda and my grandson Steve.

To Mr. and Mrs. Goodman Ace

July 30, 1954

Dear Aces:
    This is just to notify you that I got married.

Groucho

From *The Groucho Letters*

The wedding took place at Sun Valley, and the lucky girl was Eden Hartford. I'd been introduced to her by her sister, Dee, who was one of the top models of the time, and who appeared with me on several television shows.

493 Back in Hollywood, we had a night on the town with Marie Wilson, her husband Bob Fallon, Violet Vaughan and George Jessel. Eden sits at right.

494 In 1954 Arthur's book, *Life with Groucho*, was published. It was very successful, and I was pleased. The book was later made into a movie. Its title: *Lies My Father Told Me*.

495 Miriam, in April of 1955, married a young man named Gordon Allen. The marriage soon ended, and Miriam went to work on the writing staff of *You Bet Your Life*.

496 With Harpo and Gummo in Palm Springs. We all had houses there.

497 Other guests on the quiz show were Jean Simmons and Stewart Granger, then married to each other.

498 A campaign shot, taken when I ran for president of the National Dunking Association. I was defeated by Wilt Chamberlain.

499 I was a guest panelist about this time on *What's My Line?* with Arlene Francis, Dorothy Kilgallen and Bennett Cerf.

500 Another guest appearance in early 1955 was on Jack Benny's show.

501 We did a takeoff of *You Bet Your Life* in which Jack disguised himself as the first violinist of the Los Angeles Philharmonic in order to win the jackpot.

502 Jack guesses the secret word. It was "telephone." We'd been discussing Stradivarius violins, and I asked him how one could authenticate them. Jack airily replied, "You can always tell a phony."

He was tripped up on the jackpot question, however: "For $3,000, can you tell me how old Jack Benny really is?" He answered thirty-nine. Later, I asked Jack why he didn't give the real answer.

"Where else can you buy twenty-two years for $3,000?" he asked.

ONE MAN ON A CHAIR

Has Drawn More Viewers
Over the Last Six Years
Than Any Other Attraction
On Television.

504 With Eden at the premiere of *High Society*.

505 At another premiere, of *Around the World in Eighty Days*, in December 1956. The lady with us is Sophie Tucker.

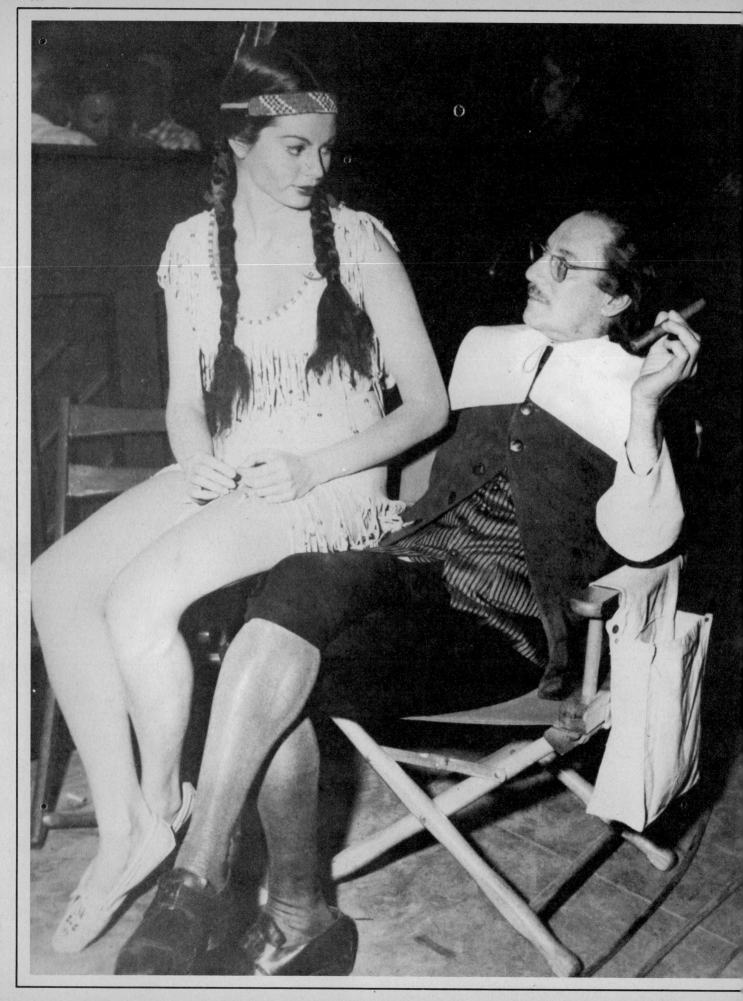

THE STORY OF MANKIND

Producer Irwin Allen, in 1957, thought Harpo, Chico and I should get together for one last movie. Once he convinced us, he put us in different segments of the all-star film, so that we had no scenes together. I played Peter Minuit, buying New York from the Indians for twenty-four dollars in beads. Harpo played Isaac Newton discovering the law of gravity. Chico was a monk. Others in the cast, made on the heels of the popularity of *Around the World in Eighty Days*, were Hedy Lamarr, Francis X. Bushman, Edward Everett Horton, Virginia Mayo, Peter Lorre and the ever-popular Helmut Dantine.

506 Eden played an Indian maiden in the film.

507 My old friend Harry Ruby also was an Indian.

508 During this period, Norman Krasna and I mounted a new production of our play, *Time for Elizabeth*. For three summers—1957 to 1960—I trod the boards all over the country.

Returning to the stage, acting in a comedy-drama for the first time, was a lesser risk than usual. For I had extreme faith in the playwrights, Norman Krasna and Groucho Marx.

The play had a simple message: to be out of work isn't healthy for a man.

I relished the challenge of one-nighters, acting the part of Ed Davis, the man who retires too soon to Florida and finds himself climbing up the bougainvillaea. He becomes so bored by his inactivity and so exasperated by the other retired people around him that his wife fears he'll commit suicide. "Kill myself?" he replies. "You know we're only covered for fire and theft." At the end of the play, he has consented to return to his old job as general manager of a washing machine company.

One of the high spots of those three summers of touring was our playing in Phoenix, Arizona. A distinguished man came backstage to see me. His name was Thornton Wilder. What did one of America's greatest playwrights think of the newest member of his fraternity? I waited, awe-struck, for his answer. "You should have ad libbed more," he advised.

From *The Secret Word Is Groucho*

"Groucho sent me."

"I'd rather see a good imitation of his weekly pay check."
THE SATURDAY EVENING

510

509 A scene from *Time for Elizabeth,* taken in 1958. The young man at center is Wyatt Cooper, who later married Gloria Vanderbilt.

510 Mickey Hargitay and Jayne Mansfield were my co-stars in *Will Success Spoil Rock Hunter?* The film was made at Twentieth Century–Fox in 1957. I played a surprise guest star, supplying the picture's denouement. At the end of the film, Jayne is delighted to hear that her childhood sweetheart, Georgie Schmidlapp—her real love—has come for her. I was Georgie Schmidlapp. Here the three of us are seen at a cancer telethon.

514 While visiting New York, Phil Silvers and I made a visit to find out who really was buried in Grant's Tomb.

515 Dancing with Audrey Hepburn.

516 With Milton Berle and Carl Sandburg. You'll note my humble attitude. I always respect my elders.

DEAR GROUCHO,

As I was reading Jack O'Brian's recent column headlined "Groucho Still The Best Bet," I started to reflect on your remarkable record as an entertainer. Twenty-five years in radio, seven in television, with dozens of awards, including an Emmy. A consistent spot over the years among the top-rated programs in both media. And today an audience of thirty-six million viewers weekly. It's been a long-term love affair, Groucho, between you and the American public. And so, with this note, I'd like to send congratulations and my warm personal endorsement of Jack O'Brian's tribute to "A Clown with Class... the immovable object of our television admiration."

Cordially,

Bob Sarnoff

518

520

517-
520 In 1958, after four years of planning, Eden and I
moved into our new house in the Trousdale section
of Beverly Hills. The house was designed by
architect Wallace Neff. Eden wanted a round bedroom and a sunken tub. I wanted an office bedroom, and Melinda wanted to be excused so she
could see *Maverick* on television.

521 Edgar Bergen was a guest on the quiz show during the 1958 season.

522 So were daughters Candice and Melinda. The show was at the height of its popularity.

Even so, I knew I wasn't everyone's cup of tea. A case in point was Phyllis McGinley, whose couplet appeared in *The New Yorker*:

I'd rather sleep in public parks
Than be on the show with Groucho Marx.

During part of the summer of 1958 Eden, Melinda and I took it easy in the hills of Nevada and on various California beaches. We chose to spend some time in Nevada because Harpo and Chico were opening there.

523

524 One of the last pictures of the five brothers together, taken in Las Vegas: Zeppo, Chico, myself, Harpo and Gummo.

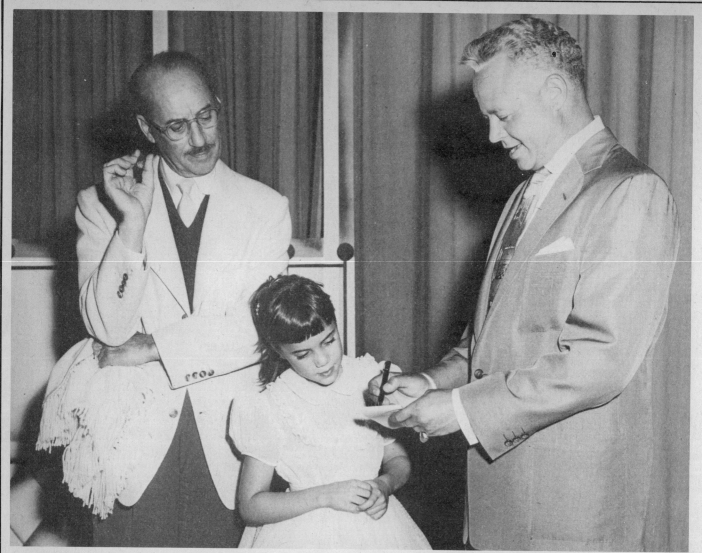

525 Melinda got Billy Daniels's autograph.

526 At Frontier Village with Melinda.

527 Eden, Melinda and me on the beach.

528 I know I'm at camp, because I'm sitting on a camp chair.

529 The following winter, Eden was cast by our friend, Irwin Allen, in *The Big Circus*, a movie he produced. She played a showgirl.

530 Melinda dancing on *You Bet Your Life* with Gene
Nelson—

531 —and Bobby Van.

533 In the NBC dressing room before the show.

534 My son Arthur took this picture of his wife Irene,
Eden and me. Irene was Pacific Palisades chairman
for the Red Cross.

535 Pointing out my caricature at the Hollywood Brown
Derby.

534

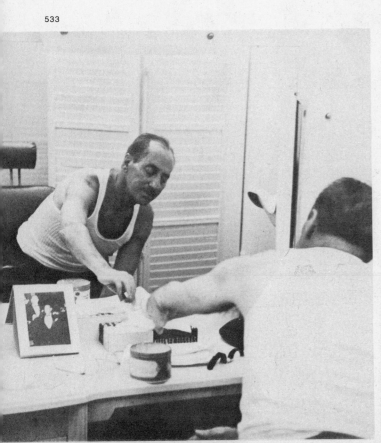

533

535

*To Groucho,
in memory of our
many campaigns together
in the Sudan,
Sid Perelman*

GROUCHO
AND ME

536 In recent years the press has concocted a feud between S. J. Perelman and me, but no such feud ever existed. Sid has often been asked about writing for the Marx Brothers, and I have often answered questions about his contributions to our films. What Sid and I both agree on is that he is a great writer with a brilliant comic mind that didn't always mesh well with the lunacies of the Marx Brothers.

537 In 1959 my autobiography—*Groucho and Me*— was published. It was a bestseller and was condensed in several magazines.

538 -39 Harpo and Chico had been playing nightclubs and county fairs with a dual act, while I'd been soloing on *You Bet Your Life*.

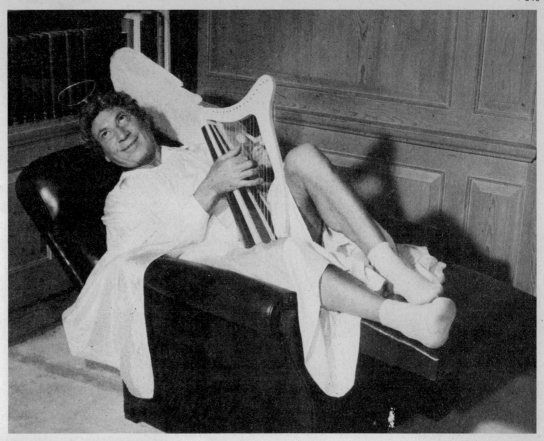

538

539

541 When we agreed to appear together for the last time on the *General Electric Theater* in March of 1959, I felt it should have been promoted as a momentous occasion. *G. E. Theater*, however, was a CBS show, and I was under contract to NBC, so my appearance couldn't be advertised.

Al Hirschfeld drew a caricature of Harpo and Chico, in costume for their roles in *The Incredible Jewel Robbery.*

542 In a publicity photo for the show, Harpo tried to get the point across. Over his blond wig he placed Groucho eyebrows and mustache, and Chico as the cop seems to be trying to figure out who he actually is.

543 Harpo appeared with his son Bill on a television anthology series. Bill at one time wanted to be an actor, but music has been so much a part of his life that he now is happily working at what he does best: music arranging and composing, plus an occasional gig.

544 This never happened. How could I bite the duck that was feeding me?

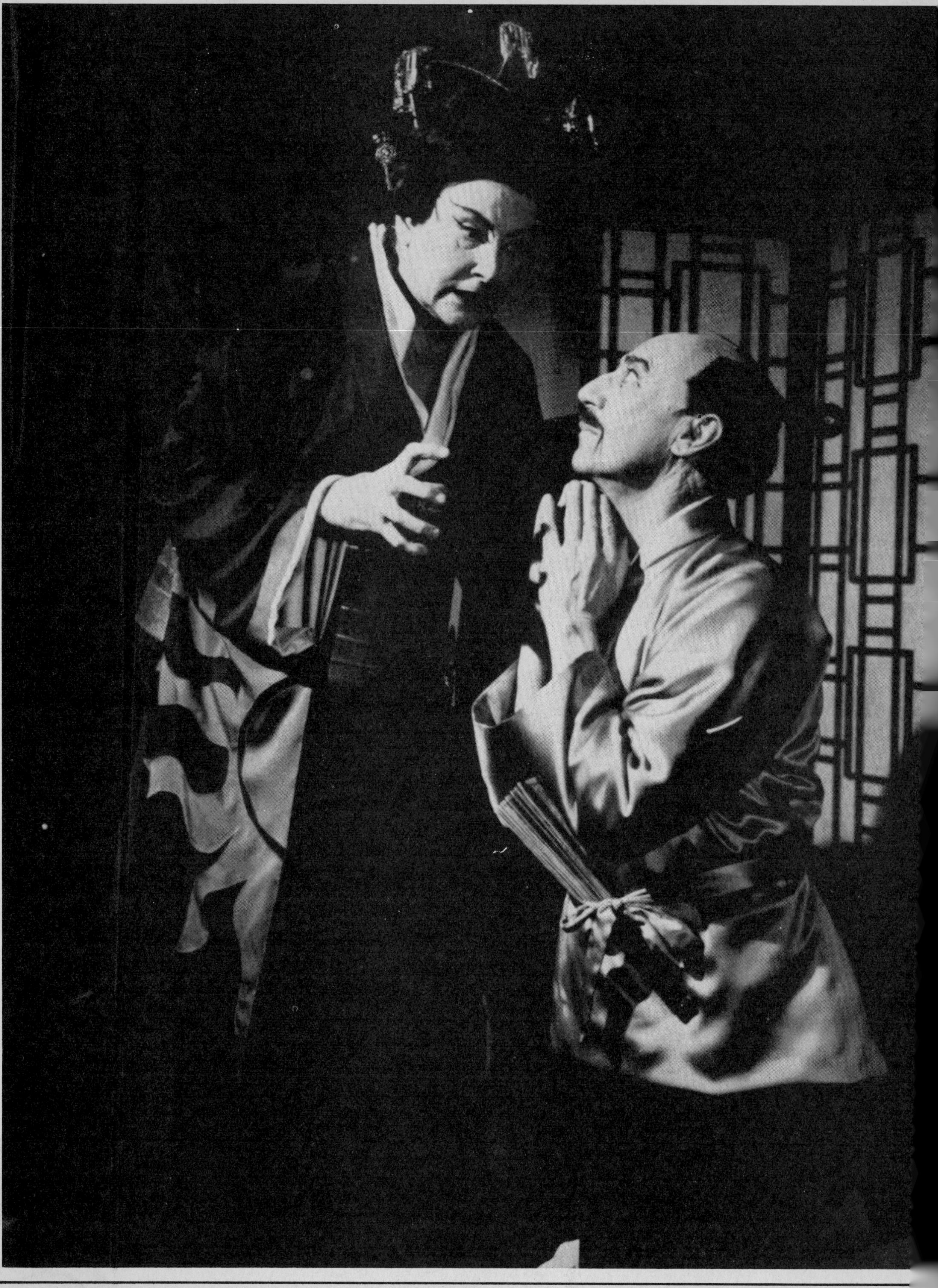

THE MIKADO

There were greater talents around to perform the famous operetta, but certainly no bigger Gilbert and Sullivan fan than myself. In April of 1960, I starred as Ko-Ko the Lord High Executioner on the *Bell Telephone Hour* presentation produced by my dear friend Goddard Lieberson.

545 Going over the script with Martyn Green, the great exponent of Gilbert and Sullivan.

546 Helen Traubel as Katisha and myself as Ko-Ko.

547 Melinda, then thirteen, played Peep-Bo, one of the three little maids from school.

548 The following fall, we started our eleventh year of *You Bet Your Life.*

549 During all that time, Gummo had been my agent and Robert Dwan the co-director of the show, along with Bernie Smith, who functioned as the show's producer and head of the writing staff. All are incredibly decent men, and I'm lucky to have been associated with them for such a long time.

550 Chico died of a heart attack in October of 1961. He was a rogue and a scamp. Money flowed through his fingers. Someone once asked Chico how much money he'd lost gambling. "Find out how much money Harpo has," he replied. "That's how much I've lost." I'd always looked at Chico with a mixture of envy and exasperation—envy at his devil-may-care attitude and exasperation at his refusal to think about tomorrow. Yet they were the same side of the coin. Had the Lord spared him and allowed him a few more years, Chico wouldn't have changed. I can imagine that after being rescued from death's door, he would look God straight in the eye and ask, "What odds will you give me on another ten years?"

LM-5-65

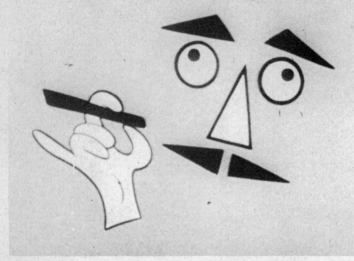

551 Just as the run of the quiz show ended, I appeared in *The Hold-Out*, another *G. E. Theater* presentation, in a serio-comic part. I played a father who refused to finance both his daughter's education and her marriage, feeling she should finish one before embarking on the other. I liked doing a dramatic part, and didn't find it difficult. I can assure you that it's much easier for a comedian to play drama than it is for a serious actor to play comedy. All good comedians are good dramatic actors. What actor could create the pathos of a Chaplin? For many years I've said that Charlie is the greatest comedian of the century, and yet no one has brought a bigger lump to my throat through the heart and soul of his performances. There was, however, a need in him to accomplish such effects. This was a need my brothers and I seldom felt.

My changeover to acting, I must admit, came at an opportune time. The quiz show at NBC had ended, and the spinoff at CBS—*Tell It to Groucho*—folded within a short time. We were trying to create something new out of basically the same old format.

552 Through syndication, I appeared on television over the next three years. More than half of the nearly five hundred *You Bet Your Life* shows were re-shown during this period under a new name, *The Best of Groucho*. This is the caricature that appeared at the beginning of the show.

553 Melinda rehearsed a dance step with Ann-Margret in June of 1962. The two were in the movie *Bye Bye Birdie*, in which Melinda was featured as a teenage dancer and Ann-Margret starred.

554 In 1962, on Harpo's advice, I applied for Social Security, though I'd been eligible to draw it since 1955. Harpo told me that he had once gone to the Indio office of the Social Security Administration to register. He was asked his name. "Arthur Marx," Harpo answered. Without the blond wig he could have been Karl Marx as far as the Social Security employee was concerned. "And have you worked in the last month?" the clerk asked.

"Yes," Harpo replied. "I worked one day."

The clerk continued, "How much did you make?"

Harpo looked him in the eye and answered, "Fifteen thousand dollars." He had filmed a commercial.

555 -56 Though he didn't know how to spell Groucho, one of my most illustrious correspondents was T. S. Eliot. His autographed picture and letter are prominently displayed on my gallery wall at home.

557 With Steve Allen, rehearsing for a television appearance.

558 A later appearance with Bob Hope.

Sir Geoffrey Faber, President

Richard de la Mare, Chairman. P. F. du Sautoy, Vice-Chairman

T. S. Eliot, W. J. Crawley, Morley Kennerley (U.S.A.), Alan Pringle, David Bland, Charles-Monteith

FABER AND FABER LTD

PUBLISHERS

24 Russell Square London WC1

Fabbaf Westcent London Museum 9543

TSE/AM   26th April 1961

Mr. Graucho Marx,
c/o Bernard Geis Associates,
130 East 56th Street,
New York 22,
N.Y., U.S.A.

Dear Graucho Marx,

This is to let you know that your portrait
has arrived and has given me great joy and will soon
appear in its frame on my wall with other famous friends
such as W.B. Yeats and Paul Valéry. Whether you really
want a photograph of me or whether you merely asked for
it out of politeness, you are going to get one anyway. I
am ordering a copy of one of my better ones and I shall
certainly inscribe it with my gratitude and assurance of
admiration. You will have learned that you are my most
coveted pin-up. I shall be happy to occupy a much
humbler place in your collection.

And incidentally, if and when you and Mrs.
Marx are in London, my wife and I hope that you will dine
with us.

Yours very sincerely,

P.S. Eliot

P.S. I like cigars too but there isn't any cigar in
my portrait either.

⁵⁵⁹ Eden and I had a party at the time *My Fair Lady* was being filmed at Warner Brothers. In the group were Phil Silvers, Carl Reiner, Eddie Robinson, Harry Ruby, Frederick oewe (our neighbor from Palm Springs) and Rex Harrison.

⁵⁶⁰ Zeppo and his wife Barbara in 1964. They were divorced in 1973. Barbara is now married to Frank Sinatra.

To Betty Comden

October 15, 1964

Dear Betty:

I want you to know how much I appreciated your lovely letter of condolence and love—

Having worked with Harpo for forty years, which is much longer than most marriages last, his death left quite a void in my life.

He was worth all the wonderful adjectives that were used to describe him.

He was a nice man in the fullest sense of the word. He loved life and lived it joyously and deeply and that's about as good an epitaph as anyone can have.

My best to your family and my love to you.

Groucho
From *The Groucho Letters*

562 In the spring of 1965, I played host on *The Hollywood Palace*. Within a few days I'd be leaving for London to start a new television series. Melinda was to sing a song on the show and a duet with me. When I introduced her, I said to the audience, "If you give her a big reception, I'll give her a very small wedding." We decided to revive the "Captain Spaulding" number from *Animal Crackers*, shown here, along with its past incarnations on stage and in films.

563 We engaged Margaret Dumont to reprise her role as Mrs. Rittenhouse. We'd tried to get her on the quiz show, but she wouldn't come on unless we paid her. This, according to the rules of the show, we couldn't do. Now I was glad that we could appear together again. She came to lunch at my house while we were rehearsing, and brought a book by Russell Baker as a gift. I'll always be grateful for the gift, for Margaret introduced me to one of my favorite writers. Melinda introduced the number that Margaret and I did, and it went off without a hitch.

564 A few days after she taped the show, Margaret died of a heart attack. She'd appeared in pictures with such great comedians as W. C. Fields, Jack Benny, Abbott and Costello, Laurel and Hardy, and Danny Kaye, and on television with Bob Hope and Dean Martin. But if the public chose to associate her solely with the Marx Brothers, it was an association which had long been indelibly imprinted on our own hearts.

Eden and I were quite the couple about London town when we arrived there to do our television series. The social life was nonstop. We met fascinating people. At one party, I was introduced to Lee Radziwill and her then husband, a Polish prince. That reminded me of a story, which I shared with them: A girl picks up a Polish officer and takes him home. She feeds him and takes him to bed. The next morning, he rises first and puts on his uniform. "Didn't you forget something?" the girl asks.

"What?" the Pole asks.

"The money," the girl replies.

The Pole stiffens. He's insulted. "A Polish officer doesn't accept money."

563

81

106

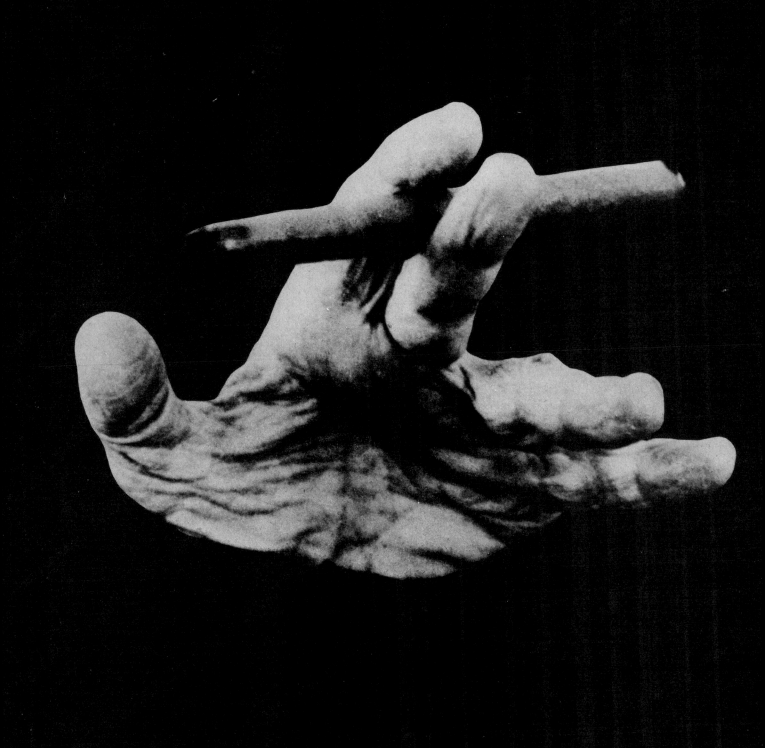

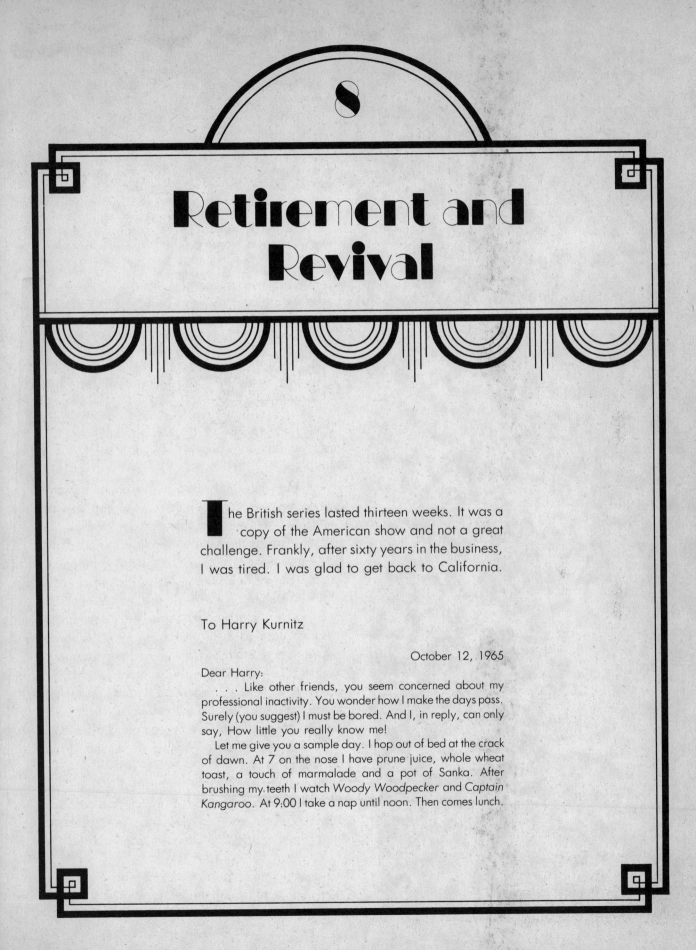

8

Retirement and Revival

The British series lasted thirteen weeks. It was a copy of the American show and not a great challenge. Frankly, after sixty years in the business, I was tired. I was glad to get back to California.

To Harry Kurnitz

October 12, 1965

Dear Harry:

. . . Like other friends, you seem concerned about my professional inactivity. You wonder how I make the days pass. Surely (you suggest) I must be bored. And I, in reply, can only say, How little you really know me!

Let me give you a sample day. I hop out of bed at the crack of dawn. At 7 on the nose I have prune juice, whole wheat toast, a touch of marmalade and a pot of Sanka. After brushing my teeth I watch *Woody Woodpecker* and *Captain Kangaroo*. At 9:00 I take a nap until noon. Then comes lunch.

Some where in United States of America

I have a can of Metrecal and a slab of apple pan dowdy. After lunch I take a nap until 2; then I watch *Huckleberry Hound* and, if my wife is out shopping, I watch *Divorce Court.* After that I brush my teeth and take a nap until 5:30. Five-thirty is the hour I look forward to. We call it the cocktail hour. We each have a glass of cranberry juice, a cheese dip and a package of Sen-Sen.

At six we eat our big meal, Yami Yogurt, apple jack and a sprinkling of sunflower seeds. At 6:30 we watch Soupy Sales and his madcap friends entertain each other with zany antics. At 7 we take two straight-back chairs and, face to face, give each other a manicure. At 7:30 we watch *Supermarket Sweep* and *Social Security in Action.* Then we play some old record-ings of Lawrence Welk and his half-man, half-girl orchestra. At 8 we take two Seconals, three aspirin, and a shot of LSD and fly to slumberland, eagerly looking forward to what thrills the next day has in store for us.

And now—I'm off to the dentist.

Be of good cheer and hurry home.

Groucho

566

From *The Groucho Letters*

On my birthday in 1966, Irving Berlin sent me a congratulatory poem:

The world would not be in such a snarl
If Marx had been Groucho instead of Karl.

Nice sentiment, but I wonder. In creating my comic character, I've often seemed rude and brusque and indifferent. Now that my career was slowing down, I could afford the time for mellow reflection. I'd been the most garrulous of all the brothers, and the pivotal character in virtually every routine we'd ever done, whether on stage or in films. When silent pictures started talking, I interrupted. It seemed as if I hadn't stopped talking since. In 1967, following my seventy-seventh birthday, I had occasion to tell of this reservation when I was interviewed by *The Los Angeles Times.* "Years ago, I tried to top every-body," I said, "but I don't anymore. I realized it was killing conversation. When you're always try-ing for a topper you aren't really listening. It ruins communication."

566 Even though I was largely retired, I hadn't made any formal announcement to that effect, and occasion-ally accepted a television guest star spot, such as my stint on *Hollywood Palace* with Eden's sister, Dee Hartford.

568 One of my most persistent and most entertaining letter writers through the years has been Nunnally Johnson.

MEMO

TO: Dear Grouch: You were asking me not long ago Lord Boothby's position on sheep. I feel that the attached answers the question much more clearly than any words of mine could.

As for Lord Morrison, he clearly has the God damndest anatomy I ever heard of.

Live and learn, chaps!

Nunnally

Now in residence at
33 Grosvenor sq.,
London, W.1.

From the Pickled Pine Desk of
NUNNALLY JOHNSON

Lord Boothby puts sheep in their place

Lord Boothby told Britain's champion hill-sheep farmers in London yesterday: "Sheep are not my favourite animals. I prefer them to birds but not much. I find them unsympathetic, not very bright in the head, and wholly lacking in initiative.

"On top of that, they seem to me to be incapable of any real affection," he added, amid a cry of "Shame." "Well," said Lord Boothby, "I think so. No sheep has ever loved me."

Lord Boothby, who was presenting the prizes at the Golden Fleece national hill-sheep competition, later said mutton was his favourite meat. He had a greater admiration for hill farmers and shepherds than for any other type of men, with the possible exception of fishermen:

The supreme championship—contested by the champions of England, Scotland, Wales, and Northern Ireland —was won by the Welsh champion, Mr Thomas Morris, of Cardiganshire, with his Welsh mountain hill-type breed. The reserve championship went to two brothers, John and Eric Barrie, of Hawick, Roxburghshire, the Scottish champions, with a North Country Cheviot breed.

the start

BUT LORD MORRISON FINDS PURE JOY AT ST TRINIAN'S

THE jolly man with a quiff taking a long, hard look at the schoolgirls of St. Trinian's yesterday was Lord Morrison

In 1967 *The Groucho Letters* were published . . . was published? The Library of Congress had requested I donate my correspondence to them, and in compiling letters from over the years, I was persuaded there was material for a book. I agreed to the suggestion, provided that royalties would go to charity. The Reiss-Davis Study Center was the charity that benefited from the proceeds of the book's sales.

nunnally johnson

flat 6, 33 grosvenor square, london w.i. telephone: grosvenor 2952

December 17

Dear Grouch:

Hundred Dollar Misunderstanding is simply marvellous.
It's a classic comedy. John Steinbeck was here last night and I passed
it along to him. (I'm like you, when I like something I want everybody
else to read it too.) Also I've ordered a couple of copies to pass along
to others. I thank you.

(male)*

John was on his way back from getting the Nobel Prize
in Stockholm. He says he holds one record anyway, he's the only American
winner to be both sober and perpendicular when he accepted the
prize. He said Red Lewis was in such a state that he forgot the acceptance speech he'd worked so hard on and ad libbed an entirely different
one. The committee, after observing Faulkner at work on the local booze
for a couple of days, resorted to deception to assure his being
sober. They shook him into listening and then told him that he was due on
the platform that afternoon. But Faulkner, whom they don't call the Old
Fox for nothing (in fact, they don't call him the Old Fox), just smiled.
Even while the Swede double-domes were explaining to him that it was
Thursday, the Big Day, Bill could hear the church bells ringing;
it was Sunday, not Thursday, and either he had three more days of wassail
or he had skipped the whole affair on the previous Thursday. In either
case, all was well and he ordered up schnapps for all. John
said the Swedes had great admiration for Faulkner, the way he was propped
up and spoke slowly but indistinctly. John said he spoke slowly too, he
said he had to, to make the speech last six minutes, which they had suggested as the minimum acceptable. It's the only speech he has ever made.
I've only made one. This was at the opening of a picture in Augusta,
Georgia. I live in such fear of people being bored by what I've got to
say that I devised an opening to hold them in their seats for a minute
or two anyway. I began, "And now in conclusion," etc. Even so, there
was already quite a bit of restlessness. What you really need sometimes
is a gun of some sort. Steinbeck said some fellow wired him, "At last
justice has been done." John replied, "You misunderstand. I wasn't after
justice. I wanted the prize." He said John O'Hara wired him: "Dear John,
you were my second choice." So much for Nobel Prizers.

Again thanks, and Merry Christmas God damn it, and our
best to you.

Nunnally

** Pearl Buck got it but I have no idea how she drinks.
If she doesn't, she's probably got some secret unspeakable vice.*

NUNNALLY JOHNSON
Via di Trasone, 76
ROMA, ITALY

July 29

Dear Grouch:

I will not lie to you. I don't care very much
for this. (I take it for granted that it will get worse.)
You and Phyllis McGinley are quite right. And I got a hint
of what I had let myself in for when I discovered that in
Italy they call DDT BPD. That's pure nastiness and you know
it. They needn't even try to explain it to me. That happens
to be just about all I want to know about Italy.

But what I setout to send to you is the following headline from the Syracuse (NY) Herald, issue of June 17,
1959, sent to me and sworn to before a legal judge by Joe
Bryan III.

FREED FUCHS
DUCKS BEHIND
IRON CURTAIN

What we want to know is, is this Arthur Freed?

My wife and I send love to you and your sainted

wife.

Nunnally

MORE GROUCHO LETTERS

To Woody Allen

March 22, 1967

Dear WW:

Goodie Ace told some unemployed friend of mine that you were disappointed or annoyed or happy or drunk that I hadn't answered the letter you wrote me some years ago. You know, of course, there is no money in answering letters—unless they're letters of credit from Switzerland or the Mafia. I write you reluctantly, for I know you are doing six things simultaneously—five including sex. I don't know where you get the time to correspond.

Your play, I trust, will still be running when I arrive in New York the first or second week in April. This must be terribly annoying to the critics who, if I remember correctly, said it wouldn't go because it was too funny. Since it's still running, they must be even more annoyed. This happened to my son's play, on which he collaborated with Bob Fisher. The moral is: don't write a comedy that makes an audience laugh.

This critic problem has been discussed ever since I was Bar Mitzvahed almost 100 years ago. I never told this to anyone, but I received two gifts when I emerged from childhood into what I imagine today is manhood. An uncle, who was then in the money, presented me with a pair of long black stockings, and an aunt, who was trying to make me, gave me a silver watch. Three days after I received these gifts, the watch disappeared. The reason it was gone was that my brother Chico didn't shoot pool nearly as well as he thought he did. He hocked it at a pawnshop at 89th Street and Third Avenue. One day while wandering around aimlessly, I discovered it hanging in the window of the hock shop. Had not my initials been engraved on the back, I wouldn't have recognized it, for the sun had tarnished it so completely it was now coal black. The stockings, which I had worn for a week without ever having them washed, were now a mottled green. This was my total reward for surviving 13 years.

And that, briefly, is why I haven't written you for some time. I'm still wearing the stockings—they're not my stockings anymore, they're just parts of my leg.

You wrote that you were coming out here in February, and I, in a frenzy of excitement, purchased so much delicatessen that, had I kept it in cold cash instead of cold cuts, it would have taken care of my contribution to the United Jewish Welfare Fund for 1967 and '68.

I think I'll be at the St. Regis hotel in New York. And for God's sake don't have any more success—it's driving me crazy. My best to you and your diminutive friend, little Dickie.

Groucho

To Goodman Ace

July 11, 1967

Dear Goodie:

The last time I saw you was in some crumby restaurant in New York where you told me about the blueberries that you keep extracting from the muffins at the counter and how this enrages the counterman. You had seen the *Today* show, you were wearing a raincoat, and I was flattered that you had arisen so early that morning to see your ex-friend exhibit himself with Hugh Downs. Although I had been on five shows in New York, so many people have told me about that one. It seems this was the first day that Hugh Downs wore a toupee, and he was self-conscious about it. He is a good-looking man and personable. I wasn't sure it was a toupee, but it looked peculiar and I kept staring at it and he kept shifting uneasily in his seat. But everyone I spoke to who had seen that show kept bringing up the look on Downs's face. Everyone else was laughing—the cameraman and the girl assistant on the show.

The Israeli War is over for the moment, and Melinda, my young one, is on a Kibbutz at present, allegedly picking fruit off the trees that weren't shot down by the Syrians. She'll be there in July and August, and I told her that if she found time to whip over to Switzerland and see how the Swiss people live.

I have nothing to tell you. Things at Hillcrest are about the same as always, except they raised the price of all their food, and to hear those rich Jews moaning that whitefish is now $3.50 a throw would make your heart melt. There is hardly anyone left young enough to play golf, so it's whitefish (anti-cholesterol, by the way) and then off to the card room, each one with his own deck of cards.

Burns has invited me to go to Vegas next Friday to see the opening of Ann-Margret, and I asked him if he couldn't possibly rephrase that statement because this letter, such as it is, does have to go through the mails. He said he would try, but that he was accustomed to saying it that way. If it's true, it will be a hell of an opening.

I'm doing a show with William Buckley this Friday, which will be shown in the next three or four weeks. It's one of those television companies called Metromedia and their shows go on whenever they find an opening to stick it in. Everybody expects me to discuss politics with him, but I'm no fool. I'll plunge right into old-fashioned vaudeville. In fact, I might even invite him to join me in a song of liberation for Abba Eban and his crowd. By the way, I don't know whether you heard his speech but I think it compared favorably with anything that Churchill said during the last war. I was so thrilled by it I bought a copy of the record. It was a wonderful week, those seven days. That was really the week that was, and it proved conclusively that the Jews have more heroes than Sandy Koufax.

I'll make this short. I just want you to know that I'm still active and that I thrive on the smog. I read somewhere that smog is good for you. This was said to me not by a doctor but by my plumber. I guess it's an improvement over the stuff that he smells on his 8-hour day at $10 an hour or more . . . my secretary says $13. She always participates in my letter writing, and someday I may have to take up shorthand and let her dictate the letters.

I have to knock this off now because I am in a one-hour parking spot and I've been up in this office 5½ hours. Hope you enjoyed the "4th" because since the race riots I have taken to hanging a flag in front of my house. Next week I am going to a meeting of the American Legion in Chicago and fill a lot of paper bags with water and drop them out of the windows of the Sherman House. They'll damn well find out someday that I'm a hunnerd percent Amurrican.

What is your relationship at present with the counterman in the drugstore? Have you resolved the problem of the blueberries in the muffins or have you switched to another drugstore? Perhaps you should have your attorney talk to him or maybe you should talk to him. This is the way the Israeli problem is going to be resolved, and maybe this could also be worked out at the corner drugstore. Would you consider switching to a waffle for breakfast? I know it's difficult to get maple syrup these days because so many trees have dried up—just as I have. This is a serious problem for the farmer. The sap is running low, new trees are not being planted. You must remember that planting a new maple syrup tree is the equivalent of an elderly man discarding his current wife and getting a young one. The waffle solution may be worth thinking about. So be of good cheer and perhaps you should try pouring maple syrup on your blueberry muffins.

Groucho

To the *Beverly Hills Courier*

December 7, 1967

Editor
Beverly Hills Courier
9414 Wilshire Boulevard
Beverly Hills, California

Dear Sir:

On the front page of your paper the headline for an item read, "Actor Held on Drunk Driving." When a lawyer gets arrested for drunk driving or some other misdemeanor do you say, "Lawyer Arrested for Drunk Driving"? Or if it happens to be a scientist, do you say, "Scientist Arrested for Drunk Driving"?

Why in the hell do you mention "Actor"? Why don't you just give his name and leave his profession to himself? Since you publish this paper in a village which probably has more theatrical people in it than any city in the whole world, why do you identify some and then mention the profession in a case like this? I thought your paper was brighter than this.

My first impulse was to send this clipping to the Screen Actors Guild and have them make a complaint to you, which they certainly would because they would resent it the same as I do.

I'm surprised at you and your paper.

Groucho Marx

572 With Alexandra Hay in a scene from Otto Preminger's 1968 *Skidoo*. I played God, the head of a crime syndicate. Both the picture and my role were God-awful.

573 In 1969 Eden and I were divorced. She was still a young woman, and the great difference in our ages had become even wider during our fifteen years of marriage. The grounds were the usual: mental cruelty. Her attorney was Marvin Mitchelson.

313

577

574 At the Academy of Motion Picture Arts and Sciences with Gregory and Veronique Peck, after a screening of *A Night at the Opera*. The Pecks lived next door to us in London. I'd taught Greg how to smoke a pipe, a trick he needed to learn for a role he was playing.

While in London we hired an Irish couple. Every weekend, they'd go to Dublin with one hundred condoms. It was illegal to sell them there. They made more money selling condoms than we paid them.

575 576

575 My good friend Sidney Sheldon was the producer of *I Dream of Jeanie,* and he hired me to play with Barbara Eden in the show . . . let me put it this way . . . I performed with Barbara . . . oh, forget it.

576 Sidney Sheldon. Would you believe I once bought a used car from this man? In recent years Sidney has turned novelist. Fellow television producers wished him great success in his new field, by a vote of fifty-two to forty-seven. Nevertheless, Sidney writes a good story. He dedicated his last book to me.

577 Steve and Phyllis and Adolph and Betty . . . or Kyle and Newman and Green and Comden. If they're the East Coast branch of the Groucho fan club, I'm the West Coast branch of theirs. Whenever I have this couple of pairs, I have a full house, and a happy one too. Our mutual admiration society started when I saw Comden and Green at the Trocadero in 1850.

574

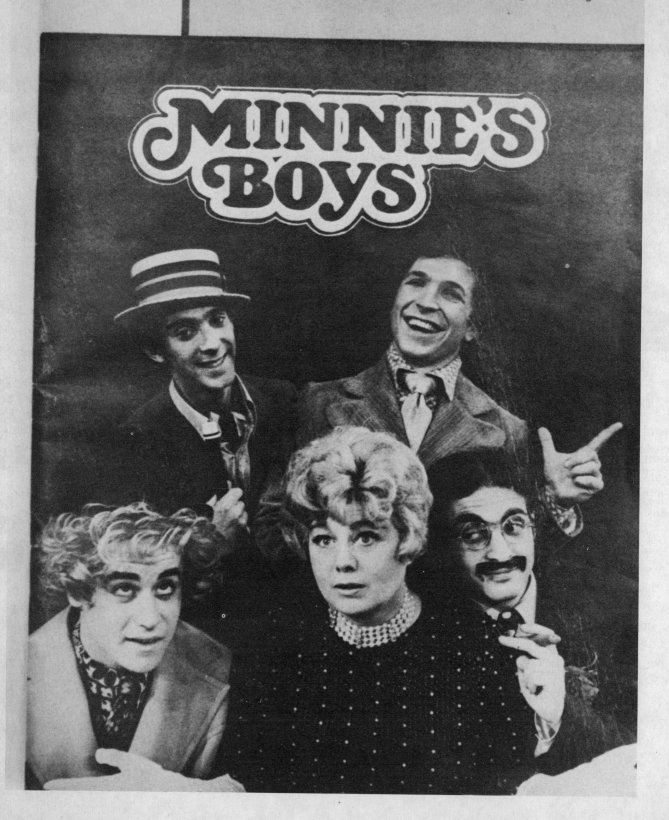

Imperial
Theatre

PLAYBILL

the national magazine for theatregoers

MINNIE'S BOYS

MINNIE'S BOYS

When I was approached about doing a musical
based on my mother and the five Marx Brothers, I
jumped at the chance. Lewis J. Stadlen, the fellow
who played me, was very good. I told him opening
night that he was better than I ever was . . . and
younger.

579 Doing "the walk" with Stadlen.

580

580 The curtain call. Shelley Winters stands behind me, bigger than life.

581 Arthur Whitelaw, who produced the show, is a dear friend of mine. He says that at the curtain call I turned to Shelley and said, "I never thought when I saw you at Saks buying sweaters for your big boobs that someday you'd wind up playing my mother." Arthur is quite wrong. I never use that kind of language. What I said was "big knockers."

If Walter Kerr is one of my favorite critics, it may be because the feeling is nicely reciprocated. He's a Marx Brothers freak, as he proved in his review in *The New York Times* on April 5, 1970:

Nobody ever just *liked* the Marx Brothers. The Marx Brothers didn't leave room in their toe-to-toe challenge on the edge of the handiest abyss for so tepid an emotion. It was one for all and all for nothing with them, an attitude that engendered as much passion, one way or another, in the beholder as there was in Groucho's swallow-tailed backward flips—he looked like a seagull doing entrechats—onstage.

And, as with all true love, the emotion was exclusive, accepted no substitutes. Whoever wanted a girl who looked sort of like his girl? Or a Harpo who was only a half-Harpo, a Groucho who flicked his cigar ash frequently but much too furiously (Groucho never had anything against cigar ash or carpets, he simply put in all his commas in a kind of skywriting), a paler Chico (when Chico was already monochromatic, gray on gray), a blander Zeppo (impossible)?

As a result I have gone my long life never seeing an acceptable imitation of any Marx brother in full sail. Where *Minnie's Boys* was smart, unbelievably bright really, was in starting them all out in birch-bark canoes, sans wigs, sans mustaches, sans tricks. This may seem obvious and even necessary if you're going to do a musical about the problems Mother Minnie had in figuring out a future for her five unemployable sons, but it's not, not at all. There must have been a strong temptation to underscore early, to plug for recognition instantly, to borrow their best bits in a hurry in order to get going, to press. That would have put us all off, right off. What they've done, instead, is to let the mannerisms grow casually, almost absent-mindedly, even to the point where for quite a while you feel they may have forgotten a few.

. . . *Minnie's Boys* is partly patchwork, here and there conscienceless, stuck with its gags-to-riches formula. I had a perfectly good time because those four boys onstage honored the men they were not trying too hard to become, and because I still go all helpless when I see even two Marx Brothers toasting marshmallows over their hard-hearted employer's wastebasket, to which they have set fire.

582 With Woody Allen's diminutive friend, little Dickie. I appeared on the Cavett show about a dozen times. He's a bright man and a wonderful friend. When George Kaufman died in 1961, I struck up a conversation with a young man as I left his funeral. Walking back to my hotel, we had quite a talk. He was a bright fellow with a lot of moxie and knowledge. When we arrived at my hotel, I invited him to join me for lunch. Dick Cavett and I have been friends ever since.

583 While in New York, I also appeared with David Frost. He wanted me to teach him "the walk."

584 Dick Cavett's diminutive friend, Woody Allen. Woody Allen is the most important comic talent around. One of his lines is a favorite of mine: "I don't mind dying. I just don't want to be there when it happens."

585 Erin Fleming was directed by Woody in *Everything You Wanted to Know About Sex but Were Afraid to Ask.*

⁵⁸⁶ How I hired Erin is a story in itself. I was divorced, living alone with a housekeeper, thinking the world had forgotten me. I'd recently run into Maurice Chevalier on the streets of Beverly Hills. No one had been a bigger star. "Do you get invited out much?" I asked him.

"Not so much," he answered. "The world has passed me by." I knew what he meant. My children had all made lives for themselves, and I didn't see them often. Zeppo and Gummo were living in Palm Springs.

There were hundreds of unanswered letters in my office, and I really needed someone to sort them out. I phoned Jerry Davis one day and asked him if I could borrow his secretary for a few days. "There's a girl in my office right now who used to be a great secretary to a friend of mine in New York," he said. "Her name is Erin Fleming." My ears perked up. Fleming has always been a lucky name for the Marxes. Harpo's wife was Susan Fleming. Catty Fleming had danced with us in vaudeville. Erin was now an actress, auditioning for a part in *The Odd Couple*, which Jerry was producing on television. She didn't want to work as a secretary anymore, but I persuaded her to do so.

She said, "I'll go through all this mail for you, but after that you'll have to find a regular secretary." She wouldn't accept a salary for the first two years because she didn't want to work full-time. She treated the assignment as a duty she'd taken on as a volunteer. As she went through the house, Erin discovered dozens of cardboard boxes filled with thousands of unopened letters . . . including an offer to play Carnegie Hall. Eventually, she became a full-time employee, and she's worked for me for seven years. Our relationship has been much talked about and much misunderstood. I love her, of course, and I know that Erin loves me. That love, however, is the love one has for a daughter and the closest of friends.

⁵⁸⁷ Jerry Davis is a good friend, but I wasn't planning to use his photograph in this book until I discovered he was smoking one of my favorite pipes. Consider this a picture of the pipe.

323

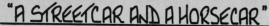

© COPYRIGHT · 1972 · HARRY RUBY MUSIC CO.

```
                        1 9 7 2

Dear Groucho:
        Hein  as how you get all your
mail now care of Nate' N Al's... I, too,
will be writing to you care of that ad-
dress..
The attachd  -attached - is a brand new
copy of the thing I recited to you and
Erin.. when we had lunch -at this place. You
all seemd to get a kind of kick out of it...
so I want you to have the very fisrt copy
of it.. which , if you can get me to sign it
-will be worth a fortune some day.
Why dod I keep on dashing off these silly
 things/ What else is there to do these days
in the music or  movie business? Anyway,
a man has got to do seomthing -or sit on his
posterior and whish he had never been born..
Enough said.. so..
        Sincerely...
```

```
        from the desk of...

                        April 26..1972
        HARRY RUBY

Dear Groucho:

When I told you, the other night, on
the phone, that I would write you..
you said something about whether it
would be a funny letter.. Well, I think
it only fair to tell you that this is
not a funny letter... because if I
didn't tell you.. you would laugh your
head off while reading it - and make
a fool of yourself.

All I want to say is that I am sorry I
couldn't make the trip with you....
I know it will be a big thing for you...
and that you will come off, as you al-
ways do.. in flying colors..

And this does it for now.. Best to
E rin and Marvin..

        As ever,

P.S.: You said something, when we talk-
     ed about that lwire I sent:
     "Better luk next time.."It was
     not sent, as you thought, at
     the out-ot-town opening of our
     show, Helen of Troy, New York.
     Isent it to Rufus Lemaire.. (
     Rufus Lemaire.. that is.. when
     a show of his opened in Philly.
     It was to get even with him on
     something he did to me..
     He was, as you may have heard..
     not quite as nice a guy as I am.
                                GUY
```

Harry Ruby was one of the few constants in my life. We'd been friends for over forty years. He was lovable, a character, and a bright man. He appeared on the quiz show a couple of times, but he never won the big money, which humiliated him. He was an inveterate writer of notes, whether on a song sheet or on that sappy stationery he used. He was also a bit odd. He'd walk the streets of Beverly Hills, head down, looking for coins. When he died in March of 1974, he had $360 in pennies, dimes and quarters saved up. One day, he even picked up a tomato on the street, which he took home, washed, and ate. He never learned how to drive a car. He was about to marry a woman who could when he died. And when he passed on, part of me died too. He was a gentle man, a funny man, a nice man.

Poor Russell's Almanac

By Russell Baker.
Illustrated. 212 pp.
New York: Doubleday & Co. $6.95.

Groucho Marx

BEVERLY HILLS, CALIFORNIA 90210

January 1, 1972

The New York Times Book Review
Times Square
New York, New York 10036

Dear Editor:

Since the day one of your hirelings from the Book Review
Section of the New York Times nailed me in the bathtub to
write a review on Russell Baker's new book, the world has
changed. Christmas came, I got stuck with a twelve dollar
tree; New Years came, I got stuck with a forty-eight
dollar check; and twenty of your stooges wrote me a pleading,
sniveling petition begging me to write one thousand terribly
funny words on "POOR RUSSELL'S ALMANAC" for roughly thirty-
eight dollars in Polish money. Then I got the flu,
my girlfriend ran away with another girl, and I was stuck
here in a three-hundred-thousand dollar mansion all by
myself with no one to talk to except a few rats (all of
them relatives from Nixon Country). Briefly, that's the
situation.

However, I did manage to read the book, and I liked it
enormously. This book is an almanac, just like it says in
the title. It's about the various weeks and months of the
year and the changing seasons, and it is written with great
wit and insight. This is from a guy who was brought up
on Lardner, Benchley, Stephen Leacock, Perelman, E.B. White,
and a few others too humorous to mention. I react to the
well-written word like a cat having its back scratched.
I think the book will be a big success -- despite all the
books on the market attacking Nixon.

Give my regards to all those flunkies who signed the
petition. And my thanks to Russell Baker.

Forever,

Groucho

GM:ef

592 When *The New York Times Book Review* asked me to write a critique of Russell Baker's new book late in 1971, I was happy to comply. He's a great writer, and I look forward to reading his work every Sunday in the *Times* of New York, just as I look forward to reading Art Buchwald every week day in the *Times* of Los Angeles.

593 Another great favorite of mine is Jules Feiffer. He's a brilliant and astute observer of contemporary life, and I'm one of his biggest fans.

593

GROUCHO IS BETTER THAN EVER

The Marx Brothers as a team have never gone away. We've been viewed and dissected in college theaters for many years. In 1972, however, the full impact of my personal popularity hit me. It was a great thrill to discover that you're loved and appreciated. All of a sudden, I was seeing the Seven Ages of Groucho everywhere I turned. Some said I had become a cult hero. Personal appearance offers came in by the dozens. Merchandising tie-ins were dangled in front of our noses by manufacturers. Soon *The Best of Groucho* would be syndicated for the second time, the television audience being offered twenty-five-year-old shows in living black and white. You can't call it a comeback, because I never really retired. You might say I was getting my second wind. Erin went over the offers I got and picked the spots I would do. Sometimes, to break in a new piece of material, she would book me into places where the exposure would be minimal. I wanted to perform again, as much as possible, but after I had a major heart attack and several small strokes, she wanted to protect me if I stumbled. After living like a hermit for three or four years, I was out socially again, doing whatever town I happened to be in.

594 With Lauren Bacall after the opening of *Applause* in Los Angeles.

In the spring of 1972, Charlie Chaplin came to Hollywood from his home in Switzerland to accept a long-overdue Honorary Academy Award. We'd met in 1914, when we were both in vaudeville, and I told my brothers then and there that he was the greatest comedian I'd ever seen. Time hasn't changed that opinion.

595 Walter and Carol Matthau had a party for the Chaplins, and Candy Bergen photographed it. Here I am with Erin and Cary Grant.

Charlie and I were happy to see each other. A few years back, he'd paid me the ultimate compliment. "I wish I could talk like you," he said. He felt his greatest successes had been in silent pictures and that his talking pictures weren't nearly as good. This time, he passed on a piece of advice to me. Since I'm a bit younger, the words came from Charlie's older perspective: "Keep warm."

596 When I decided to appear at Carnegie Hall in May of 1972, I wanted to try out the act at some obscure location. It turned out to be at Iowa State University. An impresario from the Midwest, with terribly impressive stationery, had written me an offer I couldn't refuse. The impresario—Thomas Wilhite—turned out to be a nineteen-year-old kid who'd put the deal together with a shoestring. Tom has since come to California, and he is now my public relations man. We rehearsed for months before we got the act into shape. Marvin Hamlisch graciously accompanied me at the piano.

597 Arriving at the airport in Iowa with Erin.

598 With Iowa State cheerleaders. Every time the steeple bell rings, the girl standing next to you must kiss you. It is a campus tradition . . . which I instituted. The concert was a success. We were now ready for New York.

599 I hadn't performed in New York since 1930, forty-two years previously, and the press turned out en masse to find out why I chose to come back. I said it had taken that much time for New York to forget about my last performance there.

600

"Some years back, after a childhood of preoccupation with comedy that led to observing the styles of all the great comedians, I came to the conclusion that Groucho Marx was the best comedian this country ever produced. Now I am more convinced than ever that I was right. I can't think of a comedian who combined a totally original physical conception that was hilarious with a matchless verbal delivery. I believe there is a natural inborn greatness in Groucho that defies close analysis as it does with any genuine artist. He is simply unique in the same way that Picasso or Stravinsky are and I believe his outrageous unsentimental disregard for order will be equally as funny a thousand years from now. In addition to all this, he makes me laugh."

—WOODY ALLEN

Opal

HAPPY 80th BIRTHDAY
FROM GROUCHO AND A&M RECORDS.

MINISTÈRE DES

Affaires Culturelles

Le Ministre

3, RUE DE VALOIS, PARIS-1ᵉʳ

Cher Monsieur,

On pourrait se demander si l'attribution d'une
distinction honorifique à GROUCHO MARX se justifie tout
à fait : non que votre carrière ne mérite d'être honorée,
mais c'est la forme choisie pour le faire qui pourrait ne
guère convenir au personnage que vous avez rendu célèbre.

Cependant, il faut en prendre son parti : les Etats
ne disposent que d'un nombre limité de moyens pour manifes-
ter leur estime. Du moins pour les personnes vivantes :
pour les autres, il y a les statues, les noms de rues, voire
de villes. Comme nous n'en sommes heureusement pas là, et
que la République française ne décerne pas de titres de no-
blesse, force nous est de vous attribuer une décoration.

Si nous avons choisi l'Ordre des Arts et Lettres
c'est parce que les deux arts où vous avez excellé relèvent
de la tutelle du Ministère des Affaires Culturelles,qui at-
tribue cet Ordre. Il nous est apparu que l'homme de théâtre
et de cinéma que vous êtes, a sa place parmi les personnali-
tés du spectacle que le Gouvernement français a nommées, au
rang le plus élevé, dans cet Ordre, spécialement conçu pour
reconnaître un apport à l'Art, sous quelque forme que ce soit.

Ce qu'a été cet apport, en ce qui vous concerne, il
m'appartient d'autant moins de le préciser que le monde entier
applaudit vos films et sait ce qui, dans le domaine du rire
- si difficile, si rare, si précieux - n'appartient qu'à vous.

Mais je tiens à associer à l'hommage qui vous est rendu,
les artistes qui ont conquis la gloire en même temps que vous
et qui, dans l'histoire du cinéma, demeureront inséparables :
vos frères.

Aux félicitations du Gouvernement et aux miens propres,
je joins, Cher Monsieur, l'expression de mes sentiments de
sympathie et d'estime.

Monsieur GROUCHO MARX
aux bons soins de Monsieur
FAVRE LE BRET, Président du
Festival International du Film
Hôtel Carlton
06 - CANNES

Jacques DUHAMEL

600 At Carnegie Hall.

601 The performance was later released as an album by A&M Records.

602 Later a fan sent me this typewriter tribute based on the album's sketch of me.

603-04 In the summer of 1972, Robert Favre Le Bret, head of the Cannes Film Festival, presented me with the French Government's Commandeur des Arts et Lettres. Charlie Chaplin, Alfred Hitchcock and I are the only foreigners to receive the honor.

605 Gina Lollobrigida showed up at a luncheon later. Our exchange, as reported by Rex Reed and Charles Champlin , among others, went like this:

GROUCHO: Aren't you the Italian babe I met twenty years ago on the biggest turkey ever seen on Perry Como?
GINA: I vas jus' a chile at ze time.
GROUCHO: Now you shave twice a day?
ERIN: (Aghast) He means you have a very beautiful complexion.
GROUCHO: Yeah, but you can't see it under all that makeup.
PRESS AGENT: This reminds me of Elaine's.
GROUCHO: What's Elaine's?
PRESS AGENT: A restaurant in New York. Very social, with a big turnover.
GROUCHO: I had a girl like that once.
FAVRE LE BRET: Mr. Marx, how do you like your first trip to Cannes?
GROUCHO: Where is it? Hey, Gina, what do you hear from the Pope?
GINA: (Huffily) Zee Pope ees a very beeg star, and I, Gina Lollobrigida, am a very beeg star. Two very beeg stars together is very boring!

Shooting daggers at me, Gina got up to leave. Had I said something to offend her? I like a girl with spirit. When I caught up with her, I planted a kiss on her cheek, and our picture was taken. It was the smooch heard round the world.

606 Now that I'd conquered both continents, I prepared to come home with a concert at the Music Center. Before that, I'd given my best concert on August 11, 1972, in San Francisco. It was produced by a wild man, Bill Graham, of Fillmore fame. I made him sing a duet with me. The picture was taken at the press conference announcing my Los Angeles appearance.

608 A guest shot on the Bill Cosby show. Once I was watching Bill's show with George Burns. He turned to me and said, "Sorry he's not a Jew." The highest compliment.

609 In 1973 I was invited to come visit with Barbra Streisand on the set of *The Way We Were*. She was dressed as Harpo in a scene from the Columbia picture.

610 The film version of a real-life picture (photo 420). I can now reveal that Robert Redford in Groucho makeup was playing a part and auditioning for another at the same time. The boy wants to play me when my life is made into a movie. Unfortunately, he's just not handsome enough.

Our second film, *Animal Crackers*, hadn't been publicly seen in almost twenty years because of several contractual disputes. Title to the picture had passed to Universal Pictures when Paramount sold them their film library. A group of students at UCLA, led by Steve Stoliar, circulated a petition —they gathered 18,000 signatures—which was presented to Universal. The tactic convinced the studio. They obtained the necessary clearances to re-release the picture. I was so impressed with young Stoliar (seen with Erin and me at center) that I hired him as keeper of the Marx Archives, which are being donated by request to the Smithsonian Institution after my death.

GROUCHO MARX

1083 Hillcrest Road
Beverly Hills, California 90210
February 8, 1974

Mr. Patrick Riley
L.A. Valley College
Van Nuys, California

Dear Mr. Riley,

I am writing to ask you to please excuse Jeff Gelberg
from class on February 7th which was yesterday
unless you are reading this tomorrow.

I was in dire need of his services for a Press Conference
at U.C.L.A. You see, Mr. Gelberg possesses a unique
talent, namely, he plays me better than I do.
So, I asked him to cut class, dress up as me, and
pretend to be a U.C.L.A. student all at the same time
(which calls for more acting than the average script)
all for a very worthy cause --- the demonstration
on campus for the re-release of my early now-buried
film ANIMAL CRACKERS.

To say that he was successful is but to illustrate
the poverty of my vocabulary. He had more minutes
on the NBC news than I did, and it would make me
very unhappy if he is chastised for missing class.

I understand that the only acceptable excuse is a
note from a doctor. Therefore I must warn you
that I have conducted a thorough examination of
the inflammation of his glomac region and I came
to the conclusion that he has knokus on the comocus.
Which is, fortunately, infectious.

Yours truly,

Groucho

Dr. Hugo Z. Hackenbush

HZH:ef
Encls. 704
CC: 36-24-37

From E. B. White

March 29, 1974

Dear Mr. Marx:

Thanks for your letter of recent, but not excessively recent, date. Thank you for the kind words.

Shenker, who put together *Words and Their Masters*, came here for an interview with me, but I clammed up. So he sent me a questionnaire afterwards, and I took a morning off and wrote the piece. I have now given up interviews, as I don't see why anybody should badger an old white-haired man. Or make him write anything. I am not a master of words, I am their slave.

. . . I have studied your signature and deduced from the quavering hand that you are even older than I am, which is lamentable. I am not enjoying the twilight years much. The only real fun I get out of them is that my hearing is failing and my ears pick up some mighty odd sentences, in which a word has magically been changed into another word. Just the other morning, on radio, I heard a newscaster say: "Maine's first covered bridge, which was destroyed a year ago by an optimist, is going to be rebuilt." That made my morning. Then, some time ago, I heard another thing on radio that pleased me—it was a commercial of a building supply company: "There's nothing like the warmth of Mable to make a room a home."

Except for my ears, I'd rather be a whole lot younger.

Sincerely,

E. B. White

When I consented to do a *Playboy* interview, which was published in March of 1974, photographer Charles W. Bush asked me to tell him one of my favorite jokes:

612 "A fat lady walks into a drugstore."

613 "She asks the druggist, 'Do you have any talcum powder?' "

614 " 'Certainly, madam,' the druggist says. 'Walk this way.' "

615 "So the fat lady answers, 'If I could walk that way, I wouldn't need the powder.' "

Nunnally Johnson

1108 Tower Road
Beverly Hills, California
February 1, 1974

Mr. Walter Mirisch
President
Board of Governors
Academy of Motion Picture Arts and Sciences
9038 Melrose Avenue
Los Angeles, California 90069

Dear Mr. Mirisch,

A part of what makes the Academy such a superior
professional body is its flexibility. While it has
rules and regulations that must be properly observed
it has never failed to give its attention to a member
that it felt was entitled to exceptional recognition
regardless of the polls. More than once, obviously,
our Academy has paused and said, see here, we can't let
an artist like so-and-so be continually overlooked
simply because the eccentricities of circumstance have
failed him. An actor or actress of distinction has not
come in first because he has not been well served
by either script or director or both. A director
of unquestioned superiority never won, because chance
robbed him of a script or cast that would have enabled
him to exhibit his great talents. It is the same with
more than one writer. A script that might have won him
a triumph never found the proper artists to bring out
its true value. In a business or art of so much complexity
we all know that many laurels are lost through the
vicissitudes that we all run.

But more times than I can remember the Academy has
stepped in to bring about a correction of such a mischance.
We all remember a director, or an actor, or an actress
who was in time presented with the award that they had
been deprived of by the electoral mathematics. And,
never has the Academy shown itself in a more admirable
and becoming light than when it has risen above the
rigidity of rules, and honored this artist who
deserved it. I daresay the culmination of this generous
and understanding practice was the brilliant awards
made so deservedly to our great artists Charlie Chaplin
and Edward G. Robinson. These were salutes that also
added stature to our Academy.

In this same spirit I hereby propose such an award
that I believe would maintain the same high standard
of its precedents. Obviously these extraordinary awards
can never be made to any but the truly greatest of

2.

our company of players. Any lessening of the very
highest standards would utterly destroy their value.
My proposal now is an award for the Marx Brothers.

It would be possible, of course, to support this
proposal with an account of their achievements, but
I don't believe I can think of anything less called
for. Everyone already knows them. Their maniacal comedy
has trespassed all geographical divisions and made
all races laugh at the same thing at the same time.
The very mention of their name would be enough to
brighten the entire membership of the United Nations
General Assembly with smiles and chuckles. Indeed
it may be that there is no other name in the noble
business of making people enjoy themselves that is
so widely known in the whole world. Originally
there were four of them. Then Zeppo retired, and
the great Harpo and the incorrigible Chico succumbed
to time and are now angels. But the greatest of them
is still with us, Groucho, the last of those immortal
clowns, the Marx Brothers.

Respectfully yours,

Nunnally Johnson

620 On April 2, 1974, I was taken by Stutz Blackhawk
to the Los Angeles Music Center for the Academy
Awards. Erin and I were to arrive in style, but the
car broke down. We had to hitchhike a ride. It was
a crazy start to a wonderful evening.

622

621

621 There's no one I'd rather have give me an Oscar than Jack Lemmon. A great actor and a nice man. Actors normally didn't belong to the Algonquin Round Table or the Thanatopsis Reading and Inside Straight Club or the West Side Writing and Asthma Club—much as they longed to—but if Jack had been around in those days, he would have been welcomed with open arms. He's a man with style and wit and grace. What's more, I'm in love with his wife, Felicia.

622 Jack in his presentation said the Academy was honoring me for my "brilliant creativity and for the unequaled achievements of the Marx Brothers in the art of motion picture comedy." Being so honored by friends and colleagues was heartwarming, as was the standing ovation. I knew exactly what I wanted to say:

623 "I only wish that Harpo and Chico could have been here—and Margaret Dumont, who never understood any of our jokes. She used to say, 'Julie, what are they laughing at?' But she was a great straight woman and I loved her. And then, I'd like to thank my mother, without whom we would have been a failure. And last, I'd like to thank Erin Fleming, who makes my life worth living and who understands all my jokes."

625 I was delighted to pose with Jack, who that year won as Best Actor for his role in *Save the Tiger*.

⁶²⁴ Oscar felt pretty good.
⁶²⁶ On the same night my brilliant accompanist, composer Marvin Hamlisch, kept going back for more awards. He won one Oscar for his adaptation on *The Sting,* one for Best Score and another for Best Song for "The Way We Were."
⁶²⁷ The Oscar on display on my hall table.

628

628 A few weeks after the presentation, three very good friends hosted a celebration to commemorate my getting an Oscar: Bill Cosby, Jack Nicholson and Marvin.

629 Even Zeppo was there, having driven up from Palm Springs.

630 With Bill and George Fenneman.

346

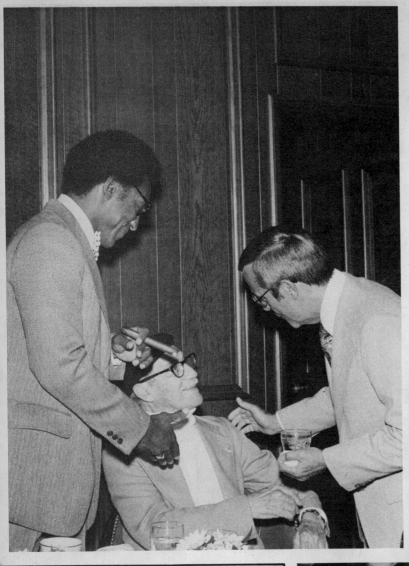

630

629

631

631 Robert Blake and William Peter Blatty. Bill Blatty was a contestant on *You Bet Your Life,* where he won the $10,000 jackpot. With the money he was able to turn to full-time writing. He eventually wrote *The Exorcist.*

632 Hugh Hefner, Barbi Benton, Elke Sommer and Joe Hyams.

633 Mr. and Mrs. William Wyler.

634 Marvin's mother, Lilly Hamlisch, and his sister, Terry Liebling, among the guests.

632

633

634

635 Later on in the evening, a few of us put on an entertainment.

636 George Segal accompanied me on the banjo.

637 Harpo's son Bill and his friend Marilyn Berglass.

638 Bill and I did an impromptu routine.

639 Jack Nicholson read telegrams.

640 Cass Elliott.

641 Carl Reiner.

642 George Burns.

643 Steve Allen, and Milton Berle.

644 Robert Klein and Alice Cooper.

353

645 When *Animal Crackers* re-premiered in New York forty-four years after its original release, I flew back for the opening. The crowds were extraordinary. There were policemen on horses holding back the crowds, but even then the people streamed through. One of the horses asked me for my autograph. All I gave him was a horse laugh.

646 While in the East, Marvin and I appeared on *The Mike Douglas Show.*

647 One of the novelty items, part of the Groucho merchandising boom, is this dollar bill with my picture on it, a steal at $5.00.

647

648 Hanging in my secretary's office are sketches drawn by fans and sent to me. Dozens arrive every month, and the display changes constantly.

649 When Lucille Ball was honored by a charity group, a bunch of oldtimers came along for the ride. Standing behind Lucy: Milton Berle, George Burns, Jack Benny, Bob Hope, myself and Gale Gordon.

651 Though I love them all, I'll never understand the kids of today. They say they're doing their own thing, then hundreds of them come out of coffeehouses and fraternity smokers dressed like Groucho Marx. These young men, and some girls too, were competing in a Groucho look-alike contest sponsored by a Boston television station promoting *You Bet Your Life*.

652 When *The Best of Groucho* began its third life on television in New York in 1975, television station WNEW-TV commissioned a poster for the event. Artist Emilio Grossi generously inscribed one of them for me.

THE BEST OF GROUCHO

WNEW-TV METROMEDIA TELEVISION

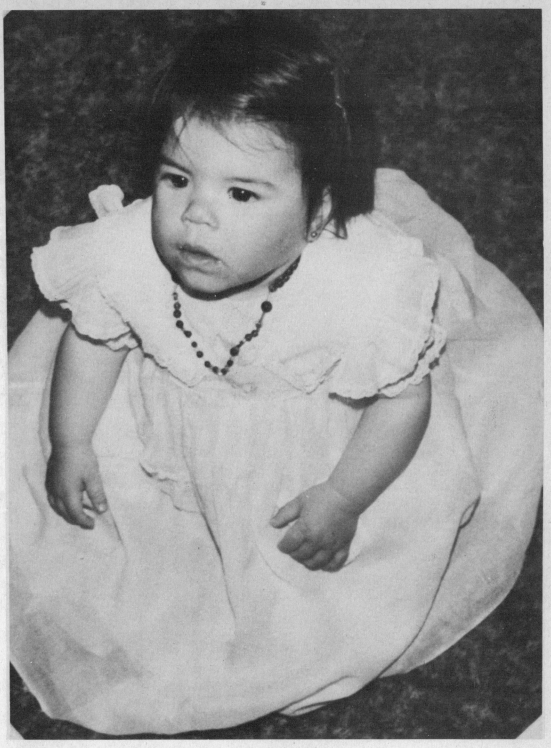

⁶⁵³ My daughter Melinda is now a wife and mother living in northern California. Despite my efforts to get her into show business, Melinda had other ideas. In retrospect, I can't say I object, considering the two great treasures she's given me. Here she is with one of them, my grandson Miles.

⁶⁵⁴ The other treasure, of course, is Melinda's daughter, Jade.

655

656

May 20, 1975

Mr. Groucho Marx
1083 Hillcrest Road
Beverly Hills
California 90210

Dear Groucho:

May I express my own personal pleasure that you have joined our Temple. I earnestly hope that you will avail yourself of the facilities and services of the Temple and come to regard Emanuel as your spiritual home.

I hope you will agree with me that the Temple exists for the deepening of our faith, the enlarging of our knowledge, the enhancement of our appreciation for the enduring values, and the ever greater commitment of all of us to justice.

B'ruchim Ha-baim B'shem Adonai'!

"Blessed are you who come in the name of the Lord!"

Welcome to Emanuel!

Faithfully,

Rabbi Meyer Heller

RMH:gaw

Welcome to you and Erin and to all your family!

657

655 Here's another Groucho look-alike, at the American Film Institute dinner honoring James Cagney. The fellow with me is Russell Fleming, Erin's brother, who teaches at the University of Toronto.

656 Mae West is a wonder. I don't know how she does it. I understand she's in her eighties. With us is Paul Novak, Mae's general factotum.

658 When I celebrated my eighty-fifth birthday in October of 1975, Los Angeles Mayor Tom Bradley declared it Groucho Marx Day. He sent over this proclamation.

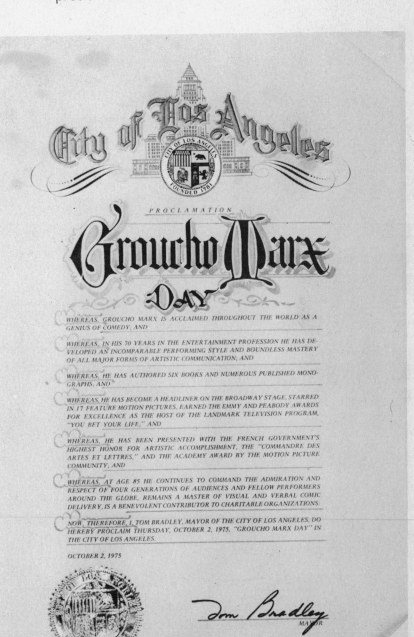

City of Los Angeles

CITY OF LOS ANGELES
FOUNDED 1781

PROCLAMATION

Groucho Marx Day

WHEREAS, GROUCHO MARX IS ACCLAIMED THROUGHOUT THE WORLD AS A GENIUS OF COMEDY, AND

WHEREAS, IN HIS 70 YEARS IN THE ENTERTAINMENT PROFESSION HE HAS DEVELOPED AN INCOMPARABLE PERFORMING STYLE AND BOUNDLESS MASTERY OF ALL MAJOR FORMS OF ARTISTIC COMMUNICATION, AND

WHEREAS, HE HAS AUTHORED SIX BOOKS AND NUMEROUS PUBLISHED MONOGRAPHS, AND

WHEREAS, HE HAS BECOME A HEADLINER ON THE BROADWAY STAGE, STARRED IN 17 FEATURE MOTION PICTURES, EARNED THE EMMY AND PEABODY AWARDS FOR EXCELLENCE AS THE HOST OF THE LANDMARK TELEVISION PROGRAM, "YOU BET YOUR LIFE," AND

WHEREAS, HE HAS BEEN PRESENTED WITH THE FRENCH GOVERNMENT'S HIGHEST HONOR FOR ARTISTIC ACCOMPLISHMENT, THE "COMMANDRE DES ARTES ET LETTRES," AND THE ACADEMY AWARD BY THE MOTION PICTURE COMMUNITY, AND

WHEREAS, AT AGE 85 HE CONTINUES TO COMMAND THE ADMIRATION AND RESPECT OF FOUR GENERATIONS OF AUDIENCES AND FELLOW PERFORMERS AROUND THE GLOBE, REMAINS A MASTER OF VISUAL AND VERBAL COMIC DELIVERY, IS A BENEVOLENT CONTRIBUTOR TO CHARITABLE ORGANIZATIONS.

NOW, THEREFORE, I, TOM BRADLEY, MAYOR OF THE CITY OF LOS ANGELES, DO HEREBY PROCLAIM THURSDAY, OCTOBER 2, 1975, "GROUCHO MARX DAY" IN THE CITY OF LOS ANGELES.

OCTOBER 2, 1975

Tom Bradley
MAYOR

658

659

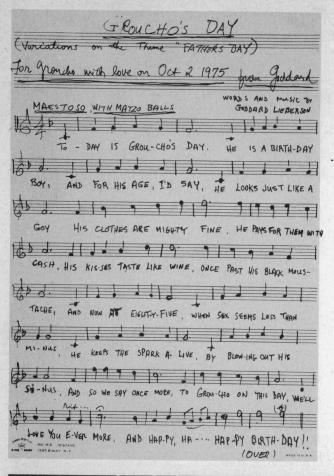

660

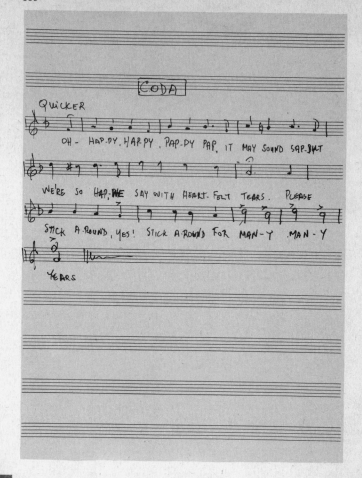

661

659 -60 A proclamation of another sort was also sent to me by Goddard Lieberson. He called his composition "Groucho's Day," a takeoff on Harry Ruby's song, "Father's Day."

662 At my birthday party—the surviving Marx Brothers, Zeppo, Groucho and Gummo.

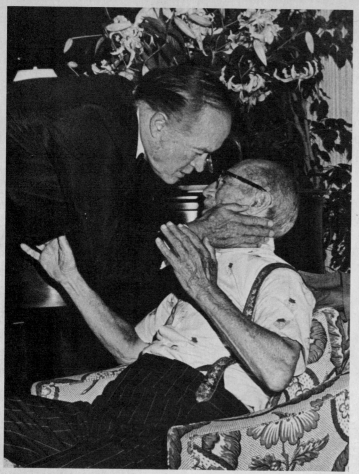

663 Bob Hope.

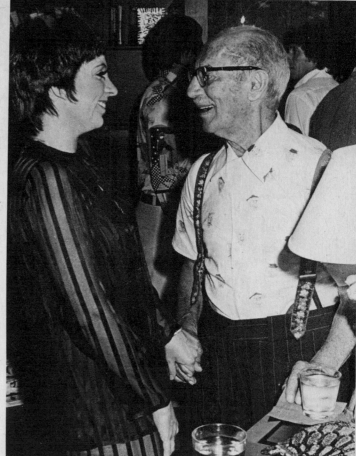

664 Liza Minnelli.

665 There's a world of show business in this picture. Sitting on the floor next to me is Sally Kellerman. We're an item. Behind her is Grace Kahn, Gus's widow. Standing in back, in the print shirt, is Peter Sellers.

667 A week after my birthday, the Friends of the Libraries at the University of Southern California hel a literary luncheon honoring me for my writings. was an SRO audience.

668 George Fenneman, seen here with his wife Peg moderated a panel which read selections from m six books.

669 They included Roddy McDowall, Jack Lemmon an Lynn Redgrave.

667

668

669

670

671

670 When this "Broom-Hilda" cartoon appeared in *The Los Angeles Times*, I wrote cartoonist Russell Myers and asked for the original. He delivered it in person, and I found him as delightful and amusing as his strip.

671 With my friend Irwin Allen. I taught him everything he knows about disaster pictures. This picture was taken either at his wedding or at mine.

672 The new year of 1976 seemed to be a celebration for old comedians. Jayne and Steve Allen kicked it off in January with a party honoring comics. They included Jean Stapleton, Norman Lear and Carroll O'Connor.

672

673 In the spring, Bobbs-Merrill reissued my first book, *Beds*, and new pictures were shot. I posed with a not-so-old comedienne who got her first national exposure on my quiz show, Phyllis Diller—

674 —and Burt Reynolds—

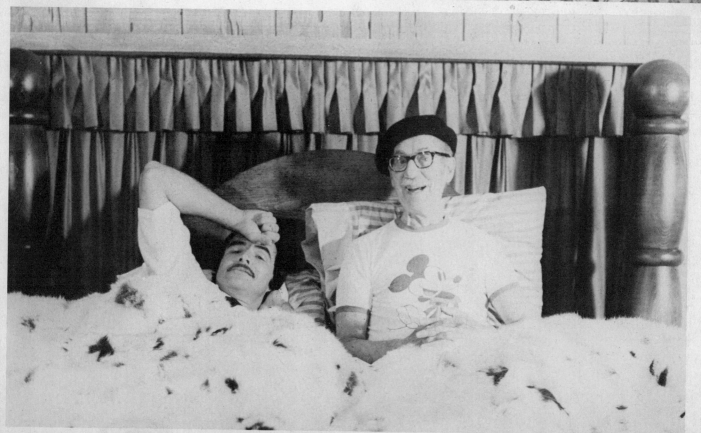

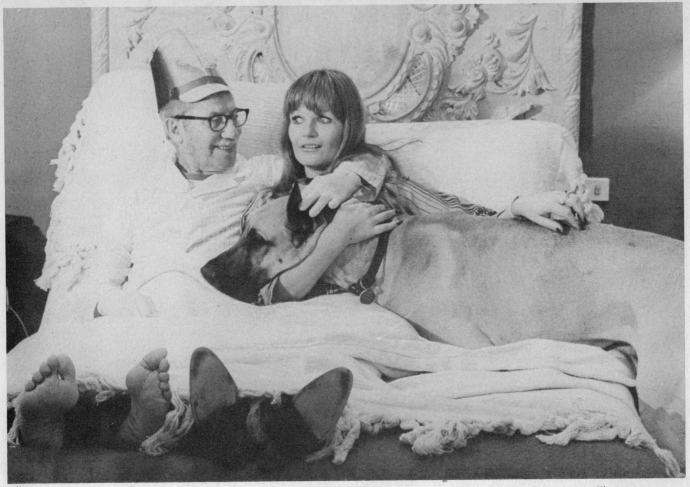

675

676

675 —Valerie Perrine and her Great Dane. . . . There is nothing like a Dane—

676 —and Elliott Gould.

For Groucho, who al[ways]
laugh. with affect[ion]

677 Bob Hope did a ninety-minute special in March, *Joys*, about a human shark that commits crimes against comedy. Here are three master criminals: George Burns, Bob and me.

679 Hal Kanter, at right, produced the show, and Billy Barty, the miniature Groucho, was one of the forty-six guest stars. Unfortunately, it was not our finest hour-and-a-half.

680 Another old comic dropped by to see me while in California doing a television special—Dick Cavett.

681 His visit was good for a round or two.

682 George Jessel came to dinner with his good friend Edy Williams.
683 Goddard Lieberson came to lunch.
685 As did Morrie Ryskind.
686 The back hallway of my house has a poster from my Carnegie Hall concert. Guests write their names on it. Displayed are my Emmy, my Oscar and other cherished mementoes.

688

689

690

688 I received the Sunair Humanitarian Award for 1976, as have Jack Benny and Lucille Ball in previous years. Some of the last survivors of the Marx family get together: Zeppo; my grandson Andy and his friend, Jacque Jones; Susan and Steve Marx, Steve being another grandson; Grace Kahn and myself. Grace is the maternal grandmother of Steve and Andy.

689 Sitting on the dais were Jane Fonda, George Jessel, Zeppo and Jack Lemmon. Those not pictured were Red Buttons, Redd Foxx, George Fenneman, Rosalind Russell and Earl Wilson, who has yet to quote any of my quips correctly.

690 George Jessel was toastmaster for the evening.

691 I'm in love again. When I met the First Lady at a reception in Beverly Hills recently, I knew Betty Ford was the real thing. She's a wonderful woman with enormous charm and great warmth. I told her she reminded me of my mother, and that's the greatest compliment I can pay.

691

To Groucho Marx
With great admiration to a wonderful person
and warm personal regards,

Betty Ford

692 Hello, I must be going.
   I cannot stay.
   I came to say
   I must be going.
   I'm glad I came,
   But just the same,
   I must be going.
   For my sake you must stay,
   For if you go away,
   You'll spoil this party I am throwing.
   I'll stay a week or two,
   I'll stay the summer through,
   But I am telling you,
   I must be going.

PHOTO CREDITS

Photos numbered:

1–6, 661–666. Frank Diernhammer
36. San Francisco Academy of Comic Art
44. Shaun Considine
45, 84, 200–202. Lester Glassner collection
65. Gene Andrewski collection
77–79, 178, 276, 390, 542. The Los Angeles Times
80, 82, 83. The White collection, Performing Arts Research Center, The New York Public Library at Lincoln Center
88–97, 104. From the Paramount release, The Cocoanuts, © Universal Pictures
101–102. Hal Phyfe
103–114. From the Paramount release, Animal Crackers, © Universal Pictures
129–153, 402. From the Paramount release, Monkey Business, © Universal Pictures
154–170. From the Paramount release, Horsefeathers, © Universal Pictures
179–184. From the Paramount release, Duck Soup, © Universal Pictures
198, 282, 384, 397, 599. Wide World Photos
212–237, 401. From the MGM release, A Night at the Opera, ©1935 Metro-Goldwyn-Mayer Corporation. Copyright renewed 1963 by Metro-Goldwyn-Mayer Inc.
241. The Museum of Modern Art/Film Stills Archive
243–274, 402. From the MGM release, A Day at the Races, ©1937 Metro-Goldwyn-Mayer Corporation. Copyright renewed 1964 by Metro-Goldwyn-Mayer Inc.
281, 480, 493, 495, 651. Associated Press
284–300. From the RKO release, Room Service, © RKO Radio Pictures, Inc.
301, 302. Walt Disney Productions
303–321, 406. From the MGM release, At the Circus, ©1939 Loew's Incorporated. Copyright renewed 1966 by Metro-Goldwyn-Mayer Inc.
329–344, 403. From the MGM release, Go West, © 1940 Loew's Incorporated. Copyright renewed 1963 by Metro-Goldwyn-Mayer Inc.
345–354, 404. From the MGM release, The Big Store, © 1941 Loew's Incorporated. Copyright renewed 1966 by Metro-Goldwyn-Mayer Inc.
358, 359. O. Soglow, © Simon and Schuster
385–389, 405. From the United Artists release, A Night in Casablanca, ©1946 by Loma Vista Films. Copyright renewed 1973 by National Telefilm Associates, Inc.
407–416. From the United Artists release, Copacabana, © 1947 Beacon Productions. Copyright renewed 1975 by National Telefilm Associates, Inc.
420, 421. Mr. and Mrs. Bert Granet collection
423, 443, 447, 448, 451, 477, 483, 484, 485, 497, 498, 521, 522, 530, 531, 532, 533, 539, 548, 552, 667, 668, 669. National Broadcasting Company

429. Ralph Levy collection
432–439. From the United Artists release, Love Happy, ©1950 Artists Alliance Inc. Copyright renewed 1975 by National Telefilm Associates, Inc.
441–442. From the Paramount release, Mr. Music, © Universal Pictures
445, 486, 487, 499, 500, 501, 502. Columbia Broadcasting System.
456–459. From the RKO release, Double Dynamite, © RKO Radio Pictures Inc.
460–469. From the RKO release, A Girl in Every Port, © RKO Radio Pictures, Inc.
470–473. © 1952, Harry Ruby Music Co.
479, 505. Pictorial Parade
482, 541. Al Hirschfeld
506, 507. Irwin Allen collection
512. Saturday Evening Post
513. Reprinted by permission of Bil Keane and The Register and Tribune Syndicate, Inc.
545–547. Bell Telephone Company
565. Sidney Sheldon collection
572. From the Paramount release, Skidoo, © Universal Pictures
574, 620–626. Academy of Motion Picture Arts and Sciences
577. Betty Comden collection
578–581. Arthur Whitelaw collection
586. Ron Scherl
589–590. © 1972, Harry Ruby Music Co.
595. Candice Bergen
596–598, 680–681, 683, 684, 686–690, 692. Steve Schapiro
600–601. A & M Records
605. United Press International
609–610, 656. Columbia Pictures
611. Howard Rosenberg
612–617. Charles Bush, Playboy magazine
628–644. Stan Adams
645. New York Post photograph by Leonardo, © 1974, New York Post Corporation
652. Copyright WNEW-TV, E. Grassi, artist
670. © 1975. The Chicago Tribune. All rights reserved
671. Irwin Allen collection
672. Steve Allen collection
673–676. Ellen Berman
682. Ed Begley, Jr.
685. Hal Kaufman

Index

Page references for pictures refer to captions.